CAR AND DRIVER AMERICAN ROAD WARRIORS

CAR AND DRIVER AMERICAN

ROAD WARRIORS
Classic Muscle Cars

Edited by Ted West

filipacchi
publishing

CONTENTS

You can get a set of five big, full-c

We call it GTO. Purists call it names. You'll call it fantastic.

GTO means *Gran Turismo Omologato*. In Italian, th
about twenty thousand bucks. The way we say it is
pronounce and it costs less besides. For a better
you have to ask the owners of Pontiac GTOs. They sa
a beautiful car with a swift, smooth 389-cubic in
suspension that makes it handle like our ads say i
brakes that stop it right here and now. Why would
this make the purists mad? Maybe we should raise

6

Pontiac GTO—first to pick the fight.

1962-1965
Setting the Stage

Car and Driver discovered the American muscle car—and a minute later, America discovered *Car and Driver.*

The magazine began as *Sports Cars Illustrated*, polite, circumspect—most of all, little. But little wasn't good enough. Renamed *Car and Driver* and re-staffed under new editor David E. Davis Jr., the magazine laid its finger on the white-hot, outta-here pulse of American V-8 performance. A raging youth culture of tire-burning late-night drag racers was milling about, just waiting for a revolution.

And with the magazine's—some would say, outrageous—1964 Pontiac GTO vs. Ferrari GTO comparison test, *Car and Driver* declared Pontiac's the better GTO. The revolution was on. Nothing was sacred, not even Ferrari.

Growing by leaps and bounds, *Car and Driver* became the largest, most influential—and hippest—car magazine on Earth. As the voice of early American Muscle, it proclaimed proto-hotties like the Pontiac GTO, Shelby GT-350 and Dodge Hemi icons of pure American performance.

From Detroit's Woodward Avenue to L.A.'s Van Nuys Boulevard, the cruise was on. And leading further into the night, hot American Muscle went street racing wherever and whenever it could evade Officer Beedle.

The night was ours....

PONTIAC TEMPEST GTO

Ferrari never built enough GTOs to earn the name anyway—
just to be on the safe side though, Pontiac built a faster one.

Most knowledgeable enthusiasts reacted negatively when Pontiac announced that their new Tempest sports model was to be called the GTO. They felt, as we did, that Pontiac was swiping a name to which it had no right. Like Le Mans, Grand Prix, Monza, Spyder and 2+2, this was another of those hard-to-digest bits of puffery from the Detroit/Madison Avenue axis. Our first look at the car made us feel a little better, because it is handsome, and then we got a call from correspondent Roger Proulx, raving about the car's acceleration and handling, so we arranged to test a Pontiac Tempest GTO.

This was the most exhaustive and thorough road test we have ever done. We used two nearly-identical cars, the differences being that one car had the shorter-ratio manual steering while the other had power; the manual steering car was also equipped with metallic brake linings. We drove our two cars unmercifully.

One was driven from Detroit to New York City, used for ten days by every member of the staff, and then driven from New York to Daytona Beach, Florida, carrying the managing editor, his wife, and three active children. This car—the manual steering, metallic brake version—was driven over 3000 miles. The other car was driven about 500. We ran dozens of acceleration tests on the two cars, plus many, many laps of the Daytona International Raceway's tri-oval and road circuit.

It was our original intention to borrow a Ferrari GTO and to run the two against each other at Bridgehampton's road racing circuit and on the drag strip at Westhampton. We had engaged Walt Hansgen to drive the Pontiac and Bob Grossman to run his own Ferrari. Unfortunately Grossman's Ferrari was tired from a season of racing, and was not considered fast enough to really be a match

for our Tempest. We then canvassed all the GTO owners in this country and simply could not get one of those lucky gentlemen and the weather to cooperate simultaneously. As a result, we drove two Ferrari GTO's, but we were never able actually to run the Tempest against either one of them.

Although it would have been great fun and quite interesting to run the Ferrari racing car against Pontiac's similarly-named touring car, our tests showed that there really was no effective basis for comparison—the Pontiac will beat the Ferrari in a drag race, and the Ferrari will go around any American road circuit faster than the stock Tempest GTO. We are positive, however, that a Tempest like ours, with the addition of NASCAR road racing suspension, will take the measure of any Ferrari other than prototype racing cars or the recently announced 250-LM. We should also point out that our test

car, with stock suspension, metallic brakes and as-tested 348 bhp engine will lap any U.S. road course faster than any Ferrari street machine, including the 400 Superamerica. Not bad for an actual delivered price of $3,400, wot?

It was a shade over ten years ago that events in Detroit took a turn for the better and started the trend that ultimately resulted in the Tempest GTO. At that time, GM announced the Corvette. It was a funny car, hooted and jeered at by enthusiasts and by-passed by the great unwashed in favor of its more understandable competitor, the two-seater Thunderbird.

From those humble beginnings (with the late-fifties prompting of a robust and growing imported car market), came a host of better, more interesting cars from Detroit. The success of the Corvette and the sports-type Corvair Monza led the other GM divisions to build similar cars, particularly in the B-O-P compact lines. Buick and Oldsmobile leaned toward the concept of "Little Thunderbirds," cars with bucket seats and floor-mounted shift levers, but little else of a sporting nature. Pontiac, God love'em, went the hairy-chested route and came up with our test car, the best American car we have ever driven, and probably one of the five or six best cars in the world for the enthusiast driver.

Obviously, personal preference must come into play here. There are many of our readers who think that a Sprite is the absolute epitome of grand touring, while others feel that no car should have a displacement greater than 1500cc. Add to these the purist who wouldn't drive an American car if his life depended on it, and you have a pretty fair-sized body of opposition. We respect their differing opinions and will defend to the death their right to express them, but we will stand or fall on our enthusiasm for the Tempest GTO.

In 1963 we were a bit stunned by a Mercury Marauder that had 427 cubic inches, 425 horsepower, good handling, and performance that, to us, was absolutely breathtaking. The Tempest GTO is better. First of all, its smaller outside dimensions make it a lot more fun to drive; and, second, it goes faster.

Our test car was equipped with the 389-cubic-inch, 348 horsepower, V-8 engine with hydraulic valve lifters and a compression ratio of 10.4 to one. It had the new GM "Muncie" four-speed transmission and Pontiac's Saf-T-Trak limited-slip differential. The rear axle ratio was 3.90 to one, and the brakes had metallic linings. The car had standard Tempest GTO suspension (slightly stiffer valving in the shocks) and manual steering with an overall ratio of 20 to 1, substantially faster than the standard manual steering ratio of 26 to 1, but slower than the power steering's 17 to 1. We preferred the power steering—not because the manual set-up was too stiff, but because it still wasn't quite fast enough.

A word of caution here: Pontiac is forced by the realities of commerce to build cars for little old ladies and GM executives as well as

enthusiasts. It is quite possible to go to your dealer's for a demonstration drive and find yourself in a GTO of infinite dullness—an automatic-transmission-, power-operated-seat-, tinted-window-car with little to distinguish it from a Chevelle, a Buick Special, an Olds F85, or any other semi-visible American car. The GTO that delights the executive from the fourteenth floor of Detroit's General Motors Building is not going to be the rabid enthusiast's dish of tea. To buy a car like our test car you should either get hold of a catalog and memorize the options you want, or seek out a livewire dealership like Royal Pontiac in Royal Oak, Michigan, the firm that loaned us our GTO.

Royal is run by a man named Ace Wilson, who must be what regional sales managers ask Santa Claus to bring them for Christmas. His dealership is big and bright, with clean modern architecture and a whole staff of knowledgeable salesmen and mechanics. Royal is Pontiac performance head-quarters, and a Royal license plate frame on your GTO or Grand Prix is enough to send teenagers into orbit anywhere in the United States. Royal even has its own line of accessories and speed equipment, certain combinations of which give the proud GTO or Catalina owner the right to call his car a Royal Bobcat, and to fit it with small black and white emblems to that effect.

Our test cars were Bobcats. This means that they were basically stock Tempest GTO's with the following changes:

1 The main jets were changed to .069 in on all three carburetors for maximum acceleration. Normally, the center carburetor runs lean (.066 in) for cruising economy, with rich jets (.073 in) on the outboard carburetors for occasional bursts of speed. The Royal treatment gives a more even mixture distribution at a slight increase in steady-speed gas consumption.

2 A progressive-action throttle linkage is installed to calm the beast down for boulevard use; it's also more accurate than the stock linkage.

3 The distributor is modified to limit centrifugal advance to 7° (14 crankshaft degrees) and initial advance is set at a whopping 20-22° (total advance, 34-36°, is reached at 3600 rpm). This makes a tremendous improvement in low-end response (i.e., below 3600 rpm) but substantially raises the octane requirement.

4 The heat riser is blocked off, a special (thin) head gasket from the Super-Duty 421 engine is installed and still more compression is gained by installing Champion J-10Y plugs without gaskets.

5 Finally, special fiber-insert rocker arm retaining locknuts are installed which permit the hydraulic lifters to function as a solid lifter—operating at 90% bleed-down.

As you can see, these changes are neither extensive nor complicated, and fall more into the area of maximum tuning than that of modification or "hopping up." The net result is an enormously strong engine with the capacity to spin its rear wheels in every gear, in spite of a limited-slip differential! The only penalty we noticed was that the car would knock like twenty-five poltergeists at a seance when anything but Sunoco 260 premium fuel (about 102 octane) was used.

Were we to buy a GTO (and there's a good chance at least one of us will), our selection might go something like this. A GTO is basically a $2,480 Tempest Le Mans with a $296 extra-equipment package that includes a floor shift, 389 engine, dual exhaust, stiffer shocks, "exterior identification" and a choice of super-premium tires or whitewalls. The four-speed, all-synchro transmission is $188 extra, and we'd gladly pay $115 to get the hottest (348 bhp) engine. The shorter axle ratios are only available with metallic brakes, HD radiator and limited-slip differential ($75 for the lot). Quick steering (20:1) is part of the handling option, though HD shocks and springs alone are only $3.82. The "wood"-rim steering wheel is $39, and from there on in, it's trimming the window with fuzz (like $36 for custom wheel covers). With every conceivable option on a GTO it would be difficult to spend more than $3,800. That's a bargain.

We find the GTO quite handsome, except for those phony vents that GM Styling's Bill Mitchell insists upon hanging on everything.

Unlike the Sting Ray, the GTO has only the ones on the hood, so we can say it could be much, much worse. Our test car was a rich dark blue with black U.S. Royal Red Line tires and very conservative wheel covers. There was nothing to give away the presence of the ferocious beast concealed inside, and yet the car would draw admiring glances wherever it went. Whether it was the car's restrained good looks or the threatening grumble from the four (count em, four) shiny tail pipe extensions, we never learned.

Once inside, everything seems to be just about where you would have put it in a car of your own design. The optional steering wheel is wood-looking plastic that had us completely conned. To our embarrassment, some smart aleck who'd read the catalog pointed out

our mistake and made us feel like General Motors had really taken us. Wood or not, it's handsome as hell and an excellent piece of fakery. The instruments are all well-placed and legible, except for the tachometer, which is terrible—it's too far to the right to be glanced at during a hard run, and, worse, it's the wand type that sweeps horizontally across a four-inch quadrant and is practically impossible to read anyway. The speedometer is just slightly left of center in the panel and it has a typical 270 degree clock-type face. Our choice would be to swap the tach and speedometer locations, substituting a Sun SST (270°) tach for the factory's $53.80 optional tach.

The transmission lever is nicely placed immediately next to the driver's thigh. It has the now famous Hurst linkage which is amazingly

short and unerringly accurate. The sports car driver's first tendency is always to try to make the gate wider than it is, and the shift pattern more complicated. After a little time in the car, however, the brutal simplicity of that great tree-trunk of a lever begins to reassure you and you start throwing shifts with the same slam-bang abandon as the drag racing types. Our photographer drove the car and commented that he was used to driving imported cars and he had a hard time getting used to the extreme closeness of the GTO's gate. Kismet.

The so-called bucket seats in the GTO are the same as those in the Corvair Monza or any of the B-O-P compacts. That is to say they are not buckets at all, but actually individual front seats with a modicum of lateral support. We'd like the car better if the seats wrapped around farther and were more firmly constructed, but that's the breaks. In one way, the softness is a good deal, because anybody who's a middleweight or bigger will compress the seat cushion all the way anyway, and then it becomes quite satisfactory. Fore and aft adjustment on the front seats is excellent provided you have the manual adjustment—the power assisted system limits travel enough to preclude any kind of straight-arm driving technique for would-be heroes. Rear seat room is cramped for three—it is, strictly speaking, a four seater.

Driving this car is an experience no enthusiast should miss. Unfortunately, few Pontiac dealers will have GTO demonstrators with the proper equipment on them, but if you can get your hands on one like we tested, it's almost worth stealing it for a few minutes of Omigod-we're-going-too-fast kind of automotive bliss. One expects the acceleration to be spectacular in first and second, but none of us were ready for the awful slamming-back-in-the-seat we got when we tromped on it at 80 in fourth.

This car does what so many others only talk about—it really does combine brute, blasting performance with balance and stability of a superior nature. The managing editor, for instance, was cruising through a pitch black Florida night on a road that skirted the Atlantic. He was traveling at about 90 when he got into a series of ess-bends marked for 45 mph—he found himself going in at about 75 and coming out at 100, so he choose

PONTIAC TEMPEST GTO

Ferrari never built enough GTOs to earn the name anyway—just to be on the safe side though, Pontiac built a faster one

95 as a comfortable median and negotiated the entire series, including bumps, camber changes and nasty, narrow little bridges without ever touching the brakes or changing the position of his hands on the steering wheel. The car does not handle particularly well in a 35-mph right-angle turn because of its large size, but as the speed rises the quality of the handling goes up by the square.

Charlie Kolb helped us wring the cars out at Daytona and he liked them so well that he wanted us to promote a team of them for the 2000-kilometer Daytona Continental race in February. Lapping the track at Daytona with Kolb driving was quite interesting because we were able to sit back and examine the car's behavior under really extreme conditions. It was totally forgiving, and always stayed pointed. Its handling starts as understeer at very low speeds, becomes neutral at moderately fast speeds, and gradually—quite pleasantly in fact— becomes oversteer when pressed to its limit. Two staff members managed to spin the car in the same 80-mph corner, and both times the tail came out, stayed out, and led the way off the road. It is, incidentally, a very pleasant car to go off the road in, provided you don't catch a finger in the whirling spokes of the steering wheel.

Obviously, the GTO as we drove it, without the $16.82 heavy-duty suspension option, is not suitable for road racing. It rolls too much and the steering, even with the 20 to 1 ratio manual installed, is too slow. But what a road car! The metallic brake linings pulled the car down from speeds as high as 120-125 over and over again without grabbing or pulling one way or the other. The car would vibrate viciously on the rough banking at 125 mph, but never showed any indication that the suspension was being overtaxed. We used Goodyear Blue Streak Stock Car Specials (7.10-7.60 x 15 rear, 6.70 x 15 front) for the road circuit and the tri-oval, but found them absolutely unable to handle the wheelspin on the acceleration runs.

We didn't like the U.S. Royal Red Line tires on a car this powerful. We would like to have had Dunlop SP's. We prefer belted tires in all high speed cruising situations, and we feel that a tire like the SP, which has proved in rallying that it can hold up and give maximum stability under the wildest power-input and wheelspin conditions, would be just right. An interesting sideline here is that we got more miles per hour in the quarter mile with the Red Lines, while we got better elapsed times with huge drag racing slicks. The times quoted in our data panel were obtained with the standard tires and are spectacular enough, but when we ran the slicks we got down as low as 12.8 seconds at 112 mph. Now that's what we'd call pretty fair acceleration. It was only ten years ago that we were all pretty impressed when a Cadillac Allard cut a 15-second quarter at the Santa Ana Drag Strip. A production Cobra won't go that fast.

So, in winding this up, how do we classify this car relative to other GT cars, and particularly to the car from which it stole its name? The Ferrari GTO is a racing car that costs upwards of $20,000 new. Therefore we are not surprised that it will go around a road racing circuit several seconds faster than our Tempest GTO. What does surprise us is that we found the Tempest GTO a better car, in some respects, than most current production Ferraris. It is not as refined, the quality of the materials and the workmanship is not as good, it feels bigger, and it is bigger, but cars are to drive, and when you drive a Tempest GTO with the right options on it, you're driving a real automobile. Can Pontiac help it if they're too dumb to know that a car can't go that fast without a prancing horse decal on the side?

C/D AND WALT HANSGEN ROAD TEST

THE PONTIAC 2+2
AGAINST THE FERRARI 2+2

Exactly one year ago, we published a road test of the Pontiac GTO. We liked it enormously, said so, and opined that Pontiac had earned the right to the name—whether Ferrari had it first or not. The subsequent response proved that it is possible to love both wisely and too well. Now we present the next round—the Pontiac 2+2 versus the Ferrari 330/GT 2+2. Racing driver Walt Hansgen joined us at the Bridgehampton road circuit, drove both cars under the same conditions, and gave us his most candid impressions of each. We have woven Walt's observations into our own, and he had some pretty cogent things to say. For the benefit of those who are about to compose blistering attacks upon us for our Letters column, our address is One Park Avenue, New York 16, and we have wives and mothers, so watch it.—Ed.

It's doubtful if Pontiac had any idea of the conflict that would erupt when they started naming their cars after various Ferraris and European tourist attractions. Even though the controversy is limited to the rarefied atmosphere of automotive enthusiasm, it is loud and bitter enough to give pause to a parent corporation that has made a few billion dollars from non-wave making.

Numerous individuals and publications have levelled savage attacks upon Pontiac for model names like LeMans and Grand Prix, but those were nothing compared to what happened last year when they called their big-engined Tempest the GTO. To make matters worse, we liked the car and approved of the name, and thus started a civil war among our readers that rages on to this day.

Obviously, Pontiac's decision to market their 1965 2+2 as a larger version of the GTO was certain to add new fuel to the year-old fire. You can imagine our delight. We contacted Ace Wilson's Royal Pontiac in Royal Oak, Michigan, and asked for a properly set up 2+2 as soon as possible. At the same time, we asked Mr. Luigi Chinetti for a Ferrari 330/GT 2+2. Both parties agreed without hesitation and provided us with cars that were the very best of their respective kinds—the Ferrari was, in fact, Luigi Chinetti, Jr's personal car, set up by the same mechanics who prepare the North American Racing Team machinery.

The Pontiac 2+2 is a Catalina sport coupe with a 421 cu. in. V-8 (hydraulic lifter) engine, stiffer suspension, and special interior and exterior trim. As we tested it, it was equipped with the hottest (376-hp), three carburetor version of the big V-8, a four-speed transmission with long, close ratios, power steering, power brakes with metallic linings, limited slip differential with 3.42 final drive ratio, and the stiffest shocks, springs, and stabilizer bar offered in the Pontiac catalog. Its wheelbase is 121 in., its overall length 214.5 in., and its test weight 4400 lbs.

Walt Hansgen: "My basic impression of the Pontiac is that it's a tremendously large car to be driving around a road circuit. The hood seems very, very wide and very, very long and when you first get in and drive off down the track—just sort of getting used to it—you get the feeling that it's going to go straight at the first corner. Surprisingly enough, it doesn't just go around the corner, it does a mighty fine job of it! It leans considerably, but it seems to lean to a certain point where it decides that it just isn't going to lean anymore—and at that point it's quite controllable. The steering response is very good."

The Ferrari 330/GT 2+2 is essentially the same car as the old 250/GT 2+2 with a 4-liter (242 cu. in.) engine and new styling. The 330/GT designation is based upon Ferrari's traditional system of naming his V-12 engines with the cubic centimeter displacement of a single cylinder. The Ferrari has a wheelbase of 104.2 in., overall length of 189 in., and a test weight of 3430 lbs.

Walt Hansgen: "I thought the Ferrari was just a nice size for two people with occasional use for the rear seats—very occasional, I'd say. It's a perfect size for American roads and conditions and so forth—about like the Pontiac GTO, not too big. I think the Ferrari would be an absolutely perfect car. It's extremely smooth on the track. The handling is better than you'd expect from a road machine."

2+2—A fistful of Pontiac!

The Pontiac 2+2 and the Ferrari 2+2 are similar in many respects. Both represent ultimate automotive performance as interpreted by their respective industrial philosophies and the economies that spawned them. If one totalled their relative strengths and weaknesses and took an average for each car, the net result would be nearly equal. Both are good cars. They are fast, safe, and luxurious. They provide their drivers with a brand of automotive excitement seldom experienced off the race course. However, the existing differences are important ones, and they're the kind that make owners and would-be owners give each other bloody noses and smouldering grudges.

The basic difference between them is one of personality—like the one we've noted between New York and San Francisco. San Francisco is probably just as good as New York. It is, however, a little insecure about its status and has an unfortunate tendency to fish for compliments—to beg strangers for approval and reassurance. New York, on the other hand, doesn't give a damn whether you like it or not.

New York knows that it's Number One, the Top Dog, and for all it cares, you can drop dead tomorrow.

By this definition, Pontiac's 2+2 is like San Francisco and Ferrari's is like New York. The Pontiac longs to be loved, and its designers have worked hard to make it live up to all of its performance publicity without sacrificing American-style good looks and shiny, super-car interior comforts. The Ferrari couldn't care less. It is almost arrogantly self-confident in its refusal to compromise, and if you don't like it, it seems to infer that you are a person lacking in taste, virility, and intelligence.

To further define this difference, it could be said that the Pontiac is a Car in the accepted American sense, while the Ferrari is a Machine. The Pontiac was designed to cause a series of sensual impressions in the onlooker and prospective buyer. First, it is flamboyantly good-looking, with great swooping curves and erotic distribution of masses within its total configuration. Second, it is extremely easy to drive and very comfortable for both front and rear seat occupants. Only when the

full force of six carburetor throats is applied is it anything like a handful, or in any way demanding to drive. It is smooth on all but broken surfaces and only rarely does its suspension betray the stiffness that makes it possible to hurry through corners at really respectable speeds. Crosswinds blow it around some, but not too badly.

The Ferrari is something else. Its styling is not going to start any riots. It is only comfortable for the man who loves it and is willing to adapt himself to it. It is hard to drive, in that the controls are stiff, heavy, and hyper-accurate. The effort required and the neophyte's tendency to under-control have an intimidating effect upon the faint-of-heart. The engine occasionally spits back through the carburetors in a snort of contempt when the clutch is not engaged smoothly or the revs are allowed to get too low. It knows it was meant to go fast and it sulks and surges and overheats when it gets balked in heavy traffic. The ride is harsh as hell on any surface at any speed under 75, but smooth as glass at anything over 80.

If the Ferrari was a woman, she'd be about thirty-five with an athletic figure and sad eyes. She'd be a lousy cook, sensational in bed, and utterly unfaithful.

The Pontiac would have an enormous bosom and the pretty-but-empty face of an airline stewardess. She'd be earnest but uninspired in both kitchen and boudoir, and your friends would think you were the luckiest guy in the world.

Our test was a two-part affair. First, we ran them against each other at Bridgehampton with Walt Hansgen driving. Then we used them both as normal family transport—as we do all of our test cars—to evaluate them under the specific conditions for which their designers had conceived them. Both suffered through the worst traffic New York City has to offer, both were driven on long turnpike trips, and we took them well off the beaten track and onto some pretty dismal little lanes as well.

For the track testing, the Firestone people very graciously sent us an engineer and a racing technician and a jazzy little Ford Econoline van jammed full of their superb new Indy-based road racing tires. With this enormous contribution we were able to fit both cars with tires that offered the best-possible compromise, limited only by rim widths and body clearances. Since both cars were

geared for their respective optimum speeds on Bridgehampton's 0.7-mile straight, they were starting as evenly matched as a $4,000 car and a $14,000 car can be.

We drove the Ferrari out from Manhattan on a busy Friday afternoon, loaded with one wife and three children, and had to fight the ghastliest traffic imaginable. The water temperature soared clear off-scale, while the oil temperature inched upward in the same frightening direction. We had been assured that this was no cause for concern, but that didn't keep us from being concerned. Down the road, when traffic began to thin and air started to ram through the grille again, the water cooled to its normal 190°, and the oil levelled off at about 160°.

That night, the Ferrari spent its time screeching up and down the deserted little roads that criss-cross the eastern tip of Long Island as sundry staff members and Firestone people sampled the delights of Italian machinery. Meanwhile, the Royal Pontiac lads—three of them—were pushing through from Michigan in the big red honker, having been unable to leave beautiful downtown Royal Oak until after work.

Next morning the Ferrari got its Pirelli Cinturato tires changed to the new Firestones and after a few more enthusiastic

demonstration rides, went to the Westhampton drag strip. It turned a fastest quarter-mile of 96 mph in 14.61 seconds. It should have gone faster, but the rear suspension simply couldn't handle the massive loads of full-throttle, drag racing starts and the axle bounded up and down furiously, hammering away until we lifted slightly or changed to second gear. On a good run, the car would peak in third at the end of the quarter. It is the fastest Ferrari street machine in our experience.

The Pontiac, conversely, came off the line like a Navy Crusader off a catapult, wheels spinning, rear end down, and no axle tramp at all. Even with the standard equipment 3.42 axle ratio, the Pontiac's best quarter-mile was 106 mph in 13.80 seconds—plenty spectacular enough for us, but the cause of some headshaking and excuse-making from the Royal mechanics, who'd wanted us to use a 4.11 ratio and slick tires.

Back at Bridgehampton, everybody bashed around the track in the Ferrari and various other machines, and when the Pontiac was ready to go, Walt Hansgen climbed aboard and went out for a quick warm-up tour, throwing a fan belt in the process. He coasted back into the pits, expressed some amazement that anything so big could go so fast, and waited for a new belt. Three more times he roared off, and three more times he coasted in with the belt dangling under the front end. On two of these occasions the belt took a water hose with it, and the intrepid Hansgen disappeared into the weeds, having spun in his own coolant.

While mechanic Milt Schornak was sorting out the Pontiac's fan belt troubles, Walt took the Ferrari and after a couple of quick laps pronounced it everything one expects a Ferrari to be. For most of the afternoon, the Ferrari just sat around looking bored while the Pontiac got all the attention. Occasionally, some staff member would leap in and go screaming off down the race track, but mostly it just sat and awaited Walt's pleasure.

Milt finally came up with an ingenious fix for the fan belt problem—he removed a heater hose bracket and fashioned a fan belt keeper from it. It worked like a charm, and we were off and running again. (This fan belt business evidently only happens to the hottest 421 and 389 engines

when used with the four-speed transmission, but it's still an annoyance that should have been fixed before the cars ever got into the public's hands. We understand that Pontiac Engineering is fixing it now, and cars sold by the time this article appears should be cured.)

Now the timed tests began. Walt went out in the Pontiac and turned a series of four laps—the fastest a pretty respectable 2:01.33. He then took the Ferrari and repeated the four lap series—this time with a fastest lap of 2:00.85. The Ferrari was less than half-a-second faster on the Bridgehampton circuit than the Pontiac! The Pontiac was faster on the straight, hitting its 5500 rpm red-line top speed of 127 without any trouble and flashing past the start-finish line like that Navy Crusader we talked about. The Ferrari had more trouble reaching its peak in fourth, and was only just touching the limit as Walt flew past his shut-off marker for the first turn. The Ferrari was driven without engaging the electric overdrive, as there was no place on the circuit where it could be used to any advantage.

Walt Hansgen: "The Pontiac—for a street machine—is an excellent car by American standards. It's quite safe and the handling is excellent. This is something we haven't had in American cars for some time and I think the 2+2 is a good approach. I'm

sure that it would handle very well on a wet road under touring conditions, and the limited slip differential—I don't know what make or type it is—is really a good one. The brakes were very good too, but the decorative metal trim on the pedals made heeling-and-toeing difficult. Bridgehampton isn't the sort of course that's very hard on brakes, but these were certainly more than adequate. And it has plenty of performance to get you out of any trouble you might get into. Man, if you ever need power, it's available!"

The American car was very impressive and great fun to watch as it slammed around the course with Hansgen at the helm. He drove the whole track in fourth, except for the 55 mph hairpin, which he took in third. He could actually have spent more time in third and perhaps gone faster, but the morning's fan belt troubles made him reluctant to shift gears any more than necessary. He drove with his right foot on the accelerator and his left on the brake, often cornering hard with the throttle wide open, jabbing the brake simultaneously—sometimes to steady the car, but more often to break the rear end loose and scrub off speed with the resultant slide.

Walt Hansgen: "The Ferrari lapped faster than the Pontiac by a very small margin. I'd say that this was due somewhat to better

handling and a little bit to its brakes. The limited-slip was good, but I wouldn't say it was any better. Of course, it didn't have the work to do that the Pontiac's did. I don't think the Ferrari would be quite as good in the rain as the Pontiac, but that's largely because of the disc brakes—disc brakes are generally pretty poor in the rain, until they're hot. In general road conditions the Pontiac would be quite a bit more comfortable, although its size would bother me. The Ferrari is a perfect size for American driving."

As one might expect, the Ferrari was considerably less spectacular to watch than the Pontiac. It was very quiet and arced around the corners with none of the Pontiac's dramatic slides or smoking wheelspin. Since it was slower on the straights, it obviously made up a lot of time in the corners, which is exactly what you'd expect a $14,000 GT machine to do. It was an object lesson in the old adage that "class will tell."

It occurred to us the next morning that the Ferrari's hood hadn't been opened since we picked it up. We finally opened it after breakfast to replace a blown fuse and while we were at it we checked the oil. It had used less than a quart. Like we said, class will tell. Its only other problems were a broken exhaust-pipe hanger—repaired by the Royal mechanics—and

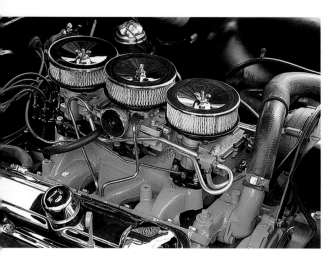

a ferocious juddering in one front brake. This vibration occurred only when the brakes were hot and being used hard, and went away when they'd cooled. Walt Hansgen allowed as how it was not atypical for such things to happen, that they usually stemmed from a slightly warped disc, or foreign matter of some kind trapped in the caliper mechanism.

Off the race track and on the road, where cars like these are most effectively tested, they're both marvelous. The Pontiac is an outstanding example of what can be done with the traditional, much-maligned American sedan. The Ferrari is the finest possible example of what can be done when exciting transportation is the designer's only goal and cost is no object.

Walt Hansgen: "I think that it would be pretty hard to ever accept the Pontiac as a sports car. Sports cars have traditionally been small two-seaters, and the Pontiac—even though it will do practically everything that the Ferrari will do—is just too big. I'd like to have the 'feeling' of the 2+2 in the GTO-size package.

"Probably the best category for the 2+2 is something like the European 'sports sedan' because of its size and the number of people it will carry comfortably. On that basis, the European sedan would be so far overshadowed by the Pontiac that there wouldn't be any contest. I just don't think the Europeans can build a car as cheaply as this, with this kind of performance and—quite frankly—with this kind of handling. Of course, all this would be dependent upon the fact that you're not concerned with how much fuel you're going to use.

"The Ferrari costs about $10,000 more than the Pontiac, but if you have the price in your pocket, it seems to me that you'd have to go a long way to beat the quality you'd get, regardless of the model. I don't think there's another car on the road like it. You get an awful lot of snob appeal. You're not going to see one on every corner and—forgetting that side of it—you're also getting a fine, precise machine that has proven to be very satisfactory and reliable. We just never hear of a Ferrari breaking down."

There are several levels of snob appeal, and both cars have it. The Ferrari is the ultimate snob's car, because it really only impresses the most knowledgeable man-in-the-street and the luxury-oriented jet-set crowd. The Pontiac is very gratifying for the more typical snob, because it stops everybody. Small boys, truck drivers, women, even sports car people and the outer-fringe upper classes cannot resist a second look—and in many cases, a thorough examination and a lot of questions. This might be called "useable status." The status achieved with a Ferrari has very little trading value until you start to move with the international bunch.

Driving the Ferrari is a very refined thrill. For any man interested enough in cars to buy this magazine, it is a moving, emotional experience. Sitting in that seat, holding that lovely Nardi steering wheel at arm's length, looking at all those perfectly round, over-informative instruments, the keen type knows that he's sitting where Phil Hill sat—that he's sharing this moment not with the hoi polloi, but with Alberto Ascari, Peter Collins, Mike Hawthorn, Fon de Portago, and a lot of other giants. He wants it to ride hard. He wants the steering to be too heavy. He wants a stiff clutch. He wants to be uncomfortable until he squirms around and finds exactly the right position. Nothing worth having ever comes easily, and the Ferrari-lover is actually reassured by the machine's non-compliance. He may never drive at those speeds at which it becomes twitchy and light and scalpel-accurate to control, but he knows that it will, and he knows that other cars won't, and that's all he needs.

Philistines and Rambler-drivers will find fault with all this, and perhaps wonder aloud why anybody would want such brute performance in a land where it is absolutely illegal and non-functional, but we don't really care what they think, do we gang?

If the Ferrari never tries to put anybody on, never tries to be any more or any less than it is, the Pontiac is one wild put-on from beginning to end. It is—to all intents and purposes—a perfectly straightforward American two-door sedan that rides a little hard and is a little unstable in a cross wind. That's on one carburetor. When the throttle is suddenly pressed home and all six throats snap open, the effect is a stunning transformation. The noise level rises from near-silence to a hard, flat roar. The pressure on the nape of the neck and the pit of the stomach is almost unbearable. The acceleration is phenomenal—the car is literally launched from a stand-still to a hundred-miles-per-hour faster than you can absorb the sensations—so fast that you don't even look at the instruments, just listen for the peaking point and slam the lever into each new gear as hard and as fast as you can. (This latter sensation could forever silence those rapturous purists who go on and on about the old Mercedes SSK and the sublime effect of opening the throttle and engaging the supercharger. Compared to this fully-appointed American passenger car, the SSK was a mild-mannered pick-up truck.)

It was our pleasure to be rumbling along at about 3000 rpm in second gear with a full load of passengers, when a sudden burst of acceleration was called for. We banged the pedal to the floor, squirted out to pass, and a beautiful, non-enthusiastic girl in the back seat threw her arms over her face and let out a long, piercing scream, which subsided only when the driver's right foot was lifted. Nobody can dislike a car that'll do a thing like that.

Aside from high quality materials, the Ferrari's interior is spartan in the extreme—even to black crackle-finish enamel on all un-upholstered surfaces. Any feeling of luxury comes only from the prior knowledge that this is indeed a $14,000 automobile—there are no easy clues for the philistines. The Pininfarina styling is not particularly elegant either—bearing an unfortunate resemblance to Bertone's efforts for the Iso-Rivolta and being nearly invisible in a

Above: The 421-CID V8 in our Pontiac 2+2.

crowd. The front end is positively dumb with its four superbly bright, but very awkward Marchal headlights. Somehow though, that prancing horse emblem and the discreetly emblazoned name are enough to offset any styling mistakes. As in some people, there's an inner fire that shines through and makes it beautiful in spite of itself.

The Pontiac enjoys no such advantage—it looks like a lot of other Pontiacs and Buicks and Oldsmobiles and it has to work hard with small details to make its point. Fortunately, the point is made. Even to the tyro, the car seems somehow laden with high-speed menace. To the initiated enthusiast, that first impression of high performance could be phony, but a closer examination still bears it out. In spite of all the shiny vinyl and chrome and metal-edged pedals and tinted glass, the Pontiac 2+2 lets you know that it isn't a car to trifle with. And once it's running, all bets are off. The idle is pure race car, and the exhaust note is quite enough to discourage anybody from trying to kick sand in your face at the beach. It makes us think of The Scarlet Pimpernel, a noticeably effeminate Englishman who composed poems by day and was a great duelist and lady's man and Champion Of The Underdog by night—sort of a walking Q-ship. Somebody commented after it had been running for a while that it still didn't look like a race car, but it sure smelled like one.

In the area of sound the two cars are as different as night and day. Cruising in the Pontiac is practically silent, while the Ferrari makes all that threshing machine noise we've come to expect and love from overhead-cam V-12s. At full throttle the Ferrari's sound gets louder and smooths out to a high-pitched moan, while the Pontiac lets out a bellow of rage that drowns out everything inside the car and can be heard for about four blocks outside.

Also on the subject of noise, the Pontiac was fitted with an AM-FM radio with their reverberator system—a pair of speakers wired so that the car is filled with a kind of stereo "echo-chamber" sound. Our staff is equally divided on whether the effect is best suited to the Mersey Beat and a little mobile frugging, or Bach Oratorios and prayerful contemplation. In any case, it is some crazy

noise. It would be great for listening to old radio horror shows like "The Mummers" and "I Love A Mystery."

Where does all this leave us? Here's the way we feel:

The Ferrari 330/GT 2+2—We doubt that any car is worth $14,000, but the Ferrari comes closer than anything else. Besides, when the price gets beyond Eight Grand the point is academic anyway. Poor people can't afford it, and rich people don't care one way or the other. We'll say this though—if the Aston Martin DB-5 is worth $12,850, and the Maserati 3500-GT is worth $12,000, the Ferrari is easily worth any price the Commendatore should choose to ask. Is it worth $10,000 more than the Pontiac 2+2? No. At least not for what it does. But it may be worth all of that and more when you consider how it does it, and what it represents as an automotive tradition and status symbol sine qua non.

The Pontiac 2+2—Statistically, the Pontiac is as good or better than the Ferrari. It can do, and does, all the things the Ferrari does. But it's awfully big. Also, it took a team of three talented mechanics and a lot of hard work under the hood to make it do what the Ferrari did all day with its left hand. But maybe that's not the way to evaluate it. It's not a road racing car—what it's really supposed to do is provide the one-car man with a true multi-purpose road machine. One car that he can buy very reasonably. One car that will give him a combination of performance and road-holding and passenger comfort that he'd normally need three cars and a huge bank account to get.

We had originally planned to use a Pontiac GTO—our first love—as a comparative benchmark for the test of the other two cars, but our only GTO had a deformed piston due to excessive amounts of timing-advance and drag racing enthusiasm. Even so, it lapped Bridgehampton at 2:05—within four-and-a-quarter seconds of the Ferrari! Not bad for an ailing V-7.

For some reason, nobody in General Motors management—and Pontiac is no exception—is very comfortable about small and intermediate-sized cars. They applaud the rousing success of the GTO, but they really figure that a bigger car,

with the same characteristics, would be more palatable to the public. The 2+2 was produced for this reason, but it doesn't quite come off. It lacks the light-footed agility and compact tautness of their GTO. We're confident that a decent GTO would have blown off both the Ferrari and the big Pontiac, but we won't know 'til next year, will we?

Walt Hansgen: "I believe that cars like the Mustang, the Barracuda, and the GTO will open up a whole new group of sports car-type people, and change a lot of people's thinking. When they realize the amount of money they're spending, and the kind of performance they're getting, there'll be a definite move toward cars like this. Then the foreign car people will do a counter-reaction and come up with cars that will compete more favorably in this light.

"The American public will buy American cars, regardless of what else is available. The Pontiac 2+2 is no sports car or GT car, but it really is an excellent automobile. If we could get every American car on the road to handle and perform this well, I think we'd be doing a tremendous job toward having safer American highways. But I sure wish that GTO had been running better."

Above: Typical narrow-stripe muscle-car 14-inchers on our Pontiac.

PONTIAC CATALINA 2+2

Manufacturer: Pontiac Division
General Motors Corp.
Pontiac, Mich.

Price as tested: $4221

ACCELERATION

Zero to	Seconds
30 mph	1.7
40 mph	2.2
50 mph	3.0
60 mph	3.9
70 mph	5.5
80 mph	7.0
90 mph	9.5
100 mph	12.0
Standing ¼-mile	106 mph in 13.8

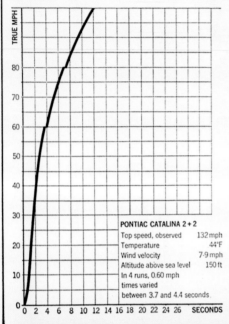

PONTIAC CATALINA 2+2
Top speed, observed   132 mph
Temperature   44°F
Wind velocity   7-9 mph
Altitude above sea level   150 ft
In 4 runs, 0.60 mph
times varied
between 3.7 and 4.4 seconds.

ENGINE

Water-cooled V-8, cast iron block, 5 main bearings
Bore x stroke ...4.09 x 4.00 in, 110 x 101 mm
Displacement ....421 cu in, 6918 cc
Compression ratio ....10.75 to one
Carburetion ...Three twin-throat downdraft
  Rochester
Valve gear ..Pushrod-operated overhead valves
Power (SAE) ....376 bhp @ 5000 rpm
Torque ....461 lbs-ft @ 3600 rpm
Specific power output....0.89 bhp per cu in,
  54.2 bhp per liter
Usable range of engine speeds.750–5700 rpm
Electrical system...12-volt, 66 amp-hr battery,
  a.c. generator
Fuel recommended..................Premium
Mileage......................8–12 mpg
Range on 26.5-gallon tank.....212–318 miles

DRIVE TRAIN

Clutch...........10.4-inch single dry plate
Transmission....4-speed all-synchro gearbox

Gear	Ratio	Over-all	mph/1000 rpm	Max mph
Rev	2.27	7.77	–10.2	58
1st	2.20	7.52	10.5	60
2nd	1.65	5.64	14.0	80
3rd	1.27	4.34	18.2	104
4th	1.00	3.42	23.1	132

Final drive ratio..................3.42 to one

CHASSIS

Perimeter frame with torque boxes, all-steel body.
Wheelbase......................121 in
Track.......................F 63 R 64 in
Length......................214.5 in
Width.........................79.5 in
Height..........................55 in
Ground clearance................6.0 in
Dry weight...................3955 lbs
Curb weight..................4155 lbs
Test weight..................4400 lbs
Weight distribution front/rear...56/44 %
Pounds per bhp (test weight)........11.7
Suspension F Ind., unequal-length wishbones
  and coil springs, stabilizer bar.
  R Rigid axle, four-link control arms
  and coil springs.
Brakes......11-inch drums front and rear,
  329 sq in swept area
Steering....Recirculating ball (power assisted)
Turns, lock to lock......................4.2
Turning circle.......................43 ft
Tires......................8.55–14
Revs per mile......................745

CHECK LIST

ENGINE
Starting.........................Fair
Response......................Excellent
Noise..................Excellent-Poor*
Vibration........................Good

DRIVE TRAIN
Clutch action ....Excellent
Transmission linkage ....Excellent
Synchromesh action ....Excellent
Power-to-ground transmission .....Good

BRAKES
Response ....Good
Pedal pressure ....Good
Fade resistance ....Good
Smoothness ....Good
Directional stability ....Good

STEERING
Response ....Good
Accuracy ....Fair
Feedback ....Fair
Road feel.......................Poor

SUSPENSION
Harshness control ....Poor
Roll stiffness ....Good
Tracking ....Fair
Pitch control ....Fair
Shock damping ....Good

CONTROLS
Location ....Good
Relationship ....Good
Small controls ....Fair

INTERIOR
Visibility ....Good
Instrumentation ....Good
Lighting ....Good
Entry/exit ....Good
Front seating comfort ....Excellent
Front seating room ....Excellent
Rear seating comfort ....Good
Rear seating room ....Good
Storage space ....Fair
Wind noise ....Good
Road noise ....Fair

WEATHER PROTECTION
Heater ....Excellent
Defroster ....Excellent
Ventilation ....Excellent
Weather sealing ....Excellent
Windshield wiper action ....Excellent

QUALITY CONTROL
Materials, exterior ....Good
Materials, interior ....Good
Exterior finish ....Good
Interior finish ....Good
Hardware and trim ....Good

GENERAL
Service accessibility ....Fair
Luggage space ....Excellent
Bumper protection ....Excellent
Exterior lighting ....Good
Resistance to crosswinds ....Fair

*Excellent cruising, noisy at full throttle.

FERRARI 330/GT 2+2

Importer/Distributor: Luigi Chinetti Motors, 780 Eleventh Avenue, New York, N.Y.

Price as tested: $14,200

ACCELERATION

Zero to	Seconds
30 mph	2.5
40 mph	3.4
50 mph	4.7
60 mph	6.3
70 mph	8.1
80 mph	10.6
90 mph	12.8
100 mph	15.5
Standing ¼-mile	97 mph in 14.6

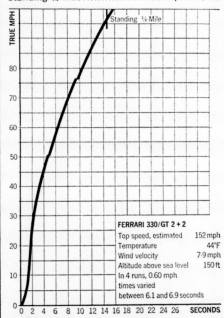

FERRARI 330/GT 2 + 2

Top speed, estimated	152 mph
Temperature	44°F
Wind velocity	7-9 mph
Altitude above sea level	150 ft

In 4 runs, 0.60 mph times varied between 6.1 and 6.9 seconds

ENGINE
Water-cooled V-12, aluminum block, 7 main bearings
Bore x stroke......3.04 x 2.80 in, 77 x 71 mm
Displacement................242 cu in, 3967.4 cc
Compression ratio....................8.8 to one
Carburetion........Three twin-throat downdraft Weber 40 DCL/6
Valve gear......Single overhead camshaft per bank with roller follower rocker arms.
Power (SAE)..............300 bhp @ 6600 rpm
Torque.................415 lbs-ft @ 5000 rpm
Specific power output......1.24 bhp per cu in, 75.2 bhp per liter
Usable range of engine speeds.1000-7000 rpm
Electrical system...12-volt, 72 amp-hr battery, d.c. generator
Fuel recommended....................Premium
Mileage..........................12-16 mpg
Range on 31-gallon tank.......360-500 miles

DRIVE TRAIN
Clutch.............10-inch dry multi-plate
Transmission........4-speed all-synchro plus overdrive

Gear	Ratio	Over-all	mph/1000 rpm	Max mph
Rev	2.60	11.06	—7.1	—50
1st	2.54	10.80	7.3	51
2nd	1.70	7.21	10.9	76
3rd	1.26	5.35	14.8	104
4th	1.00	4.25	18.5	130
4th OD	0.78	3.31	23.8	152

Final drive ratio....................4.25 to one

CHASSIS
Tubular steel frame, all-steel body.
Wheelbase.........................104.2 in
Track....................F 55 R 54.5 in
Length..........................189 in
Width...........................69 in
Height..........................52 in
Ground clearance..................5.0 in
Dry weight.....................3040 lbs
Curb weight....................3180 lbs
Test weight....................3430 lbs
Weight distribution front/rear.......52/48%
Pounds per bhp (test weight).........11.4
Suspension: F Ind., unequal-length wishbones and coil springs, stabilizer bar.
R Rigid axle, lower semi-elliptic leaf springs and upper radius rods, auxiliary vertical coil springs.
Brakes..12-inch Dunlop discs front and rear, 573 sq in swept area
Steering.................ZF worm and wheel
Turns, lock to lock....................3.3
Turning circle.........................41 ft
Tires.........................205-15
Revs per mile...................816

CHECK LIST

ENGINE
Starting	Fair
Response	Excellent
Noise	Fair
Vibration	Fair

DRIVE TRAIN
Clutch action	Excellent
Transmission linkage	Fair
Synchromesh action	Fair
Power-to-ground transmission	Fair

BRAKES
Response	Fair
Pedal pressure	Fair
Fade resistance	Excellent
Smoothness	Fair
Directional stability	Excellent

STEERING
Response	Excellent
Accuracy	Excellent
Feedback	Good
Road feel	Excellent

SUSPENSION
Harshness control	Poor
Roll stiffness	Excellent
Tracking	Excellent
Pitch control	Excellent
Shock damping	Good

CONTROLS
Location	Good
Relationship	Good
Small controls	Excellent

INTERIOR
Visibility	Fair
Instrumentation	Excellent
Lighting	Fair
Entry/exit	Fair
Front seating comfort	Fair
Front seating room	Good
Rear seating comfort	Poor
Rear seating room	Poor
Storage space	Poor
Wind noise	Good
Road noise	Fair

WEATHER PROTECTION
Heater	Fair
Defroster	Fair
Ventilation	Poor
Weather sealing	Good
Windshield wiper action	Fair

QUALITY CONTROL
Materials, exterior	Excellent
Materials, interior	Excellent
Exterior finish	Good
Interior finish	Fair
Hardware and trim	Fair

GENERAL
Service accessibility	Good
Luggage space	Fair
Bumper protection	Fair
Exterior lighting	Excellent
Resistance to crosswinds	Excellent

ENTER THE BIG BORE

Dodge Coronet R/T... with 440-Magnum

Drag fans, here's your car. Coronet R/T packs 440 cubic inches of go! The big-inch, deep-breathing 440-Magnum sports a special 4-barrel carburetor, larger exhaust valves, longer duration cam and low-restriction dual exhaust. Underneath there's a heavy-duty

suspension with sway bar and special shock absorbers for better handling, high-performance nylon cord Red Streak tires, and big 3-inch-wide brakes—front and rear—for surer stops. Front disc brakes are optional. An extra leaf in the right rear spring copes with torque and helps prevent

wheel hop. Coronet R/T comes on strong with sizzling style, too. Body side paint stripes, distinctive hood air-scoop design, bucket front seats, and special R/T insignia put it lengths ahead of the look-alike crowd. Hunting for trophy-winning performance that handles

Mopar was quick to join the fray.

1966
Heating Up

Nineteen sixty-six was a banner year for American Muscle—*Car and Driver* saw to that. And high performance in its most public form, professional racing, was hotter than a stolen girlfriend.

The brand-new Can-Am road-racing series, powered by monster American V-8s, was challenging Formula One to match it for game. Indy-car immortals Mario Andretti, Parnelli Jones and A.J. Foyt were racing sports cars—and road-racing gods Jimmy Clark, Dan Gurney and Graham Hill ran Indianapolis. Most important, the first true drag-racing giants... "Big Daddy" Don Garlits, Don "The Snake" Prudhomme, Tom "The Mongoose" McEwen... were becoming household names.

All of these racing forms had one parameter in common—awesome acceleration. In *Car and Driver* (and down at the A&W), zero-to-60 was king. Every weekend, young Parnelli wannabes drove their NASCAR muscle cars and Trans-Am pony cars to the dragstrip—and burned off all their remaining tire rubber on the way home.

American Muscle was evolving so rapidly, in fact, that even a Hemi might not be enough. A Dodge 426 Hemi is hot, *Car and Driver* agreed... but to 100 mph, maybe a non-Hemi Plymouth 440 is hotter.

Let the night roll on....

ROAD TEST
SHELBY MUSTANG GT 350H
Yipes! Stripes! Let Hertz put you in the GT 350's seat.

Cigarette butts in the ashtray of a rented car? Not when we rented a Shelby Mustang GT 350H from Hertz. No sir we found cigarette butts in the rear brake scoop. What other rent-a-car outfit can make that claim? One of the technical boys at Shelby once hinted that those distinctive scoops on the flanks of the Cobra–ized Mustang are more decorative than functional, that the rear brakes don't need any more fresh air, except when racing. Apparently, nobody realized that Shelby's ingenious crew had created the world's first external cigarette receptacle.

Seriously, the alliance between Shelby and Hertz has eliminated the necessity of owning a sports car. Now the enthusiast can have his cake and eat it too. Rates vary according to locale: in the New York area it was a moderate $17 per day (or $70 per week) and 17 cents per mile. Hertz wouldn't rent us one when there was snow on the ground; said they didn't have snow tires for it. (New York has a law that says you get towed off the roads in a "snow emergency" if you don't have approved snow tires.)

Renting a Shelby Mustang is bound to be more ego-gratifying than a no-go small-bore import or a big, blowsy "sport-type" American sedan. The GT 350 is a real guts sports car, with hair on its chest—all the way down to its navel. Shelby has contracted to supply Hertz with one thousand GT 350s, designated the GT 350H ("H" for Hertz). Most of these special GT 350s will have new high-performance automatic transmission, although a limited number will be available with 4-speed manual transmissions for the do-or-die purists. Said puristi will have to join the Hertz Sports Car Club, the qualification for membership being a demonstration of your ability to operate a manual gearbox. Hertz then gives you a little card, so the next time you want to rent a stick shift Shelby Mustang, you just flash your smile and your HSCC card.

There isn't any significant difference between the GT 350 you can buy and the Hertz version. The standard GT 350H color scheme is black with two broad gold stripes—a sensational, crowd-stopping, combination. Other color schemes are available, including the regular GT 350's white with two broad blue stripes. A trio of narrower stripes along the rocker panel are interrupted by a "G. T. 350H" nameplate behind each front wheel. All the Hertz cars have the "occasional" rear seats and "mag-type" wheels that are options on the GT 350. Incidentally, the "H" might well stand for "Homologated" if Shelby—or, for that matter, Hertz—wanted to race the car as a Group 2 sedan; the 1000 examples Shelby will produce for Hertz fulfill the FIA's minimum production requirement.

Nor is there any significant difference between this year's Shelby Mustang and last year's, although there is a whale of a difference between Ford's stock $3,500 Mustang and Shelby's version. Standard high-performance, 271-horsepower Mustangs are delivered to the Shelby American factory near Los Angeles International Airport, where they are rebuilt to GT 350 specifications. Wide-base wheels and 130-mph 7.75.15 Goodyear Blue Streaks are fitted, as are trailing arms at the rear, a one-inch anti-sway bar at the front, and Konis all around. The front suspension geometry is altered, the steering speeded up, and a chassis brace is installed across the engine compartment between the upper shock mounts. The front brakes are 11-inch Kelsey-Hayes discs with heavy-duty pads; the rear brakes are 10.3-inch drums (¾-inch wider than stock) with sintered metallic linings. Finned, cast aluminum rocker covers and sump are bolted on, as is a high-riser intake manifold and a big 4-barrel carb with 1.7-inch venturis and center-pivot floats so it won't cut out in turns. This, along with fabricated steel headers and low-restriction mufflers, boosts the horsepower figure by 35, to 306 @

6000 (vs. stock 271 @ 6000), and the torque from 312 lbs-ft. @ 3400 to 329 lbs-ft. @ 4200. Final touches include the rear brake scoops, a new hood with a big air scoop and NASCAR-style hood pins, plexiglass rear quarter windows in place of the regular Mustang fastback's vent panels, a cleaned-up grille with the Mustang emblem offset to the driver's side, and the stripes. There are about a million options for racing the GT 350 in the SCCA's B Production category, many of which were proved in competition by the Cobra 289 and Ford's racing GT 40, both of which also use the basic Fairlane V-8. Last year, in their first season of racing, the GT 350s won several National Championships, including the final play-off at Daytona.

Last year, one staffer characterized one of the first GT 350s as a "brand-new clapped-out race car" and likened it to a World War II fighter plane. For '66 the car has been considerably refined, though it's still a tough, for-men-only machine, requiring strong arms to twist the steering wheel, strong legs to push the pedals, and strong kidneys to survive the ride. The exhaust pipes, which used to end just ahead of the rear wheels (stock-car style, and right under your ear) have been lengthened and rerouted to terminate aft of the rear axle. This change has made the noise level more bearable, and almost solved the problem we mentioned last year of exhaust fumes seeping into the cockpit. The ride seems more supple, though still what the British call "gratifyingly stiff," and the noisy, ratcheting-type, limited-slip racing differential is gone (thank heavens; it used to scuff the inside rear wheel around a turn and then unlock with a crack like a breaking suspension member). A regular, street-type limited-slip is optional, but none are fitted to the Hertz cars that we know of.

Visually, a '66 is distinguished from the '65 by the rear quarter windows and the brake scoops, which weren't on last year's model.

The hood and its scoop look the same as before, but last year it was molded fiberglass, this year stamped steel. Inside, the change is more pronounced. The '65 GT 350s had standard Mustang instrumentation plus a pod atop the dash housing a tach and oil pressure gauge. The steering wheel had a wood rim and considerably less "dish" than the standard wheels, and the horn was operated by a spring-return toggle switch on the fascia. This year, the pseudo–woodrim with phony rivets, and the 5-dial instrument panel of Ford's Mustang "GT" have been adopted. The "GT" instrumentation includes an oil pressure gauge, so the tach now sits alone on top of the dash. The automatic transmission is a new feature, as are the optional rear seats. A carry-over feature is the use of USAF-style, three-inch-wide seat belts with-metal-to-metal buckles and quick release mechanisms, just like the racing cars.

The changes for '66 have made the GT 350 more civilized, and we still think it's a great sports car in the classic tradition, but there are some aspects of Shelby's metamorphosis that we criticize. Prime among them is the car's interior appearance—which, after all, is what the driver spends most of his time looking at. It looks too much like any run-of-the-mill Mustang that half-a-million average Americans are using for utility transportation.

We also found fault with the rear seats and quarter windows. Construction of both was rough-and-ready, and in poor condition after only 5000 miles. The upholstery was beginning to tear, the trim was starting to come loose, and rain leaked around the plexiglass window. The rear seats are none too comfortable, but, surprisingly, better than the last notchback Mustang we drove. But it's sports car, not a bloody bus, and besides, few of our complaints would bother the man who only rented the car.

The staff was most impressed with the looks of the GT 350H. It makes any stock Mustang look sick, particularly with those oversize tires and stylized wheels. We were also favorably impressed with the overall performance and general roadability of the car. The engine is lively and responsive, and does a much better job of getting its power to the ground than any of the six "Super Cars" we tested in the March issue.

The automatic transmission felt a bit like the one used in the Ford Fairlane GT/A of our "Super Car" test, but better on part-throttle acceleration. Shelby American modifies this transmission to shift at 5500 rpm at full throttle, although the driver can hold it in each of the three gears with the shifter. Our shifts were made at 6000 rpm, and the acceleration times compare favorably with those for the 4-speed. Starting without wheelspin, the automatic actually has an edge on the 4-speed up to about 45 mph. Wheelspin can be induced by "pumping up" the converter (using brake and throttle simultaneously), but even then the tires have the situation well in hand—there's no fishtailing or useless clouds of smoke.

Shifts are crisp and clean, probably faster than anybody but a drag racer could achieve with a manual. Fuel economy doesn't seem to suffer much, and it loses only two miles an hour of top speed. Flat-out, the car has a high, hammering note. At highway speeds, the changing pitch of the automatic shift jangled some people's nerves. The idle is lumpy, but in a way that promises good things to come.

Good things do come for the driver of a GT 350. Its cornering ability is a lovely mixture of the beast getting the better of you and you keeping hold of the tiger's tail. The taut suspension, well-controlled geometry, and big tires suffice to keep it on the road at insane speeds, and when it starts to slide, you can wrestle the slide in the direction of your choice. Its steering characteristic is pretty neutral, tending toward understeer. Driven too deep and too fast into a corner, the car can be "saved" by backing off (which scrubs off speed), by giving it part throttle (which squats the tail down for a better bite), or by full throttle (which gets the tail out and tightens up the turning radius). If steering with your right foot gets boring, you can always give the steering wheel a wrench to make the front end perform appropriate maneuvers. Needless

to say, the GT 350 is more fun to drive than anything since the Mini-Cooper S. Maybe more fun than the Mini; at least when you floor the Mustang, it moves.

The level of creature comfort on long trips is amazingly high. There is a screw adjustment for the seat back rake angle which we unbolted to let the seat flop as far backward as it would go. Head-, foot-, and hip-room are good, but the door is a little close to the shoulder. The trunk space would be pitifully inadequate, except that the rear seats fold down to provide a huge luggage platform. Even with the seat up, there's a shelf under the rear window, like the VW's. Vision all around is excellent, as is the heater (it was one of the few cars in recent memory that could warm up its occupants on a sub-zero morning within five minutes of starting), but there was one thing we worried about constantly: the NASCAR style hood pins. The normal latching mechanism is removed, so the pins are the only thing holding the lid down. When some little brat steals the pins as souvenirs, you have to start looking for a 3/8-inch twig. Moral: When driving a GT 350 through treeless country, run over any kid who even looks at your automobile with envy. And for sure, they all will.

Clockwise from top: The Shelby 289-CID small block; slick wheels and racing stripes; dash-mounted tachometer; racing-style seatbelt fasteners.

SHELBY MUSTANG GT 350H

Manufacturer: Shelby American, Inc.
6501 W. Imperial Highway
Los Angeles, Calif.
Price as Tested: $17/day or $70/week, plus 17¢/mile

ACCELERATION

Zero To	Seconds
30 mph	2.1
40 mph	3.1
50 mph	4.9
60 mph	6.6
70 mph	8.9
80 mph	10.8
90 mph	14.2
100 mph	17.9
Standing ¼ mile	93 mph in 15.2

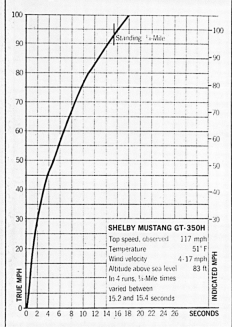

SHELBY MUSTANG GT-350H

Top speed, observed 117 mph
Temperature 51° F
Wind velocity 4-17 mph
Altitude above sea level 83 ft
In 4 runs, ¼-Mile times varied between 15.2 and 15.4 seconds

ENGINE

Water-cooled V-8, cast iron block, 5 main bearings
Bore x stroke..4.00 x 2.87 in, 101.6 x 72.9 mm
Displacement.................289 cu. in, 4727 cc
Compression ratio..................10.5 to one
Carburetion....Single 4-barrel, 1.7-in venturis
Valve gear.Pushrod-operated ohv, solid lifters
Power (SAE)............306 bhp @ 6000 rpm
Torque...............329 lbs-ft @ 4200 rpm
Specific power output.....1.05 bhp per cu. in, 64.4 bhp per liter
Usable range of engine speeds.800-6000 rpm
Electrical system..12-volt, 55 amp-hr battery,
Fuel recommended...........Super premium
Mileage......................6-12 mpg
Range on 16-gallon tank........96-192 miles

DRIVE TRAIN

Transmission..3-speed automatic with torque converter

Gear	Ratio	Overall	mph/1000 rpm	Max mph
Rev	2.80	10.29	−7.0	−42
1st	2.46	9.57	7.9	47
2nd	1.46	5.68	13.4	80
3rd	1.00	3.89	19.5	117

Final drive ratio.................3.89 to one

CHASSIS

Platform steel frame, semi-integral steel body
Wheelbase.......................108.0 in
Track..............F: 57.0, R: 57.0 in
Length.........................181.6 in
Width...........................68.2 in
Height..........................51.2 in
Ground Clearance..................5.3 in
Curb Weight.....................2884 lbs
Test Weight.....................3158 lbs
Weight distribution front/rear........52/48%
Pounds per bhp (test weight).........10.9
Suspension F: Ind., upper wishbone, lower control arm and drag strut, coil springs, anti-sway bar
R: Rigid axle, semi-elliptic leaf springs, trailing arms
Brakes, F: 11.3-in Kelsey-Hayes discs, R: 10 x 3-in drums, 408 sq in swept area
Steering....................Recirculating ball
Turns, lock to lock.....................4.0
Turning circle.......................4.0 ft
Tires and wheels.......7.75 x 15 Goodyear Blue Streaks on 6JK rims

CHECK LIST

ENGINE

Starting	Very Good
Response	Excellent
Noise	Fair
Vibration	Very Good

DRIVE TRAIN

Clutch action	—
Transmission linkage	Good
Synchromesh action	—
Power-to-ground transmission	Very Good

BRAKES

Response	Very Good
Pedal pressure	Poor
Fade resistance	Very Good
Smoothness	Good
Directional stability	Good

STEERING

Response	Good
Accuracy	Good
Feedback	Good
Road feel	Good

SUSPENSION

Harshness control	Fair
Roll stiffness	Very Good
Tracking	Excellent
Pitch control	Very Good
Shock damping	Very Good

CONTROLS

Location	Good
Relationship	Good
Small controls	Good

INTERIOR

Visibility	Good
Instrumentation	Good
Lighting	Good
Entry/exit	Good
Front seating comfort	Very Good
Front seating room	Very Good
Rear seating comfort	Fair
Rear seating room	Poor
Storage space	Very Good
Wind noise	Fair
Road noise	Fair

WEATHER PROTECTION

Heater	Excellent
Defroster	Excellent
Ventilation	Good
Weather sealing	Good
Windshield wiper action	Very Good

QUALITY CONTROL

Materials, exterior	Very Good
Materials, interior	Fair
Exterior finish	Very Good
Interior finish	Fair
Hardware and trim	Fair

GENERAL

Service accessibility	Very Good
Luggage space	Fair
Bumper protection	Fair
Exterior lighting	Very Good
Resistance to crosswinds	Very Good

ROAD TEST

PLYMOUTH 426 HEMI

Under that sedate exterior, 425 ferocious horses.

Well, all we can say to the guys at Plymouth is, "You shoulda been here last month." Had they sent us our Hemi test car in time for the March issue's comparison of the six "Super Cars," they would have taken home all the marbles. Without cheating, without hordes of expensive NASCAR mechanics, without towing or trailing the Plymouth to the test-track, it went faster, rode better, handled better, stopped better, and caused fewer problems than all six of the cars tested last month. What's more, it had been driven from Detroit to New York and used as a jitney in a solid week of bumper-to-bumper traffic during the transit strike before we ever took it to New York International Raceway for testing.

Mechanically, the Plymouth is the best car in this class. However it has a couple of strikes against it, and we should mention these at the outset. The price for the Hemi-426 engine option is a staggering $907.60—our test car listed for about $4,200 and it wasn't loaded, by any means. And at the same time, this very high price tag does not give the purchaser a particularly distinctive or good-looking automobile. Our test car was a bright red Belvedere Satellite sport coupe, and its appearance—both interior and exterior—could only be described as drab. It isn't in the same league with cars like the Pontiac GTO or the Fairlane GT, both of which make a powerful visual statement of high performance.

One more factor that weighs against the Hemi as a GTO-beater—at least in the case of our test car—is bad quality control. The righthand door never closed on the first try. The console glove-box popped open within an hour of the time we picked the car up, kept popping open, and finally had to be taped shut. The steering gearbox was not properly bolted down and its looseness made us think

that the car was virtually unsteerable, until we found the trouble and got it fixed. And finally, we had to put up with an awful lot of wind noise—a constant rumble of turbulence around the windows that sometimes became pretty tiresome.

But as a machine for sitting down in and going fast—and never mind all that jazz about what it looks like or how the windows fit—that's where Chrysler Corporation's Hemi-426 really gets the job done. It offers the best combination of brute performance and tractable street manners we've ever driven. Passengers, even knowledgeable enthusiasts, can ride around in the car and never know what a bomb it is, unless the driver chooses to unleash the might of all those big Omigawd-ferocious horses.

The Hemi-426 option—as fitted on our test car—consists of the following components: 426 cu. in. V-8 engine (425 bhp @ 5000 rpm, 490 lbs/ft of torque @ 400 rpm); heavy-duty torsion bars, rear springs, front stabilizer bar, shock absorbers, prop shaft, ring and pinion, steering gear; 7.75 × 14 Goodyear Bluestreak (police-type) Nylon tires on 5.5-in. rims, 11 × 3-in. front and 11 × 2.5-in. rear drum brakes (the biggest in Detroit) with metallic linings. That's what you get for your $907.60. Then you also have to buy the following mandatory options: heavy-duty Torque-Flite 3-speed automatic ($206.30) or 4-speed manual transmission ($184.20). Front disc brakes are optional . . . and recommended.

We think that the car will be substantially improved by the addition of the disc brakes, but the metallic lined drums on our test car stopped it like it was hooked onto an arresting cable. Their only flaw was their grabbiness when cold, which was at first dramatically accentuated by the vagueness of the loose steering gear. Once we got the steering fixed we found the brakes to be much

more effective and directionally stable—quite capable of a series of 80-0 mph panic stops without serious fade.

But the real story of our love for the Plymouth Hemi-426 is the performance of the engine. In trying to describe it, we keep falling back on words like "sporty" and "zippy,"—words that really aren't too satisfactory as an expert definition. We compare it to another all-time favorite engine, the 327 cu. in. Corvette V-8. Both the Corvette and the Hemi have a free-breathing, effortless ability to rev forever. A quick stab at the throttle pedal—in any old gear—will send the tachometer needle flying around the tach like a teeny little Fiat Abarth, or a Ferrari. It just doesn't feel like a seven-liter engine—except for the fact that you're suddenly doing 120 and you don't know how you got there.

The origins of this engine go far back into the earliest fifties, when Chrysler experimented with all kinds of sophisticated high-performance powerplant designs, ranging as far out as double overhead cam sixes, and finally settled for the tremendously successful 331 cu. in. "Firepower" V-8, which featured hemispherical combustion chambers and power potential that is still being exploited by hot rodders today. It was discontinued in 1958, because its complexity made it expensive to build, but it was so good that you'd be hard put to find one in a junkyard today. Any old Firepower engine that isn't still hauling some worm-eaten Chrysler, Dodge, or DeSoto around, is apt to be hauling some courageous youth off down the drag strip at a ridiculous speed.

It was only natural that Chrysler's 1963 return to stock car racing should revive interest in the still-unbeatable "hemi" design, and, further, that the roaring success of these new Hemis would create a vigorous demand from the performance-hungry public for a

street version. It took a couple of years for the engineers to tame the beast, but the result was well worth the trouble.

The street Hemi is available only in Plymouth's 116-in. wheelbase Belvedere, or the similar-size Dodge Coronet and Charger. It's doubtful if Chrysler will make a nickel from the sale of these engines, even at the high premium they're charging, but there's no question in our mind that the man who wants to have the hottest setup in his neighborhood, will have to opt for the Hemi—and this should have substantial "image" benefits for the rest of the Chrysler line.

The street Hemi comes about as close to being "hand-made" as any production line engine could. All critical parts are carefully chosen for perfect fit and balance, and completed engines run through a much more sophisticated test procedure than anything

short of specially-built racing powerplants.

The street Hemi differs from the racing version in several ways: the racing Hemi has aluminum heads, magnesium "ram" intake manifolding, and fabricated exhaust headers. The street version has cast iron heads and exhaust headers, and a cast aluminum intake manifold that allows two four-barrel carburetors to feed both banks of cylinders, instead of each one feeding a single bank as on the ram-induction racing setup. The engine starts and runs at normal cruising speeds on the two primary barrels of the rear carburetor. As the throttle is opened wider, the two front primaries open up, and finally, at full-throttle, the four secondaries pop open and eight large barrels are dumping fuel and air past the 2¼-in. intake valves! It takes a lot of gas and even more courage to run the Hemi at full throttle for very long, and while

the gas is fed through a fuel-line about as big around as your wrist, you have to supply your own courage. Our overall gas consumption for everything, including commuting, a 700-mile trip from Detroit to New York, and an afternoon at the drag strip, averaged 12.3 mpg—going as high as fourteen on the turnpikes and as low as eight when all those holes were opened up.

The compression ratio has been reduced from 12.5 to 10.25:1 on the street Hemi, and the valve timing is a bit more conservative too. Otherwise, the bottom-end and valve-gear layouts are exactly the same as on the racing engine, as are the dimensions. The cam is located high in the block, between the two banks of cylinders, and staggered pushrods operate the valves via solid lifters and two rocker shafts per bank—the double rocker shafts being essential to obtain the

necessary inclined intake and exhaust valves for the hemispherical combustion chambers.

The engine's power range and ultra-responsive flexibility make it more useful than anyone would dream possible with such high power outputs. Driven normally, one gets the feeling that the engine sort of functions as its own torque converter, and the four-speed transmission is there mainly to provide a choice of axle ratios. We never used all four gears around town—usually starting in first and then changing to third, or starting in second and going to fourth. Our car had the standard 3.54 rear axle ratio (with limited-slip differential) and we found that it would even take off quite smoothly from a standstill in third, but our conscience wouldn't allow us to do too much of that.

One thing is apparent. This car, with this engine, needs a four-speed box like it needs porcelain bud vases in the engine compartment. We didn't drive one equipped with Torque-Flite, but we would unhesitatingly recommend the automatic transmission to anyone who plans to buy a Hemi—even for the drag strip.

The best technique for getting good acceleration times with our test car seemed to be to run the revs up to about 12-1400 rpm and drop the clutch. Then floor it as soon as the car was off the line with both wheels getting a bite. There's still plenty of wheelspin this way, but it's much easier to control with the throttle, and we got very good times. In fact, after we'd gotten the technique worked out, we got better quarter-mile times with 35 lbs of air in the tires (we

had forgotten to lower the pressures) than we had managed earlier with a more typical starting procedure and only 18 psi.

Part of the car's ability to accelerate so well, we're sure, comes from a pretty decent suspension layout—it really does seem to get an awful lot more of the available power onto the ground. And better still, it's a more roadable car at the same time. After the engine, we'd select the shock absorbers as the car's most impressive component. We brought it back from Detroit with five people aboard, a full load of luggage and some antiques we'd purchased, and it never came close to bottoming the suspension, even when we had to negotiate the cratered streets of New York City.

Even on ice and snow, the power comes on so smoothly, and the limited-slip differential works so well, that you can bash around very comfortably at normal driving speeds when other citizens with less spirited steeds are tiptoeing around and still getting all out of shape.

On first climbing in, one finds very little to make him aware of the car's power. The tachometer is mounted on the floor, which is about as useful as wearing your wristwatch on your ankle, and it only reads to 6000 without any red-line at all. T he rest of the instruments are right out of any Plymouth taxicab, and the phony hand-tooled vinyl interior doesn't make it any easier to love. The steering wheel is one of the plastic-wood jobs, which isn't bad, but the spokes have sharp edges and there's no horn ring—you have to let go of the wheel to reach the center horn button.

Your first clue to the car's better side comes when you fire up the engine and the fast-idling rumble of the exhaust makes itself heard. Incidentally, it starts faster, with less fuss, than most cars—certainly better than any other hot machine in our experience. Your second clue comes when you depress the clutch—or attempt to, for there will be many who give up any dream of driving a Hemi right then and there—it's what you could call stiff. But once the clutch is disengaged, you grab the tree-trunk-like gear shift lever, poke it into first,

and you know everything's going to be all right.

An enthusiastic run through the gears without a thorough pre-flight checkout will utterly amaze you, and could conceivably do bad things to the valve gear, since the engine will wind right off the clock without any hesitation or warning, and you'll be much too busy driving to try to find the tachometer—much less read it. The car doesn't bawl and haul like a GTO, but when you shift to fourth and relax enough to seek out the instruments, you'll find that you're going far faster than you might have guessed.

The Hemi, with all the suspension and brake bits that make up the complete package, is an extremely civilized Super Car. So civilized, in fact, that only the most knowledgeable man-in-the-street will ever spot if for what it is. The guy in the driver's seat will have no such problem, however. It may not howl and scream and paw the air when you open the tap but there's never any doubt that you're going somewhere in a terrible hurry.

All things considered, the Plymouth Belvedere with the 426 cu. in. Hemi engine is the best machine of the entire family of hot intermediate-sized American cars. The engine, the suspension, the brakes, and the drive line, are all superb in the way they perform their various functions. The car is very comfortable for the sports car-oriented man to drive, with a very good driving position and first-class controls. But then we have to start finding fault.

If the Plymouth Hemi expects to make it in the GTO league—especially with its very high price tag—it's going to need sprucing up. It needs to look like a hot car, and it needs to have a greater feeling of quality and distinction about its interior and exterior appointments.

In the meantime, we're quite sure that those guys who want the fastest, best-handling sedan Detroit can sell them, will be happily lining up to spend $4,200 on cars identical to the one we tested. It could look like a Land Rover and it'd still be the toughest kid on the block.

Above: Plymouth's big Hemi; 426 cubic inches, 425 brake horsepower.

PLYMOUTH SATELLITE HEMI

Manufacturer: Chrysler-Plymouth Division
Chrysler Motors Corporation
12200 East Jefferson Avenue
Detroit 31, Michigan
Price as Tested: $4182.22 FOB Detroit

ACCELERATION

Zero To	Seconds
40 mph	2.8
50 mph	4.1
60 mph	5.3
70 mph	6.9
80 mph	8.4
90 mph	10.2
100 mph	12.8
110 mph	15.7
Standing ¼ mile	104 mph in 13.8

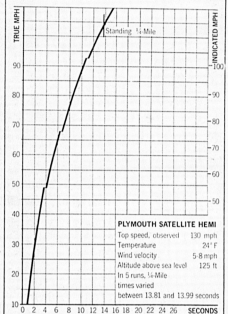

PLYMOUTH SATELLITE HEMI
Top speed, observed .... 130 mph
Temperature .... 24° F
Wind velocity .... 5-8 mph
Altitude above sea level .... 125 ft
In 5 runs, ¼-Mile
times varied
between 13.81 and 13.99 seconds

ENGINE

Water-cooled V-8, cast iron block, 5 main bearings
Bore x stroke ..... 4.25 x 3.75 in, 109 x 96 mm
Displacement .... 426 cu. in, 6983 cc
Compression ratio .... 10.25 to one
Carburetion .... 2 4-bbl, progressive linkage
Valve gear. Pushrod-operated overhead valves, mechanical lifters
Power (SAE) .... 425 bhp @ 5000 rpm
Torque .... 490 lbs-ft @ 4000 rpm
Specific power output .... 99 bhp per cu. in, 61.03 bhp per liter
Usable range of engine speeds .. 800-6000 rpm
Electrical system ... 12-volt, 78 amp-hr battery, 400W alternator
Fuel recommended .... Premium
Mileage .... 9-14 mpg
Range on 19-gallon tank .... 171-266 miles

DRIVE TRAIN

Clutch .... 11-inch single dry plate
Transmission .... 4-speed manual, all-synchromesh

Gear	Ratio	Overall	mph/1000 rpm	Max mph
Rev	2.58	9.13	−8.4	−51
1st	2.66	9.42	8.1	49
2nd	1.91	6.76	11.3	68
3rd	1.39	4.92	15.5	93
4th	1.00	3.54	21.5	130

Final drive ratio .... 3.54 to one

CHASSIS

Wheelbase .... 116.0 in
Track .... F 59.5 R 58.5 in
Length .... 200.5 in
Width .... 75.5 in
Height .... 53.2 in
Ground Clearance .... 5.8 in
Curb Weight .... 3954 lbs
Test Weight .... 4369 lbs
Weight distribution front/rear 55/45%
Pounds per bhp (test weight) 10.3
Suspension F: Ind., unequal-length wishbones, torsion bars, anti-sway bar
R: Beam axle, semi-elliptic leaf springs
Brakes .... 11-in drums front and rear, 380.1 sq in swept area, metallic linings, power assisted
Steering .... Rack and sector, power assisted
Turns, lock to lock 5.4
Turning circle .... 44 ft
Tires and wheels .... 7.75-14 Goodyear Bluestreaks on 5.5J rim

CHECK LIST

ENGINE
Starting .... Excellent
Response .... Very Good
Noise .... Fair
Vibration .... Excellent

DRIVE TRAIN
Clutch action .... Very Good
Transmission linkage .... Very Good
Synchromesh action .... Very Good
Power-to-ground transmission .... Fair

BRAKES
Response .... Fair
Pedal pressure .... Poor
Fade resistance .... Very Good
Smoothness .... Poor
Directional stability .... Fair

STEERING
Response .... Fair
Accuracy .... Fair
Feedback .... Poor
Road Feel .... Poor

SUSPENSION
Harshness control .... Poor
Roll stiffness .... Very Good
Tracking .... Good
Pitch control .... Good
Shock damping .... Fair

CONTROLS
Location .... Very Good
Relationship .... Good
Small controls .... Good

INTERIOR
Visibility .... Excellent
Instrumentation .... Fair
Lighting .... Very Good
Entry/exit .... Very Good
Front seating comfort .... Very Good
Front seating room .... Excellent
Rear seating comfort .... Fair
Rear seating room .... Good
Storage space .... Good
Wind noise .... Poor
Road noise .... Fair

WEATHER PROTECTION
Heater .... Excellent
Defroster .... Excellent
Ventilation .... Very Good
Weather sealing .... Good
Windshield wiper action .... Very Good

QUALITY CONTROL
Materials, exterior .... Fair
Materials, interior .... Fair
Exterior finish .... Good
Interior finish .... Good
Hardware and trim .... Good

GENERAL
Service accessibility .... Fair
Luggage space .... Very Good
Bumper protection .... Very Good
Exterior lighting .... Very Good
Resistance to crosswinds .... Very Good

ROAD TEST

PLYMOUTH GTX

The toughest car on the block this year may not be a Hemi

Pontiac GTO lovers better take their performance image and head for the hills. The Plymouth boys have breathed new life into the old 440 engine to produce a new monster capable of blowing off everything including a street Hemi up to 100 mph. Yes, it's another one of those cars, with a huge engine in a short-wheelbase (116-in.) body. And it has been named, appropriately we think, the GTX.

Chrysler Corporation began a tradition back in 1954 when they produced the first U.S. post-war sports sedan, the Chrysler 300. Among its contemporaries it stood alone as a good-handling, powerful and well-balanced car with adequate brakes and tough good looks. Each year since then, except for a relapse in the early '60s, Chrysler has continued to

produce at least one car of this type. Our test GTX 440 is one of their best to date. It uses the revitalized Super Commando 440 cu. in. V-8 ("New Cars 1967," C/D, Oct. '66) as standard equipment and the famous 426 Hemi is optional. Despite more mass up front it is without a doubt the best-handling big Plymouth yet, although braking ability with the optional discs seems slightly down from last year. The new 440 produces 375 hp at 4600 rpm with 480 lbs./ft. of torque at 3200 rpm. Coupled with Chrysler's excellent TorqueFlite automatic transmission, which was on our test car, it is a joy to drive.

We like the GTX for several reasons, aside from its ability to turn 0-60-mph times consistently at 6.0 seconds. There are a great

many sports sedans with similar capabilities, but the majority fall all over themselves when they arrive at their first twisting road. Not so the GTX. It sticks, and sticks well, under practically all road conditions. The front suspension uses high-rate torsion bars, heavy duty shock absorbers and a 0.94-in. diameter anti-sway bar. This heavy-duty set-up, plus excellent suspension geometry designed to keep the front wheels at right angles to the road surface, keeps the tires in firm contact with the ground at all times. The rear suspension appears, at first glance, to be a paradox. There is nothing to control axle movement other than two semi-elliptic leaf springs and heavy-duty shock absorbers. But the anticipated axle tramp, leaf spring windup and resultant poor adhesion simply doesn't happen. Instead it behaves beautifully. The secret is in the location of the axle brackets on the leaf spring. With most suspensions of this type, the axle is attached at the spring half-way point, just like on grandpa's buggy. On the GTX, and other Chrysler products, the axle is attached approximately one third of the total spring length from the front pivot. This enables the spring to act as a traction rod—at the same time, the pivot is too close to the axle's mass for the spring to flex torsionally. Thus the rear is well located without adding expensive links. In fact it is so well located that driver-induced idiocies such as jumping the car over a hill at 80 mph so it would land sideways and out of shape in a hard right turn produced no ill effects whatsoever. The car simply landed, stabilized itself, and proceeded through the corner.

The only real fault in the GTX's handling is the overlight power steering. We don't enjoy wrestling with brutally stiff steering, but the GTX is at the other extreme, with a feather-soft touch requiring too little effort and giving even less road feel. As we struck

PLYMOUTH GTX

Manufacturer: Chrysler-Plymouth Division
Chrysler Motors Corp.
12200 East Jefferson
Detroit, Michigan

Vehicle type: Front-engine, rear-wheel-drive, 5-passenger sports sedan, all-steel integral body/chassis.

Number of dealers in U.S.: 4000

Price as tested: $N.A.

(Prices for the 1967 models had not been released by the manufacturers at press time. Our unofficial estimate would be ca. $3900.00, as our test car was equipped.)

Options on test car: Disc front brakes, shoulder harnesses, AM radio, power steering, console, TorqueFlite automatic transmission.

ENGINE

Type: water-cooled V-8, cast iron block and heads, 5 main bearings
Bore x stroke..4.32 x 3.75 in, 109.7 x 95.2 mm
Displacement................440 cu in, 7154 cc
Compression ratio................10.1-to-one
Carburetion.................1 x 4-bbl Carter
Valve gear........Pushrod-operated overhead valves, hydraulic lifters
Power (SAE)........375 bhp @ 4600 rpm
Torque (SAE)........480 lbs/ft @ 3200 rpm
Specific power output....0.85 bhp/cu in, 52.4 bhp/liter
Maximum recommended engine speed....................5000 rpm

DRIVE TRAIN

Transmission:............3-speed automatic, plus torque converter
Gearshift position:.........Console-mounted (PRND₁D₂L)

Gear	Ratio	Mph/1000 rpm	Max. test speed
I	2.45	10.2	51 mph (5000 rpm)
II	1.45	16.3	81 mph (5000 rpm)
III	1.00	23.6	118 mph (5000 rpm)
R	2.20	−10.7	N.A.

Max. torque converter ratio........2.00 to one
Final drive ratio....................3.23 to one

DIMENSIONS AND CAPACITIES

Wheelbase............................116.0 in
Track...........F:59.5 in, R:58.5 in
Length.............................200.5 in
Width...............................76.4 in
Height..............................54.0 in
Ground clearance.....................5.9 in
Curb weight......................3869 lbs
Test weight......................4009 lbs
Weight distribution, F/R.........54.8/45.2%
Lbs/bhp (test weight)...............10.7
Battery capacity..........1200 H, 70 amp/hr
Alternator capacity................552 watts
Fuel capacity.....................19.0 gal
Oil capacity......................4.0 qts
Water capacity...................18.0 qts

SUSPENSION

F: Ind., unequal length wishbones, torsion bars, anti-sway bar
R: Rigid axle, semi-elliptic leaf springs

STEERING

Type:.................Recirculating ball
Turns lock-to-lock.......................5.3
Turning circle..........................41 ft

BRAKES

F: Kelsey-Hayes 11.04-in vented discs
R: 10 x 2.5-in drums
Swept area....................387.8 sq in

WHEELS AND TIRES

Wheel size and type.............5.5K x 15-in, pressed steel disc, 5-bolt
Tire make, size and type..B. F Goodrich-7.75-14
Test inflation pressures....F: 28 psi, R: 28 psi
Design load capacity 1270 lbs per tire @24 psi

PERFORMANCE

	Seconds
Zero to 30 mph	2.3
Zero to 40 mph	3.2
Zero to 50 mph	4.4
Zero to 60 mph	6.0
Zero to 70 mph	7.7
Zero to 80 mph	9.7
Zero to 90 mph	12.3
Zero to 100 mph	15.1

Standing ¼-mile..........14.4 sec @ 98 mph
80-0 mph..................318 ft (.68 G)
Fuel mileage.....11–15 mpg on premium fuel
Cruising range....................209–285 mi

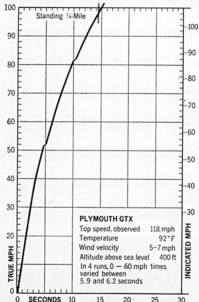

Standing ¼-Mile

PLYMOUTH GTX
Top speed, observed ....118 mph
Temperature ....92°F
Wind velocity ....5–7 mph
Altitude above sea level ..400 ft
In 4 runs, 0 — 60 mph times varied between 5.9 and 6.2 seconds

CHECK LIST

ENGINE
Starting..........................Very Good
Response..........................Very Good
Vibration.............................Good
Noise................................Good

DRIVE TRAIN
Shift linkage....................Very Good
Shift smoothness......................Fair
Transmission noise...............Very Good

STEERING
Effort............................Excellent
Response.............................Good
Road feel............................Poor
Kickback.............................Good

SUSPENSION
Ride comfort.....................Very Good
Roll resistance......................Good
Pitch control....................Very Good
Harshness control....................Good

HANDLING
Directional control..............Very Good
Predictability...................Very Good
Evasive maneuverability..............Fair
Resistance to sidewinds...........Excellent

BRAKES
Pedal pressure....................Excellent
Response.........................Very Good
Fade resistance......................Poor
Directional control..............Very Good

CONTROLS
Wheel position.......................Good
Pedal position.......................Good
Gearshift position...............Very Good
Relationship.........................Good
Small controls...................Very Good

INTERIOR
Ease of entry/exit...............Very Good
Noise level (cruising)................Fair
Front seating comfort............Very Good
Front leg room...................Excellent
Front head room..................Excellent
Front hip/shoulder room..........Excellent
Rear seating comfort.................Fair
Rear leg room........................Fair
Rear head room.......................Good
Rear hip/shoulder room...........Very Good
Instrument comprehensiveness.........Fair
Instrument legibility ....Good

VISION
Forward..........................Excellent
Front quarter....................Excellent
Side.............................Excellent
Rear quarter.....................Very Good
Rear.............................Very Good

WEATHER PROTECTION
Heater/defroster.................Very Good
Ventilation......................Very Good
Weather sealing..................Excellent

CONSTRUCTION QUALITY
Sheet metal......................Very Good
Paint............................Very Good
Chrome...........................Very Good
Upholstery...........................Good
Padding..............................Good
Hardware.!...........................Good

GENERAL
Headlight illumination...........Very Good
Parking and signal lights............Good
Wiper effectiveness..............Very Good
Service accessibility................Good
Trunk space......................Very Good
Interior storage space...............Good
Bumper protection................Very Good

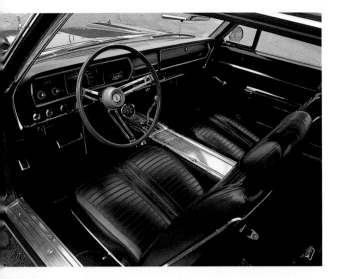

ground after our flying excursions, for example, the steering hardly reacted. With all those wild things happening around us, it was very disconcerting to get no feedback through the wheel.

When we tested the 1966 Plymouth Satellite, equipped with a street Hemi and 4-speed transmission (C/D, April 1966), we were rather upset that the car didn't look like anything special. A Plain-Jane car sometimes fits well into life's order, but when a buyer forks over extra money for a fast car at the top of the line, he wants it to have a distinctive identification. That complaint has been remedied in the GTX, even though the sheet metal is essentially the same for 1967. Our test car stood out in traffic like George Lincoln Rockwell would in Watts. The car's special identity is dramatized by detail chrome strips around the fender lips, twin simulated air scoops on the hood and contrasting racing stripes that run the length of both front and rear decks. A special grille provides instant recognition at the front, and a similar trim panel between the tail lights does the job for the rear. A final touch is provided by a chrome pop-open gas filler on the left rear fender.

Inside, the GTX is uncluttered but mundane with a standard Belvedere dash and a console-mounted tachometer set so far forward and so low that it's visible mainly to rear-seat passengers. The one redeeming feature of the interior design is a pair of very comfortable and attractive thin-shell bucket seats. They allow the occupant to sit high for improved comfort and visibility, and are firm enough to prevent fatigue during extended periods of driving. A new safety feature, which is incorporated into practically all American 2-door cars for 1967, is a locking front seat back to prevent the seat from folding forward during a crash. But it all felt a little loose and uncertain on our test car and there were two or more inches of play before the backrest contacted its stop. There was sharp dissent among the staff on Chrysler's optional shoulder harness (or strap, as they call it) which crosses diagonally over the shoulder to the transmission tunnel. Some felt it was comfortable, while others disputed both its comfort and its safety, since it mounts on

the rear wheel well and rises to the wearer's shoulder. (In an accident this can place a downward pressure on the spine. But there was also a strong conviction that it was better leaving the spine unprotected than the head.)

We have saved our strongest criticism for last; the brakes, despite being discs with rear drums, faded horribly. We conducted our standard 80-0 panic stop series and were unable to record a practical stopping distance on the third run of the set. The first stop came in 318 ft. at .675 gravities deceleration, the second was worse, and on the third try we wondered if it would stop at all. To re-check, we allowed the brakes to cool and repeated the procedure, with similar results. In view of the fairly good times recorded on the first stop in both test series, we would guess that the GTX brakes are not dissipating heat rapidly enough, causing the pads to glaze. The metallic-lining brakes of the 1966 Hemi seemed to work better, and are still available for the GTX. They well may be a better solution to the stopping problem than the current GTX disc option.

Overall, we were impressed with the GTX. The drive train felt really solid and reliable. It had better be—it's covered by the Chrysler 5-year, 50,000-mile warranty. Along with the manual 4-speed transmission, you will receive an additional performance package on the engine, and a heavier drive train. This includes a 9¾-in. ring gear (in place of the standard 8¾-in. unit used on the automatic). The 440 performance engine comes with an aerated crankcase that prevents oil surge away from the pickup, and reduces friction losses due to the crankshaft striking and dragging through the oil as it turns. Other items included are an unsilenced air cleaner, a dual-breaker distributor for improved high-rpm performance, and a viscous fan drive which also saves horsepower by free-wheeling when it isn't needed. Chrysler says this additional equipment is included on the 4-speed manual version primarily to ensure drive-train reliability. At the same time it practically guarantees GTX owners of being the fastest thing at the drag strip. And even if it won't slow down at the end of a run, it'll stick like sin in that high-speed U-turn. GTO owners had better look to their defenses.

Top to bottom: All business in the cockpit; 440 CID in the engine room; distinctive striping on the skin.

SPECIAL TEST REPORT

A *CAR AND DRIVER* STAFF COMPARISON OF AMERICA'S FASTEST SPORTS SEDANS

6 SUPER CARS!

OLDSMOBILE 4-4-2 • CHEVELLE SS 396 • PONTIAC GTO •
SKYLARK GRAN SPORT • FAIRLANE GT/A • COMET CYCLONE GT

Gather together six of the hot intermediate sedans and compare them? One against the other? Actually rank them on the basis of their performance on the race track, the drag strip and street? You guys are out of your minds!

And so they laughed when we sat down to play. The idea to run a bonanza six-way test on the so-called Super Cars was hatched immediately following our wildly successful test between the Ferrari 2+2 and the Pontiac 2+2 that appeared exactly one year ago. Proceeding cautiously, we established a basic format for multi-car comparisons with our evaluation of six luxury cars in July, 1965, and the stage was set for the most elaborate and possibly the most important automotive test that has yet appeared in C/D. The choice of the Super Cars was obvious. First of all, no group of sporting automobiles has made a greater impact on the American scene. The excitement started the moment the first Pontiac GTO appeared in 1963 and has steadily mounted as new cars like the Olds 4-4-2 and Comet Cyclone have arrived to compete for a share of the booming performance market. Secondly, these automobiles are tailored specifically for the American enthusiast and C/D has therefore had a great editorial involvement with them since that famous moment in March, 1963 when we alternately enraged and delighted readers everywhere by implying that the Pontiac GTO was in many ways a better car than the fabled Ferrari GTO. Two years later, we are still receiving mail about that story.

Our original plan of action called for testing eight cars, all to be driven by an expert driver on a drag strip and road course. Acceleration, braking and suspension behavior would be measured there, with the final phase of the test involving extended use of the cars on the street. From the start, it was agreed that the ultimate measure of the test cars would be their usefulness as high-performance, over-the-road vehicles, and not as potential racing machines. The eight cars included the Buick Skylark Gran Sport, Chevelle SS 396, Comet Cyclone GT, Dodge Coronet Hemi, Plymouth Belvedere Hemi, Ford Fairlane GT/A, Oldsmobile 4-4-2 and the granddaddy of the bunch, the Pontiac GTO. This would have given us a group of cars ranging in wheelbase from 115 inches to 117 inches, with engines varying in size between 389 cubic inches and 426 cubic inches. Weights would have averaged somewhere around 3700 lbs., and we would have had a chance to evaluate eight basically similar automobiles. As it turned out, the two Chrysler products were unavailable (for reasons we will recount later), and we ended up with six nearly identical cars. In fact, our test cars were within one inch of having the same wheelbase, within 12 cubic inches engine displacement and within 166 lbs curb weight!

Because it is an excellent road course, with plenty of room to shake out really fast cars, our first choice as a test site was Bridgehampton Race Circuit on the eastern tip of Long Island. We had used the track on previous occasions and knew it was the sort of course that strongly resembles a first-class, two-lane highway, with pronounced elevation changes, sweeping bends and long straightaways. It was an ideal place to evaluate cars of this sort. Because it was near the track and fully equipped with the proper electronic timing gear, we decided to use the Westhampton drag strip for our acceleration runs.

Choosing a driver was more complicated. He had to be of top caliber, with an established reputation in the United States. Ideally, he would not have contractual agreements with any of the Big Three that might prompt anything besides absolute objectivity. Masten Gregory was our man. An American who has been living in Paris for the past few years, Masten had recently ended a run of poor luck with a sparkling performance at Indianapolis and a well-deserved victory at Le Mans. He had an acknowledged ability for handling nasty, overpowered racing cars, and his ability to articulate his reactions behind the wheel had gained him favor as a test driver in Europe. Not only was Gregory completely unconnected with any of the Detroit manufacturers involved in the test, but also, he informed us by letter, he hadn't ever seen, much less driven, any of the cars! This meant that we could expect some highly impartial—and probably surprising—opinions from him.

Firestone had supplied the tires for the Ferrari-Pontiac test program and expressed their willingness to provide rubber and a crew of experts to handle operations at both Bridgehampton and Westhampton. Because this comparison would be based entirely on "streetability" and not on maximum performance, it was imperative that a high-speed passenger car tire and not an outright race tire be used. After consulting with Firestone officials, it was decided that the cars would be shod with the company's 7.75 × 14 "Super Sports 500" tire that offered high cornering power in both wet and dry weather at speeds up to 120 mph.

Realizing that some sort of inspection procedures would be necessary to ensure that stock parts were being used on the cars, we contacted the Hurst-Campbell Corporation in Warminster, Pa., and they came up with an ideal solution. They enlisted the talented group of young men who make up their performance division in Detroit. Headed by Jack Watson, they are probably as wise to hot domestic machinery as any aggregation anywhere. A number of them are former technical officials of the National Hot Rod Association, an organization which has an unequalled record for keeping their thousands of entrants abiding by the rules. The Hurst people agreed to run compression and displacement checks on the six entered cars, to check suspensions, and to generally scrutinize the automobiles to ensure that stock components were being utilized. In addition, Hurst forged aluminum wheels were offered for all of the cars. Because of the excessive strain that would be placed on the stock wheels, we had decided early in the planning that some sort of special wheels would be necessary, and the Hurst products were perfect. Having been designed and tested to be stronger than most other custom wheels offered to the public, the Hurst wheels would not only greatly increase the inherent safety of the test, but would give each of the six automobiles the same amount of unsprung weight with regard to wheels and tires.

Now all we had to do was get the cars. Late last summer we contacted the manufacturers by letter. After outlining the basic format of the test, we added a paragraph stipulating clearly the rules of the test: "We want the cars to be stock. They can be set up for absolute maximum performance using available optional components, but we don't want any NASCAR or NHRA race cars. Furthermore, we don't want any rear axle ratios or tires changed between the quarter-mile tests and the timed laps on the road racing circuit." To make sure that our position was unmistakable, we sent a follow-up letter that said, in part, "We want stock cars. Any optional equipment that can be purchased on the car from the dealer is acceptable. We do not want any non-standard shock absorbers, camshafts, stabilizer bars, carburetors, ignition equipment, exhaust headers or any other special equipment of this sort. We want these to be good examples of the cars our readers can buy, not specially-equipped competition cars." We were to discover later that not everybody was completely intimidated.

Nonetheless, our rules were tacitly accepted by the companies that consented to take part in the test. Only Chrysler Corporation notified us that they were unable to participate, and their action was prompted by several official and unofficial reasons. Publicly, both Dodge and Plymouth withdrew because no production Hemi engines would be available until after the test was completed. However, several highly-placed officials dealing in the Corporation's performance activities privately felt the test would prompt a great flurry of rules-bending and subtle cheating. "Whether you guys like it or not, you're running a race involving a bunch of very serious competitors. Frankly, we don't know how you're going to keep everybody legal," one Chrysler man said. In all, a rather prophetic observation.

Plymouth indicated that no Hemis would be available and said no more—officially. Dodge, which sometimes indicates more enthusiasm for fun and games of this sort than its sister division, tried hard to get a special pre-production vehicle prepared, but had to give up when costs became prohibitive. A convertible was available, but it was agreed that the additional weight and slightly more flexible chassis would place an undue disadvantage on the car during the handling phase of the program. Exit Chrysler Corporation.

Meanwhile, word began to filter into our office about where and how the test cars were being prepared. We heard that former race driver and sports car builder, John Fitch, was doing the final tuning on the Oldsmobile 4-4-2 and had gone to the trouble of renting Bridgehampton for a day to sort the car out. This was initially a bit alarming, but an exchange of correspondence and telephone calls with Fitch satisfied us that he was operating with completely available showroom parts. The Chevrolet people called up several times to double-check a few minor points in the rules and then disappeared to quietly prepare their machine. The Pontiac people notified us that their car would be equipped with the special Royal Bobcat conversion which includes special carburetor jetting, thinner head gaskets, blocked heat risers and advanced ignition timing. This left us somewhat less than ecstatic because the Royal kit is available only through a single Royal Oak, Michigan dealer and can therefore hardly be described as universally available. However, Pontiac was perfectly candid about the alterations which did involve stock parts and could be made by any GTO owner in his own garage, so we decided to let them run. We heard nothing from Buick, other than a letter acknowledging that they would participate and matter-of-factly stating that their car would conform to the rules. The alarming news came from the south. We heard that Holman and Moody, the world-famous stock car and drag racing car builders were "preparing" the Fairlane GT/A and checked with Ford for confirmation. "Yes," said a jaunty voice, "but only because the Fairlane is being built in our Atlanta, Georgia plant and we want Holman and his boys to check it over to be sure all the nuts and bolts are tight before we send it north." This was followed by a throaty chuckle and we knew the fun had started.

A few days later Lincoln-Mercury told us that Bud Moore, the Spartanburg, South Carolina stock car wizard, was setting up their Comet Cyclone GT. Thanks to a rather effective underground, we were aware of the fact that Moore was doing considerably more to the Comet than "tightening nuts and bolts," but all we could do was keep our fingers crossed until the car arrived.

ON THE STRIP

You don't flirt with winter in the north-eastern United States, and we were therefore genuinely concerned that we get the Bridgehampton evaluations completed before eastern Long Island was enveloped in the fog and rain that precedes the snow. We had set aside one day for technical inspections and drag strip runs and two more for the road circuit trials. As it turned out this was not sufficient, but everything got underway on a bright, if somewhat chilly day at Westhampton. The C/D staff arrived at the strip with several cars, including the SS 396 Chevelle that was Chevrolet's entry. We had picked the car up in Detroit a week earlier and, after a 688-mile trip to New York and regular duty in traffic, were absolutely assured of its stock condition. Several others inspired less confidence.

1: Comet Cyclone GT; 2: Chevelle SS 396; 3: Pontiac GTO; 4: Fairlane GT/A; 5: Oldsmobile 4-4-2; 6: Buick Skylark GS.

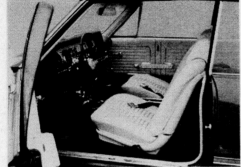  

OLDSMOBILE 4-4-2

Price as tested	$3730.97
Engine displacement (cu. in.)	400
Bore & stroke (in.)	4.00 x 3.97
Carburetion	Single 4-bbl
Compression ratio	10.5 to one
Horsepower @ rpm	350 @ 5000
Torque @ rpm	440 @ 3600
Transmission	4-speed manual
Rear axle ratio	3.55
Wheelbase (in.)	115
Track, F & R (in.)	58–59
Length x width x height (in.)	204.5 x 74.5 x 54.0
Test weight (lbs.)	3490
Suspension	F: Ind., unequal-length wishbones, coil springs, anti-sway bar
	R: Rigid axle and locating links, coil springs, anti-sway bar
Brakes F & R (type & dia.)	9.5-in. drums
Steering	Recirculating ball
¼-mi. acceleration	14.59 sec. @ 100.55 mph
Lap time (Bridgehampton)	2:06.0
Panic stop (80–0 mph)	5.1

CHEVELLE SS 396

Price as tested	$3551.45
Engine displacement (cu. in.)	396
Bore & stroke (in.)	4.09 x 3.76
Carburetion	Single 4-bbl
Compression ratio	10.25 to one
Horsepower @ rpm	360 @ 5200
Torque @ rpm	420 @ 3600
Transmission	4-speed manual
Rear axle ratio	3.55
Wheelbase (in.)	115
Track, F & R (in.)	58–58
Length x width x height (in.)	197 x 75 x 53
Test weight (lbs.)	3605
Suspension	F: Ind., unequal-length wishbones, coil springs, anti-sway bar
	R: Rigid axle and locating links
Brakes F & R (type & dia.)	9.5-in. drums
Steering	Recirculating ball
¼-mi. acceleration	14.66 sec. @ 99.88 mph
Lap time (Bridgehampton)	2:08.1
Panic stop (80–0 mph)	5.2 sec.

PONTIAC GTO

Price as tested	$3621.62
Engine displacement (cu. in.)	389
Bore & stroke (in.)	4.06 x 3.75
Carburetion	Three 2-bbl
Compression ratio	10.75 to one
Horsepower @ rpm	360 @ 5200
Torque @ rpm	424 @ 3600
Transmission	4-speed manual
Rear axle ratio	3.55
Wheelbase (in.)	115
Track, F & R (in.)	58–59
Length x width x height (in.)	206.4 x 74.4 x 53.8
Test weight (lbs.)	3620
Suspension	F: Ind., unequal-length wishbones, coil springs, anti-sway bar
	R: Rigid axle and locating links, coil springs
Brakes F & R (type & dia.)	9.5-in. drums
Steering	Recirculating ball
¼-mi. acceleration	14.05 sec. @ 105.14 mph
Lap time (Bridgehampton)	2:06.8
Panic stop (80–0 mph)	5.5 sec.

The GTO, decked out in an eye-popping coat of "tiger gold" metallic paint, was pulled from Detroit to New York via tow bar behind an identical stand-by machine. A third car in the Pontiac entourage was pulling a trailer full of spare parts. But it was on the way to the strip that we encountered the most startling sight. There it was, parked in front of a motel—a gigantic red transporter bearing South Carolina license plates, with a shiny red Comet Cyclone GT chained down on the ramps that were normally occupied by one of Bud Moore's famous NASCAR Grand National Stock cars. We didn't know whether to laugh or cry.

We arrived at the drag strip to find that the Oldsmobile 4-4-2, the Fairlane GT/A and the Buick Skylark had been driven out in normal

fashion and we immediately commenced the timed runs. Because stock car drag racing technique is highly specialized—and, we might add, not particularly related to what one normally considers either street or circuit driving—Masten Gregory was not involved in the Westhampton tests. He spent the day at Bridgehampton, learning the course (which he had never run before) while others more adept at the rev 'em up, slam-bang business of dragging took his place. It had been agreed beforehand that representatives from each car would drive with times being recorded without regard to who was driving. While the runs were going on, each car was systematically pulled out of action and run through technical inspection by the Hurst group. This

involved, as we mentioned, displacement and compression checks, weighing and a visual examination of the engine, drive-line and suspension components. In the meantime, the Comet had arrived in the company of none other than ol' Bud Moore himself, and he and his crew set about unloading the machine and taking it for a few shake-down cruises on the slightly bumpy Westhampton quarter-mile.

Both the Comet and Fairlane sounded fierce. Their mufflers had been unbaffled to reduce back pressure—though the Holman and Moody mechanic who had driven the GT/A north on one hand, and Moore on the other, both firmly maintained that the exhausts were dead stock. It was apparent from the start that considerably more than routine bolt-tightening

BUICK SKYLARK GRAN SPORT

Price as tested.................$3978.04
Engine displacement (cu. in.).........401
Bore & stroke (in.)............4.18 x 3.64
Carburetion....................Single 4-bbl
Compression ratio..................10.25
Horsepower @ rpm..........340 @ 4600
Torque @ rpm.................445 @ 3200
Transmission........2-speed automatic
Rear axle ratio........................3.36
Wheelbase (in.).......................115
Track, F & R (in.).....................58–59
Length x width x height (in.) 204 x 75 x 54
Test weight (lbs.)....................3550
Suspension...F: Ind., unequal-length
        wishbones, coil springs,
        anti-sway bar
      R: Rigid axle and locating
        links, coil springs,
        anti-sway bar
Brakes F & R (type & dia.)..9.5-in. drums
Steering....................Recirculating ball
¼-mi. acceleration
                14.92 sec. @ 95.13 mph
Lap time (Bridgehampton).........2:08.5
Panic stop (80–0 mph)...........5.0 sec.

FORD FAIRLANE GT/A

Price as tested.................$3059.34
Engine displacement (cu. in.).........390
Bore & stroke (in.)............4.05 x 3.78
Carburetion....................Single 4-bbl
Compression ratio............10.5 to one
Horsepower @ rpm..........335 @ 4600
Torque @ rpm.................427 @ 2800
Transmission.........3-speed automatic
Rear axle ratio........................3.89
Wheelbase (in.).......................116
Track, F & R (in.).....................58–58
Length x width x height (in.) 197 x 74 x 55
Test weight (lbs.)....................3640
Suspension...F: Ind., upper wishbone,
        lower link and drag strut,
        coil springs, anti-sway
        bar
      R: Rigid axle, semi-elliptic
        leaf springs, coil springs
Brakes F & R (type & dia.)..10-in. drums
Steering....................Recirculating ball
¼-mi. acceleration
                14.26 sec. @ 99.00 mph
Lap time (Bridgehampton).........2:08.1
Panic stop (80–0 mph)...........5.6 sec.

MERCURY COMET CYCLONE GT

Price as tested.................$3550.00
Engine displacement (cu. in.).........390
Bore & stroke (in.)............4.05 x 3.78
Carburetion....................Single 4-bbl
Compression ratio............10.5 to one
Horsepower @ rpm..........335 @ 4600
Torque @ rpm.................427 @ 2800
Transmission............4-speed manual
Rear axle ratio........................4.11
Wheelbase (in.).......................116
Track, F & R (in.).....................58–58
Length x width x height (in.)
                203 x 73.8 x 54.3
Test weight (lbs.)....................3474
Suspension...F: Ind., unequal-length
        wishbones, coil spring,
        anti-sway bar
      R: Rigid, semi-elliptic leaf
        springs, coil springs
Brakes F & R (type & dia.)..10-in. drums
Steering....................Recirculating ball
¼-mi. acceleration
                13.98 @ 103.8 mph
Lap time (Bridgehampton).........2:05.8
Panic stop (80–0 mph)..............N.A.

had been done to these automobiles. For openers, they sat approximately 1½ inches lower than showroom versions which we had examined prior to the test—due primarily to some clever work with the spacers that separate the rear leaf springs from the axle housing. It appeared that both machines had also received considerable attention to their front and rear shock absorbers and springs, though Holman-Moody and Moore are both such acknowledged experts in the area of "super-tuning" stock cars that challenging them on specific points was absurd.

Meanwhile, the Chevelle and the Oldsmobile were showing signs of being under-prepared. Several of the Hurst crew made runs with each car and returned to complain about the

way they ran. A check of the works indicated that the Chevelle needed its valves adjusted and the Oldsmobile had a spark plug lead that needed replacement. At the same time the two engineers who had brought the Skylark Gran Sport were standing around looking a bit baffled by the entire drag strip procedure so both the C/D and Hurst staffers pitched in to make sure the Buick got a representative number of runs.

Within an hour of running, the pattern of the test became apparent; we had three stock cars—the Chevelle, the Oldsmobile and the Skylark—and three others—the GTO, the Comet and Fairlane—that were armed to the teeth. In the case of the Royal Bobcat GTO, we at least knew what we were dealing with,

but with the Comet and the Fairlane, only the men with access to the inner precincts of the Holman and Moody and Moore shops could tell for sure how far the rules had been stretched.

The Comet bordered on the ludicrous. It came off the line like a Super Stock, surging up on its haunches under power exactly like a specially modified NHRA stocker. Its engine was an ostensibly stock 390 cubic inch Ford—the same prosaic old workhorse that has loyally powered the Thunderbird for so many seasons. Anyone who knows engines will tell you there isn't a 390 built that will turn more than 5300-5500 rpm in stock form, but the ones in our Comet and Fairlane would turn an effortless 6500 rpm.

How was this done? The expertise with

which men like Messrs. Holman and Moore tune engines is both unparalleled and undetectable, but it should be noted for the record that the valve train of the racing Ford 427 can be installed on the 390 block with relatively little effort.

After each run the Comet had its gas tank topped up in order to keep a maximum amount of weight—crucial in dragging—over the rear wheels. Not that this was in any way illegal, but it does contrast significantly with the low-key, almost casual approach being taken by several of the other entrants. We made over 200 runs during the day at Westhampton, with the Comet recording the fastest time: 13.98 seconds at 103.80 mph. This stands as some sort of unofficial world's record for a "stock" Comet Cyclone GT. (A competition magazine which specializes in drag coverage ran a previous test on a Cyclone, using a champion drag racing driver on what is known as a "high traction" drag strip. Poor fellow, he was only able to run 14.40 seconds at 99 mph using special drag racing slicks! But then he could only wind his engine to 5200 rpm.)

The GTO sounded almost as fierce as the Fairlane and the Comet while it turned the second-fastest E.T. of the day. Much of the noise was traceable to the blocked heat risers, which caused a deep resonance in the exhaust, and the optional cold air box which amplified the sound of air being sucked into the carburetors. The car turned the fastest trap time, at 105.14 mph, while clocking an E.T. of 14.05 seconds.

The GT/A, operating with Ford's new automatic gearbox, was third fastest, with a time of 14.26 seconds at 99.00 mph. The H-M representative admitted that the pump pressure in the transmission had been increased to permit faster, more positive shifts, and this, coupled with the high-revving engine and the doctored suspension helped the times considerably. Unlike the Comet, which seemed to have a kind of compromise suspension setup to make it handle on both the road course and the drag strip, the Fairlane appeared to be over-balanced toward excellence in the quarter-mile. The front shocks seemed inordinately soft, and heavy applications of throttle at the starting line would cause the nose to rear up,

dragster fashion, prompting a weight transfer to the rear for improved traction. The only other quarter-mile acceleration times that we have ever seen published on a GT/A Fairlane were 16.5 seconds at 82 mph.

Though they were less than a second slower than the Comet's top time, the Chevelle, the 4-4-2 and the Buick were out of the action at Westhampton. After some rather vigorous driving by the Hurst crew, the 4-4-2 was finally clocked at 14.59 seconds at 100.55 mph, but there wasn't a prayer of making it run any quicker in its present shape. The Chevelle ran a best time of 14.66 seconds at 99.88 mph while the Buick surprised a few people by cranking off a 14.92 run at 95.3 mph. This was better than a number of those present expected from the Gran Sport, considering its relatively unprepared condition and its two-speed automatic transmission. While the Fairlane's 3-speed automatic was a truly high-performance option, the unit employed on the Buick was unsuited for high-performance driving on any kind of race track.

During the planning stages of the test, we were approached by the people who operate the Brockway truck company in upstate New York with a proposal that we test one of their high-performance diesel tractors along with the six automobiles. The object of this effort would be to blunt some of the general criticism that trucks are sluggish, oversized traffic bottlenecks. Though we assured them we wouldn't be able to give them equal time or billing with the cars in question, it sounded like a unique opportunity to learn what sort of developments were taking place in the trucking industry and we welcomed them to come along. Operating in co-operation with the Goodyear truck tire division, Brockway announced that they were bringing a Model 359T lightweight tractor powered by a super-charged Detroit Diesel engine. Their driver would be Dutch Hoag, an outstanding veteran of modified stock car racing in the east and an expert operator of big trucks. They arrived at the strip, complete with a trailer loaded with enough weight to give the rig a total burden of 45,000 lbs. Hoag used the 15-speed transmission in a way that would bring tears to your eyes, slamming shifts home through

the non-synchro gears with lightning speed, and he finally got the gigantic unit to rumble through the quarter-mile in under 30 seconds. In all, an impressive time for the monster, though, as in the case of the six cars, the real action was being saved for Bridgehampton.

AROUND BRIDGEHAMPTON

The first day at Bridgehampton was planned as a shakedown for both Gregory and the cars. Masten was anxious to get a fair amount of practice in each of the automobiles before he began the three timed laps that would be run as an official segment of the test. At the same time, the entrants wanted the opportunity for final tuning before trying any really hot laps. The day was uneventful for the most part, except that the Comet, the Fairlane and Chevelle overheated on their initial runs, and Masten expressed dismay over the long throw from second to third gear in the SS 396. This was corrected by the Hurst guys, who shortened the lever travel with a few adjustments. After all, they're in the shifter business, aren't they?

The Comet smoked furiously on deceleration, but Moore and his boys assured us it was only because "we set her up a little loose," but still within the factory specifications, they maintained. Late in the afternoon the Oldsmobile's limited-slip differential failed, but was repaired following an emergency trip to a nearby dealership for spare parts.

The weather did not cooperate and it took us three full days of running at Bridgehampton before we completed the timed laps and the braking tests. It got foggy and then it rained and the wind blew and we sat for hours waiting for the track to dry. One of the first cars to take its three flying laps (officially timed by Heuer watches) was the Comet and it was simultaneously the fastest and the untidiest of the bunch. After turning in the top time of 2:05.8 (81.9 mph) the ever-smoking engine blew up on the back straight-away and spread a trail of oil in the groove. A connecting rod holed the block, putting the car out of the test completely and preventing us from getting any 80-0 mph brake times. The Fairlane barely made its three laps before Gregory brought it in with great clouds of smoke issuing from the exhaust. He reported that the engine was beginning to seize and felt it advisable to stop before it blew up. It did however, manage to limp through the brake tests, which put it one up on the Comet.

Although the Comet was the fastest, the Oldsmobile 4-4-2 impressed Gregory the most and he got it around the 2.35-mile course in 2.06 flat. "It's far and away the best-handling car of the bunch," he reported, and went so far as to say it was faster in the corners on a wet surface than the other five cars were in the dry! The only reason it was not fastest of all was its relatively low power, which Gregory reported was less than any of the six cars except the Buick. Conversely, the GTO had far and away the strongest powerplant, but a generally soft suspension and severe axle hop under braking prevented it from running better than third fastest, at 2:06.8. The Fairlane and the Chevelle both turned the track at 2:08.1, with the GT/A's substantial power-plant offsetting its porpoising suspension and fading brakes. The Chevelle might have lapped more quickly, had it not been for an inadequately-positioned tachometer. His view of the tach obscured by a steering wheel spoke, Gregory reported that he lost speed on several occasions by accidentally pumping up the valve lifters when he lost track of the revs. The Buick was the slowest of the lot at 2:08.5, due primarily to its two-speed automatic transmission, which was out of place on the Bridgehampton circuit. The Brockway truck and Dutch Hoag were tremendous. Carrying various members of the staff on wild laps, Hoag managed to get the 22-ton giant around the track in 3:27.4!—a truly stunning demonstration of driving and truck performance.

Although the Gran Sport was the slowest in both the quarter-mile and road circuit phases, it sparkled in the 80-0 braking tests. Running two consecutive stops to test fade, the car recorded the quickest time, screeching to a halt in 5 seconds flat. The Oldsmobile recorded the next best time, at 5.1 seconds, and the Chevelle

CHECK LIST (Cars rated numerically, with 6 as maximum)	Oldsmobile 4-4-2	Chevelle SS 396	Pontiac GTO	Buick Skylark GS	Fairlane GT/A	Comet Cyclone GT
ENGINE						
Starting	3	5	4	6	2	1
Response	2	4	6	1	3	5
Noise	5	4	2	6	3	1
Smoothness	5	4	1	6	3	2
DRIVE TRAIN						
Clutch action (manual)	6	5	3	—	—	4
Shift smoothness (auto.)	—	—	—	3	1	—
BRAKES						
Response	4	5	1	6	3	2
Pedal pressure	4	5	6	2	3	1
Fade resistance	5	4	2	6	1	3
Smoothness	3	2	1	6	5	4
Directional stability	5	4	1	6	3	2
STEERING						
Response	6	5	3	4	2	1
Accuracy	6	5	4	3	2	1
Feedback	6	5	3	4	2	1
SUSPENSION						
Power-to-ground transmission	6	4	1	5	3	2
Harshness control	5	4	3	6	2	1
Roll stiffness	6	5	2	1	2	3
Tracking	6	2	5	3	1	4
Pitch control	6	5	2	3	1	4
Shock damping	6	4	3	2	1	5
CONTROLS						
Location	3	4	6	1	5	2
Relationship	3	4	6	1	2	5
Small controls	3	5	6	2	1	4
INTERIOR						
Instrumentation	3	5	6	1	2	4
Storage space	6	5	4	3	1	2
Wind noise	3	6	4	5	1	2
Road noise	4	5	3	6	1	2
QUALITY CONTROL						
Materials, exterior	4	2	6	5	3	1
Materials, interior	4	1	6	5	2	3
Exterior finish	3	2	5	6	4	1
Interior finish	3	1	6	5	4	2
Hardware and trim	4	2	5	6	3	1
GENERAL						
Service accessibility	6	5	2	1	4	3
Bumper protection	6	4	5	3	2	1
Exterior lighting	6	4	5	3	2	1
Resistance to crosswinds	5	6	4	3	1	2
Luggage space	6	3	5	4	1	2
COMFORT (2 front, 2 back)						
Steering wheel position	4	6	5	3	2	1
Seat adjustment	4	6	5	3	2	1
Seat design, front	3	6	5	4	2	1
Seat design, rear	3	4	6	5	1	2
TOTAL	181	167	157	155	91	90

stopped in 5.2 seconds. The GTO was a bit unmannerly, but did manage to stop in 5.5 seconds. The only car of the bunch to exhibit fade on its second stop was the Fairlane (while the others improved) and it consumed 5.6 seconds in coming to a complete stop.

The formal segments of the test completed, we then took the cars for intensive testing on the street—that is, the ones that would still run. The Comet was loaded onto its transporter and trundled back to South Carolina for repairs, and the Ford was taken to a New York dealer for a checkup. Both were returned later for us to complete our evaluations. Several days following the Bridgehampton runs the GTO gave up on a Manhattan street, the victim of a broken fuel pump drive. Shortly after that was fixed, the left upper control arm of the rear suspension ruptured and it was returned to the shop a second time. Ironically, it was the three most stock machines, the Chevelle, the Buick and the 4-4-2, that gave the least trouble. All of them operated dutifully for the duration of the test, with only the Oldsmobile showing any signs of late-hour weakness when both the transmission and rear end began growling before it was returned. The other casualty of the test was the Chevelle, which lost its fourth gear synchromesh on the last day at

Bridgehampton.

After nearly two weeks of round-the-clock involvement with the cars, we sat down with masses of notes, including several hours of taped interview with Gregory, and began the difficult task of evaluating and ranking the cars. The results follow.

TEST RESULTS

OLDSMOBILE 4-4-2

When the 4-4-2 was introduced as a 1965 model, our enthusiasm was limited by what we felt was a rather ill-mannered suspension and a generally pallid performance package. One year later, we are forced to change course completely, because the entire C/D staff, as well as Masten Gregory, were in complete agreement that the 4-4-2 was the best machine of the six we tested. Our most positive impression is based on the car's handling, which, as we mentioned, surpassed the competition in every department.

Masten Gregory had this to say: "The Oldsmobile was the only car of the bunch that I genuinely enjoyed driving. If I had gotten more practice time, I'm sure I could have gone fastest in this car. It was the most comfortable

and would definitely be my choice for a transcontinental journey. Though it was too small, the 4-4-2's tach was one of the few that I could read easily, and its placement—on the left side of the dash, just below eye level—was one of the best. It was superior to the other cars in road-holding, so I naturally liked it more. It was more fun to drive at speed. I felt more comfortable in it, and I felt you could do much more with it without getting into trouble. I didn't think it had the strongest engine by a long way. Adequate—but not really what I would call the quickest by any means."

Thanks to a minor relocation of the upper rear control arms on the entire 1966 F-85 line, Oldsmobile has come up with the best-mannered car of the six. It was the only one tested that didn't bother Gregory with rear axle tramp under heavy braking, and its near-neutral handling under all high-speed conditions impressed us immensely.

If we had to register any complaints, they would center on the abrupt, on-off way in which the power comes in. Gregory found it difficult to feed in power in fast bends without going over the detent in the 4-barrel carburetor and bringing in the two additional throats with a bang. Though it is purely subjective, the looks of the 4-4-2 didn't cause much response among the staff. They are purely Oldsmobile, without any attempt to copy any other proven performance image like the GTO, but the car does come off a bit dowdy when compared to some of the flashier shapes of the competition. We found that the Hurst wheels did wonders for the exterior, and we can only try to examine our psyches to determine how much of our negativism can be traced to the Kalifornia Kustom white vinyl interior.

In all, the 4-4-2 is a beautifully balanced automobile. Our test car came to us in absolutely stock condition, and placed fourth in the drags, and second in both the timed laps and braking test. It was strong and exceedingly comfortable and it exhibited some of the most civilized handling we've found in a domestically built car. When we consider that this is only the second year the car has been produced, we can only pause to wonder just how good it will be in another 24 months.

PONTIAC GTO

This is the car that started it all, and in some ways the GTO still has a year's jump on the competition. It is certainly the sportiest looking and feeling car of the six, and it indicates an awareness on the part of its builders about what this market demands. It was the only car to have a truly legible, complete set of instruments, including a dash-mounted tachometer. Its shape, its paint, its flavor, say GO! and on the basis of purely subjective, emotional response, the GTO should win hands down. In addition, its superb, if un-stock, engine was the most powerful (though smallest) of the six cars, but it was its suspension that let it down. Only one of the other cars (the Comet) had more excessive rear axle tramp and we found them both bordering on the uncontrollable. Gregory encountered such massive rear spring windup and resultant axle tramp under heavy braking that he was forced to use both the throttle and brake simultaneously while slowing down.

Gregory's comments on the GTO are as follows: "The GTO had more horsepower than the rest of the cars. It certainly made more engine noise, and this sucking sound from the carburetors tends to give you the impression of power. It felt very strong. The suspension was certainly too soft, which surprised me—I had expected it to be quite firm—but it was so soft that it affected its time. It tends to float and bounce in the corners and the rear axle tramp is awful. In addition, the body seems noisy, with some rattles, and I encountered a bit of brake fade."

In all, the GTO with the Royal Bobcat package simply seems like too much. By that we mean it's hard to start and keep running in the cold; it tends to stall whenever the engine is slowed from high speeds; its idle is much too high—near 1000 rpm, and the gas mileage at steady turn-pike speeds is around 11 mpg. Don't get us wrong, the GTO is maybe the raciest car of them all, with genuine guts, but it seems over-balanced in the engine department. When it was first produced, we tended to forgive some of its handling foibles because of its newness and exciting originality, but now, in the face of sophisticated packages

CHEVELLE SS 396

On the record, our SS 396 wasn't a particularly impressive performer. It finished fifth in the drags, tied for fourth in the timed laps and took third in the brake test. But we must keep in mind that the car was, next to the Buick, the least prepared of the bunch, and it was therefore one of those which we could evaluate with some idea of how it would run fresh off a showroom floor. Two staff members drove the car from Detroit to New York and they still haven't stopped telling people that it was one of the most comfortable trips they ever made. The Chevelle, like the 4-4-2, scored very high with us because of its intrinsic balance. It handled very nicely and therefore was a ball to drive. Its engine, which certainly is one of the most advanced designs in the world, has great, turbine-like smoothness with tremendous power (and probably more potential power than the others by a wide margin) plus great flexibility.

Masten Gregory described the Chevelle this way: "I like it quite a bit as a road car as opposed to going fast around the course. It had a very light, sensitive feeling which I enjoyed. It was certainly not mushy in any respect—it reminded me a bit of a thoroughbred dog. The suspension felt quite good, but not as good as I would have expected. It bottomed more around the course than I felt it should have. None of the cars seemed to have as much horse-power

as their factory ratings, and the Chevelle didn't feel like it had anywhere near its claimed 360. Maybe somewhere between 280 and 300 hp. The Chevelle had the best seating position by far, but it had a six-way power seat and an adjustable wheel. On some of the cars (the GTO, the Comet and the Fairlane) I had to put a block of wood on the accelerator so that I could get the seat back far enough and still reach the pedals, but the Chevelle was almost ideal the way it was. The tachometer was big enough to read, but its position was terrible."

Adding to Masten's complaints, we found an excessive gap in the third and fourth gear ratios. With our test car geared at 3.55:1, third gear was usable only to 80 mph, which was considerably under some of the competition and probably hurt its lap times. Like the Oldsmobile, its appearance did not cause much excitement. Its simple exterior borders on being barren, though we found the Hurst wheels added a much-needed element of flashiness. Gregory locked up the inside rear wheel twice on Bridgehampton's only really tight corner, but could find no major flaws in the running gear of the Chevelle. The SS 396 is not the fastest car or the best handling, but it is possibly the best compromise of them all, especially when its relatively low price is considered. It too is a new car on the market and you can rest assured that its development has just begun. On that basis, we think the Chevelle deserves second spot by a wide margin.

Opposite: 1966 Oldsmobile 4-4-2. Above: 1966 Chevelle SS 396.

HEATING UP **43**

was just driven off the factory floor and to the test. When I first drove it around, the tires were too soft and it felt a bit mushy—but not bad. Later we blew up the tires and though it was still too soft, it was much better. I didn't like the gearbox. I don't think a two-speed automatic is adequate for a car of this type. But it is a well-balanced automobile. Definitely too soft on the suspension, but with stiffer springing it would be a very good car. Despite this, I really got to like the car and I think it might be great for regular driving."

The softness in the suspension was as bad as any we have encountered in some time. The mere presence of one person in the back seat would cause the car to bottom frequently on secondary paved roads, and we are sure that a full load of passengers and luggage would make the situation intolerable. Despite its 401 cubic inches—the largest engine in the test—Gregory and the staff agreed that it felt the least powerful. We all drove the car in the wet for rather lengthy periods of time, and were impressed with its control-lability and roadworthiness. Gregory said that it was the most forgiving of the six, and that is eloquent testimony to the car's suspension geometry. The seating is excellent, though the interior and instrumentation is pure middle-class America, with a liberal allotment of idiot lights and generally uninformative dials. It is too bad Buick doesn't really pay some close attention to the demands of this super-car market, because the Gran Sport has tremendous potential. If they ever decide to go to work, look out.

FAIRLANE GT/A

We might just as well say it right now and get it over with: it was extremely difficult to get a clear picture of the true worth of the Fairlane and the Comet because of their highly-tuned condition. Because both the engines and suspensions bore little or no relationship to what the customer will find on his dealer's floor, we can only disqualify ourselves from making really valid judgements. In the case of the GT/A, it was set up primarily to perform on the drag strip, and therefore its value as a road car practically disappeared.

like the 4-4-2, it needs improvement. Last year, in our 2+2 vs. 2+2 test, the Pontiac tended to shed fan belts; this year we encountered the same problem with the GTO at the drag strip. Pontiac officials assure us this only happens on the Tri-Power carburetor setup when it is coupled with power steering, and add that it is being corrected. But they said that last year. And of course, we had the aforementioned problems with the fuel pump drive and the rear control arm.

BUICK SKYLARK GRAN SPORT

The Skylark makes us wonder just how good it might have been if somebody had really been aware of what our test was going to demand. Sending us a car with the two-speed automatic was an unfortunate error in judgement that prevented us from

really measuring the car's potential. While everybody else was busily filling their tires with approximately 45 psi of air at the recommendation of Firestone and Gregory, the Buick men stubbornly insisted that the hot laps be run with the stock 28 psi pressure. Finally logic prevailed, but this is an indication of the laudable, if slightly naive resolve with which Buick intended to keep their car stock. The Gran Sport is in many ways good in spite of itself. Its springing is soft to the point of absurdity, but this is partly offset by an excellent suspension and chassis. You are given the impression that Buick isn't really attuned to what this performance market is all about and they aren't about to find out.

"I didn't like the car at first," said Gregory, "because I thought it was much too soft, but as I got used to it, I started liking it quite a bit. I think it had less preparation than any of the cars and it was probably the only one that

The front suspension, as we mentioned, was so limber that Gregory found that the car would leap and bound around even on the long and comparatively smooth Bridgehampton main straightaway. Gregory said that he was running through the high-speed, downhill series of bends at the end of the main chute 20 mph slower with the Fairlane than the other cars, and still had to work harder to keep it on the road. As we said, it had great power, and the three-speed automatic transmission, which can be shifted at will, was its only redeeming feature. Unfortunately, even this had been "adjusted" to make faster shifts, so a positive evaluation becomes difficult.

This is what Gregory had to say: "What impressed me most was the three-speed transmission for driving on the street. It was very quick shifting, and it felt like it was set up in different power ranges. The brakes were the least efficient of all the cars, although that may have been because of the linings— I don't think they were metallic. *(Right, the Olds, Chevelle, Buick and GTO had metallic linings.—Ed.)* I was not terribly happy with the suspension or the way the car handled. It seemed to me to be too soft for the power that was involved, and I think it needed a firmer, more level ride than it had. It seemed very comfortable on the road, but not at all comfortable speeding around Bridgehampton. Back to the transmission for a moment: it shifted very quickly, certainly much quicker than I could have shifted it manually. It was the noisiest of the bunch—with an exhaust like a racing car. In all, it has a very sporty feel, but the suspension and brakes need improvement."

Enough said.

COMET CYCLONE GT

The Cyclone was the most difficult to evaluate because it was by far the most modified. As we said, many hours of hard work had gone into making the Comet a truly hot machine, and the result was much closer to a racing car than to a representative showroom model. It was the fastest of the class on both the drag and the road course, as it should have been,

considering its modifications. The Lincoln-Mercury people who accompanied the car got a bit belligerent when we implied that their vehicle stretched the spirit of the rules. They claimed, and rightly so, that every piece was an authorized factory accessory, but forgot our stipulation that they be "generally accessible" to the general public. The Ford Motor Company, being active in racing, has volume upon volume of parts catalogues, with infinite variations in springs and shocks and valves and cams, etc., but they exist almost exclusively for their stock car and drag racing programs. Anybody trying to buy that sort of equipment from his local dealer would only get a blank stare or an indulgent smile for his trouble. Our Cyclone GT test car, sadly, just wasn't in the same league with the others and we therefore cannot take its times seriously. In addition, it blew up before the test was completed.

Masten Gregory's comments on the Comet: "It seemed to have been prepared more for racing and had quite a harsh ride. A completely different ride—much flatter and harsher, but better for racing around Bridgehampton. It had very severe axle tramp under heavy braking. So bad, in fact, that even though it had a four-speed gearbox, I had to drive it all the way around the course in fourth gear. It had a very good engine with a very good power range. It worked from 3500 rpm to 6500 rpm, which was the best power range of all the engines there. And that's the only reason I could go so quickly. It became very difficult if I shifted into third gear approaching the corners, because of this rear axle tramp."

After the blown engine had been replaced and the car returned to us for our road evaluation, we found that the very tight limited-slip differential would ratchet severely on any slow-speed corner. We can only presume that this is not standard for all Comets. Aside from the great clouds of smoke that billowed out of the engine at the race track, the interior constantly smelled of oil. The clutch was stiffer than any we had ever encountered on a production machine. Like the Fairlane, the car sat about 1½ inches lower on its suspension than other Cyclones

that we checked. However, the seats were quite comfortable, and the instrumentation and interior appointments were above average. And we're sure that you can find them in a showroom.

CONCLUSION

The man from Chrysler was right. In a certain sense we did end up sanctioning a racing event and we did encounter some wildly diverse interpretations of our rules. Nevertheless, we are convinced of the validity of the tests, and are inclined to think the results would have been much the same even if all of the entrants had enjoyed virtually the same state of preparation. As a class, we were impressed with the general quality and finish on all of the cars and certainly view them as representative examples of what Detroit can build in the way of high-performance vehicles. They are sensibly sized for our driving conditions and offer a high level of reliability with commensurately great performance. If there were to be any single area of universal complaint, it would be the brakes. Not one of the cars appeared with disc brakes, and we frankly had hoped that some of these cars, weighing no more than 3700 lbs., would be able to stop from 80 mph in under 5 seconds. Additionally, only the Fairlane and the Comet (plus the untested Dodge and Plymouth) offer three-speed automatic transmissions, while the GM intermediates offer only two-speed automatics.

But on the whole we were amazed by the cars and by the fact that we managed to get them all together in the same place at the same time.

With any luck at all, we'll do it again next year.

Pontiac raises its GTO Muscle-Car ante with The Judge.

1967-1968
Taking It Into the Street

It began with a few uppity engineers shoehorning monster motors into dumpy little "compacts." Like annoyed parents, the Detroit boardroom was shocked at the sudden popularity of muscle cars. But the skyrocketing sales of America Muscle made it impossible to ignore.

And as sales boomed, corporate concern softened and mellowed to a smug, told-juh-so grin. One way and another, Motor City would "adjust" to this unexpected, enthusiast-driven revenue stream.

In the styling studio, square edges and dumpy shapes began to melt and flow. American Muscle's sensuous new silhouette was learning to express these cars' exciting appetite for aggression. Very suddenly, high performance was beautiful.

Racing dictated that notchbacks become aerodynamically smoother—or go all the way to a dramatic fastback profile. Muscle Car shapes became more seductive. The logic was inescapable: if tire-smoking muscle was blended with gleaming chrome and handsome contemporary shapes, it couldn't miss. And it didn't.

The buying public, reacting subliminally to racing's unwritten tongue, lined up in the showroom for big V-8s in sleek new aerodynamic shapes. Against all expectation, American Muscle had gone mainstream.

Darling, don't you think a shiny new Olds 4-4-2 or Ford Torino GT 427 would look good in the driveway?

Why, yes, dear, I think it would....

ROAD TEST
DODGE HEMI CHARGER

It looks like the Chrysler Corporation is flat out in the automobile business again.

Last year, we applauded Plymouth for building what we thought was the best looking Detroit car of 1967, the Barracuda. A remarkable feat, considering the Chrysler Corporation's odd, unstable styling history which, since the Airflow, has been marked by committee-styled cars which, aside from lacking integrity of design, have oscillated between being far out to the point of vulgarity and being timid to the point of sterility—a seemingly endless series of overcompensations for each preceding year. With this background, we were pleasantly surprised by the '67 Barracuda, but quite prepared to wait years before Chrysler came up with a worthy successor. We conjured a picture of designers and stylists lying about their studios, spent from their Barracuda effort, and barely able to create so much as a new bumper for 1968.

Imagine, therefore, our surprise—again pleasant—when we saw Dodge's new Charger. Working with Chrysler Corporation's 117-in. wheelbase "B" series body/chassis, the designers that we'd imagined were worn out have not only achieved far more than a face-lift, they have easily surpassed the mark of excellence set less than a year ago.

The only 1968 car which comes close to challenging the new Charger for styling accolades is the new Corvette, which is remarkably similar to the Charger, particularly when viewed from the rear quarter. But, we give the honors to the Charger for several reasons. First, the Corvette, being a smaller car in both seating capacity and wheelbase, has a much easier time attaining the desired sporty image. Second, Dodge stylists have shown that they can create a car in the current idiom with originality, combining just the right amount of tasteful conformity with that novelty and freshness which attracts attention. Originality takes guts in Dodge's position as the smaller division of the number three automaker, but

the Charger's aerodynamic wedge theme is not only distinctly new but it is very like the new breed of wind-tunnel tested sports/racing cars which are just now making their debut in the 1967 Can-Am series. Third, while the Charger is a vast improvement over its predecessor, the 1968 Corvette is anticlimactic after the Mako Shark show cars which preceded it.

Chrysler Corporation, then, is flat-out in the automobile business again. The Marlin-like Charger of the past (really a Coronet with a hastily added fastback roof), and the similarly makeshift Barracuda were grim reminders of the Corporation's close call with financial disaster in the early Sixties. But the belt-tightening policies of Lynn Townsend—Chrysler's chief executive since 1961, and more recently Board Chairman—combined with his intense efforts to improve and increase the Corporation's manufacturing facilities seem to be paying off. The 1967 Barracuda and the new Charger, each with its own distinctive sheet metal now, are evidence of Chrysler's increasing strength and ability to meet both the financial and creative challenge of the specialty car age.

Specialty cars are conceived from a significantly different planning philosophy than that of the bread-and-butter cars which Detroit used to build exclusively. Bread-and-butter cars are built with the primary intention of offending no potential buyer, rendering the cars largely featureless and unexciting. Specialty cars, on the other hand, are built to please specific groups of customers. We like the more positive philosophy behind the specialty car, and the Charger is chock-full of features with obvious appeal for the performance-minded enthusiast.

The aerodynamic appearance of the Charger (it's as aerodynamically slippery as it looks, according to Chrysler's engineers) is accented by a rear spoiler combined with a truncated

rear end for a Kamm effect—a design approach which has become almost mandatory in modern racing cars. The Charger takes on the nose-down appearance common to both NASCAR and NHRA, and the bulging rear fenders should accommodate the racing tires used in both drag and stock car racing with a minimum of rework. The greenhouse, following the sharply curved sideglass, slants steeply towards the center of the car, very reminiscent of Le Mans Ferraris, particularly when viewed from the rear. A tunnel-type backlight is used instead of a pure fastback (a styling feature fast going out of fashion from over-use). The smaller rear window of the tunnel roof also gives much less distortion to rear vision than a steeply slanted fastback window.

Further visual performance identity is achieved by the use of a racing-style gas filler cap mounted high on the left rear quarter, and quasi fog/driving/parking and turn signal lights mounted low in the front bumper. Matte black paint is used extensively in the grille and around the tail lights. Full wheel cut-outs, fat tires on 6-inch rims, and simulated engine compartment exhaust vents in the hood (which also house turn signal indicator lights, like the Mustang GT) and at the leading edge of the doors complete the Charger's complement of visually "in" features.

The interior of the Charger carries the GT theme further, with bucket seats, map pockets in the doors, and a well-padded dash with a full complement of instruments set in a matte black background. The tachometer and speedometer are directly in front of the driver while the smaller engine instruments are to the right of the driver, but angled towards him.

With all this performance image going for the Charger, we just had to order an engine to go with it—and when you're talking a Chrysler product, the performance engine is the Hemi. There just isn't more honest horsepower

available off the showroom floor than you get from this bright orange monster. While there are larger displacement engines to be had (Dodge offers a 440 cu. in. V-8 option for the Charger for less money than the 426 cu. in. Hemi), none of them can be had with two 4-barrel carburetion.

The Hemi, despite its high performance carburetion, comes very close to meeting smog control regulations without any modifications, hence, has had only minor alterations to the carburetor and distributor calibrations to meet the new laws. The carburetors feed the hemispherical combustion chambers through huge ports and 2.25-in. intake valves with thin (.309-in.) stems, all calculated to put as much fuel/air mixture in the Hemi as possible. The exhaust system is as efficient, with 1.94-in. valves, thin stems, and cast headers leading to a 2.5-in. dual exhaust system.

The rest of the Hemi is just as tough, with cross-bolted caps for three of its five main bearings; a specially heat-treated, forged steel crankshaft; big, husky connecting rods; forged domed pistons, solid lifters and heavy duty pushrods; and a dual-breaker distributor—in short, a racing engine. And that's what it was originally designed for.

When Chrysler decided to sell the Hemi as an option, they found it was cheaper to carry over the racing parts into production, in most cases, than to tool up for cheaper, street parts. For all-out competition, about all you need is the high compression pistons (same basic design, but more pop-up), a longer duration camshaft, and a set of tubular headers. For stock car racing, there is a very special "ram-tuned" intake manifold and a giant Holley 4-bbl. carb.

Our "street" Hemi was more than powerful enough for any use an ordinary citizen might

find. Rated conservatively at 425 hp and 490 lbs./ft. of torque, the Hemi propelled the Charger through the quartermile traps at just over 105 mph, covering the distance in 13.5 seconds—not bad for 4346 lbs. test weight and a "cooking" engine. The drag racers buy a 500-lb. lighter 2-door sedan, and do some of the tuning we mentioned above, to go through the traps at close to 130 mph—just in case you had any doubts about our engine being in street tune.

Some of you may have had a Hemi before, and may have experienced some problems with it. particularly in the area of oil consumption. For 1968 the Hemi has undergone some changes to fix this problem and to insure against some others. New valve stem oil seals have cured the oil consumption problem, an oil pan windage tray has permitted the addition of an extra quart of oil to the sump to make sure that the oil pick-up never sucks air, and a fuel vapor separator has been added to the fuel line to prevent vapor lock (which can make hot starts difficult). A slightly longer duration camshaft is also new. Although the peak rating hasn't changed since 1967, the new cam improves the shape of the power curves. We suspect, however, that the camshaft and the windage tray are responsible for the Charger's extra one mph at the end of the quarter-mile, compared to the Plymouth Hemi Satellite we tested in April, 1966.

The Satellite we tested was a 4-speed manual, and we remarked at the time that we'd rather have had an automatic, so we ordered our Charger with one. We were right; the automatic is the plan. Driving through the special high-stall-speed torque convertor which comes with the Hemi, you can either shift manually, winding the Hemi right out to 6500 rpm, or leave it in Drive, where the TorqueFlite shifts for you at about 5500 rpm. If you keep your foot in it that long, the 2-3 shift has you doing well over 90 mph. If you cool it, the automatic lets you drive the Hemi like the 230-hp, 318 cu. in. (standard equipment for the Charger). It would take a fairly sharp mother-in-law to suspect that you had anything but the most docile of powerplants underneath the hood.

We were prepared to not like the brakes on our Charger, as the brakes on Chrysler's "B" body cars have previously fallen short of our standards, but things have changed. We ordered the disc brake option, wanting all the stopping power we could get to go with the Hemi's go power, and found the brakes to be very satisfactory. Directional stability was good, and our stopping distances were right around 274 ft. (.78 G), a perfectly acceptable figure, considering the mass of the car. We did encounter fade once, early in our braking tests, which we attributed to "green fade," a phenomenon that new brake pads go through once before they settle down. Afterwards, we experienced no fade in five successive panic stops from 80 mph.

Handling was dominated by the Charger's inherent understeer characteristics, a function of both the massive Hemi engine in the front of the car and the large front anti-sway bar.

The understeer tendency was strong enough that once the limit of adhesion was reached and the front end began to plow, only instant full throttle in the lower gears would get the rear end out. A gentle increase in throttle would only increase the amount of understeer. By anticipating breakaway, we could coax the Charger into a 4-wheel slide with a flick of the wheel and a simultaneous increase in throttle. This induced power-slide was fairly easy to control, but it took up a lot of the road. Generally, the Goodyear F70-15 tires gave good performance and allowed fairly fast cornering without breaking traction—the only way to go, on the street; other maneuvers we restricted to the test track. The Charger assumes a fair amount of body lean when cornering, despite the giant anti-sway bar, stiff springs, and heavy-duty shock absorbers—all of which come with the Hemi.

The Hemi Charger's ride, while harsh by most standards, will be called appropriately firm by most enthusiasts. There will be those who will argue that a Pontiac GTO or an Olds 4-4-2 handles as well without the attendant harshness. But both of these cars suffer from a certain amount of axle hop under hard braking and acceleration, something we didn't encounter with the Charger. It's all a question of how hard the rubber bushings are, and, in the case of the Charger, how many leaves the rear springs have. We'd rather suffer a harshness than axle hop, if a common solution to both problems can't be found. Much of the harshness we felt resulted from the 30 psi tire pressures that are recommended with the Hemi.

While we are discussing handling, we ought to point out that unless your Hemi Charger is going to be used strictly on the drag strip, power steering is a must, not only for it's ease of operation—you've got to be a weight lifter to park a manual steering Hemi—but also because of the faster steering ratio in the power unit. The manual steering has an overall ratio of 28.8-to-one while the power gear is 18.8-to-one—almost twice as fast.

Our main objections to the Charger were on the inside. The seats are terrible—they just don't do anything right. Our unhappiness concerned not so much the seat cushions

themselves, but the position of the seat in the car and the angle between the seat proper and the seat back. The seat is very low, relative to the steering wheel, and the seat back—not adjustable—seems to be almost perpendicular to the seat cushion, forcing us to sit bolt-upright. The guys who design seats should have to sit in them while they work at their drawing boards.

We also didn't like the shift lever in the optional console we ordered. Not only is it ugly and out of place in the context of the rest of the Charger's interior, but the detent button is directly on top, making for an unnatural motion when shifting manually. Of the levers we've seen, the T-handle with the button on the side, like the Cougar and the Mustang, or the "goal-post" shifter used by Buick and Oldsmobile, where one squeezes the crossbar to release the detent, are both excellent. We'd settle for either in place of the Charger's (which is shared by all Chrysler console shifters).

With the exception of the rear quarters, vision from within the Charger is good, and we aren't prepared to sacrifice the attractive tunnel-roof wings for visibility. We do, however, recommend a right-hand outside mirror to compensate.

We don't care for (and didn't order) optional belt-like stripes around the rear quarters that Dodge is emphasizing this year. Stripes—like fastbacks—are out in any form; matte black anti-glare paint on the hood is in now, and a good design could be worked into the Charger's hood vent sculpturing.

The Chrysler Corporation is opposed to ventless door windows, on the grounds that there really isn't a practical flow-through ventilation system. So the Charger still has vent windows, and we suspect that Chrysler might just be right. Time will tell. We were glad to have them on our Charger, because air-conditioning is not available with the Hemi engine—it just won't fit.

To add frosting to the cake, the new Charger is 165 lbs. lighter than the old one, and while at this writing prices were as unavailable as peace in Vietnam, we suspect the new Charger will be cheaper than the old one. These days, when you get something better for less, snap it up.

DODGE CHARGER

Manufacturer: Dodge Division
Chrysler Corporation
7900 Joseph Campau
Detroit, Michigan

Number of dealers in U.S.: 3128

Vehicle type: Front-engine, rear-wheel-drive, 4-passenger sports sedan with all-steel integral body/chassis

Price as tested: NA
(Prices for the 1968 models had not been released by the manufacturer at press time)

Options on test car: Hemi engine, automatic transmission, power steering, power disc brakes, HD suspension, limited-slip differential, 15-in wheels and tires, sports console, floor-mounted gearshift, AM radio, vinyl roof, rear window de-fogger, special paint

ENGINE

Type: Water-cooled V-8, cast-iron block and heads, 5 main bearings
Bore x stroke . . 4.25 x 3.75 in, 108.2 x 95.2mm
Displacement . . . . 426 cu in, 6981 cc
Compression ratio . . . . 10.25 to one
Carburetion . . . . 2 x 4-bbl Carter
Valve gear . . . . Pushrod-operated overhead valves, mechanical lifters
Power (SAE) . . . . 425 bhp @ 5000 rpm
Torque (SAE) . . . . 490 lbs/ft @ 4000 rpm
Specific power output . . . . 0.99 bhp/cu in, 61.1 bhp/liter
Max. recommended engine speed . . . 6500 rpm

DRIVE TRAIN

Transmission . . . . 3-speed automatic
Max. torque converter ratio . . . . 2.1 to one
Final drive ratio . . . . 3.23 to one

Gear	Ratio	Mph/1000 rpm	Max. test speed
I	2.45	9.7	63 mph (6500 rpm)
II	1.45	16.5	107 mph (6500 rpm)
III	1.00	24.0	139 mph (5800 rpm)

DIMENSIONS AND CAPACITIES

Wheelbase . . . . 117.0 in
Track . . . . F: 59.5 in, R: 59.2 in
Length . . . . 208.0 in
Width . . . . 76.6 in
Height . . . . 53.2 in
Ground clearance . . . . 5.7 in
Curb weight . . . . 4035 lbs
Test weight . . . . 4346 lbs
Weight distribution, F/R 55.5/44.5%
Lbs/bhp (test weight) 10.2
Battery capacity . . . . 12 volts, 78 amp/hr
Alternator capacity . . . . 445 watts
Fuel capacity . . . . 19.0 gal
Oil capacity . . . . 6.0 qts
Water capacity . . . . 18.0 qts

SUSPENSION

F: Ind., unequal-length wishbones, torsion bars, anti-sway bar
R: Rigid axle, semi-elliptic leaf springs

STEERING

Type . . . . . . Power-assisted recirculating ball
Turns lock-to-lock 5.3
Turning circle . . . . 41 ft

BRAKES

F . . . . 11.0-in vented disc
R . . . . 10.0 x 2.5-in cast iron drum
Swept area . . . . 387.8 sq in

WHEELS AND TIRES

Wheel size and type . . . 6.0JK x 15-in, stamped steel wheel, 5-bolt
Tire make, size and type . . . . Goodyear F70-15, 2-ply nylon, tubeless
Test inflation pressures . . F: 30 psi, R: 30 psi
Tire load rating . . . . 1280 lbs per tire @ 24 psi

PERFORMANCE

Zero to	Seconds
30 mph	1.7
40 mph	2.5
50 mph	3.5
60 mph	4.8
70 mph	6.0
80 mph	8.5
90 mph	10.0
100 mph	12.5

Standing ¼-mile . . . . . . 13.5 sec @ 105 mph
80-0 mph panic stop . . . . 274 ft (0.78 G)
Fuel mileage . . . . . 9–12 mpg on premium fuel
Cruising range . . . . 171–228 mi

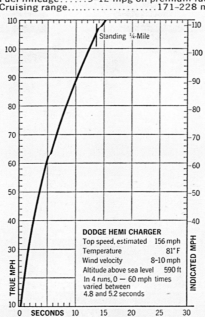

Standing ¼-Mile

DODGE HEMI CHARGER
Top speed, estimated . . . . 156 mph
Temperature . . . . 81°F
Wind velocity . . . . 8-10 mph
Altitude above sea level . . . . . . 590 ft
In 4 runs, 0 — 60 mph times varied between 4.8 and 5.2 seconds

CHECK LIST

ENGINE
Starting . . . . Fair
Response . . . . Very Good
Vibration . . . . Good
Noise . . . . Fair

DRIVE TRAIN
Shift linkage . . . . Poor
Shift smoothness . . . . Good
Drive train noise . . . . Very Good

STEERING
Effort . . . . Excellent
Response . . . . Very Good
Road feel . . . . Poor
Kickback . . . . Excellent

SUSPENSION
Ride comfort . . . . Good
Roll resistance . . . . Very Good
Pitch control . . . . Very Good
Harshness control . . . . Fair

HANDLING
Directional control . . . . Very Good
Predictability . . . . Very Good
Evasive maneuverability . . . . Very Good
Resistance to sidewinds . . . . Very Good

BRAKES
Pedal pressure . . . . Very Good
Response . . . . Good
Fade resistance . . . . Very Good
Directional stability . . . . Good

CONTROLS
Wheel position . . . . Good
Pedal position . . . . Very Good
Gearshift position . . . . Very Good
Relationship . . . . Very Good
Small controls . . . . Very Good

INTERIOR
Ease of entry/exit . . . . Very Good
Noise level (cruising) . . . . Good
Front seating comfort . . . . Poor
Front leg room . . . . Very Good
Front head room . . . . Excellent
Front hip/shoulder room . . . . Very Good
Rear seating comfort . . . . Good
Rear leg room . . . . Good
Rear head room . . . . Very Good
Rear hip/shoulder room . . . . Very Good
Instrument comprehensiveness . . . . Excellent
Instrument legibility . . . . Excellent

VISION
Forward . . . . Very Good
Front quarter . . . . Good
Side . . . . Excellent
Rear quarter . . . . Fair
Rear . . . . Good

WEATHER PROTECTION
Heater/defroster . . . . Excellent
Ventilation . . . . Excellent
Air conditioner . . . . —
Weather sealing . . . . Excellent

CONSTRUCTION QUALITY
Sheet metal . . . . Very Good
Paint . . . . Very Good
Chrome . . . . Very Good
Upholstery . . . . Very Good
Padding . . . . Very Good
Hardware . . . . Very Good

GENERAL
Headlight illumination . . . . Excellent
Parking and signal lights . . . . Excellent
Wiper effectiveness . . . . Excellent
Service accessibility . . . . Fair
Trunk space . . . . Very Good
Interior storage space . . . . Excellent
Bumper protection . . . . Very Good

ROAD TEST
CHEVY II NOVA SS

All docile and innocent… the vestal virgin-image pales slightly when you turn on the engine.

Don't think that GM doesn't know about it. As a matter of fact, that's probably why the 396 is offered in the first place—it's certainly why we tested it.

Inconspicuous to the point of being invisible—that's the Chevy II. It rivals the taxi cab as the omnipresent non-car. You don't even see it in traffic unless you search it out with Chevy II radar eyes. The Chameleon II, sneaking quietly along in the curb lane in a single color, doing a terribly earnest, terribly effective job of fading into the background.

They're seldom washed, Chevy IIs, and invariably have skinny black tires with hub caps like dog feeding dishes. The car that the concept of fleet cars was made for.

If you can isolate a '68 Chevy II, say a parked one that's been washed recently, take a look at it. Surprisingly, it's not too bad. It's got the current swoopy GM lines with kind of a half-hearted fastback and what looks like too little front overhang. Something like a drag race funny car. If the one you're looking at has lots of overhang it's probably a Chevelle. And, in fact, that's the reason for the abrupt increase in Chevy II sales this year. Signing the check for your econo-stone is a whole lot easier if the unpracticed eye of your neighbor will categorize it one rung higher on the Chevrolet status ladder.

As enthusiasts, our interest in standard Chevy II-istry is well off the bottom of the scale. We're willing to pretend it doesn't exist if you will. But also as enthusiasts, the thought of a sleeper makes sly smiles come over our faces and our eyeballs snap both right and left in a pure reflex action to check for the fuzz. The sleeper appeals only to the most secure and sophisticated performance car fancier. There are no admiring glances from onlookers to bolster the ego. The entire driver satisfaction is based on the inward confidence that you can put the hurt on a strutting GTO or Mopar

before they even realize you're a threat. Making your point in one of these street discussions by putting a fender on somebody's Super Car is pure ecstasy, particularly when you do it with an innocuous car. And to our way of thinking, a Chevy II is innocuous beyond Noah Webster's wildest dreams.

That was the plan. Order up a Chevy II with the highest output 396, the 375-hp job, and have a ball. Now, those of you familiar with Chevrolet's engine line-up are well aware that the only similarity between the 375-hp 396 and the 325-hp 396 that was in the Camaro for the Sporty Car test (March) is the displacement. The major engine parts are all different. The 375-hp engine gets the heavy-duty block with 4-bolt main bearing caps, a forged crank with special heat treatment, connecting rods of a stronger alloy and forged, 11.0 to one compression ratio pistons. And that's only part of the story. To make the 50 additional horsepower this engine inherits Chevy's high performance cylinder heads with bigger ports and valves, a high capacity aluminum intake manifold with an 800 cfm Holley 4-bbl., and a mechanical lifter camshaft with more duration and lift.

A very serious engine to stuff into an unsuspecting Chevy II.

As you can imagine, serious Chevy IIs like this have limited appeal—in fact, no appeal at all to the normal Chevy II buyer—so serious-engined Chevy IIs are not what you'd call numerous. When we asked Chevrolet for a test car they rocked back on their heels and explained that there was no way to program one into production so that we could have a new car before our deadline. If we were to have one at all, it would have to come out of their fleet. Searching turned up a cooling system test car in the engineering area which we could have as soon as its test schedule was complete. Fine with us. Detroit's Woodward Avenue is a perfect

place to evaluate a sleeper so we would just stop by the Tech Center and pick up the car.

Our device turned out to be a bright red 2-door coupe with a black vinyl top. "Nova" and "SS" appeared in chrome plated script on its exterior erogenous zones. All docile and innocent we thought. Something a single working girl might own and faithfully wash every Saturday—taking great care about polishing the "Nova" and the "SS."

The vestal virgin-image paled slightly when we started the engine. The 375-hp Chevy IIs are built with a special low restriction dual exhaust system which has larger diameter tail pipes than the lower performance models and no resonators. That's the mechanical part, which, of course, from the outside looks no different. But the sound—there's the difference—a super low pitched rumble, sort of syncopated, that sets serious cars apart

from Cadillacs and 6-cylinder stones. Every sleeper needs that for reassurance.

We weren't on the Motor City streets 10 minutes before we began to suspect that the Chevy II wasn't a sleeper after all. The mid-afternoon traffic included cars full of teen-agers making their way home or to work or wherever they go after school. Whatever they're doing they always keep a close watch on other cars. Every car is a potential adversary. Their whole, competitive, complicated, insecure teen-age lives require them to know every car in the world, and every engine and every combination thereof so nobody risks a run in with the heat for less than an interesting match. Big 427 Vettes will go against Hemi Mopars but ignore 390 Fairlanes completely. Older Pontiac hardtops, the Super Cars of the early '60s, now look for other $500 cars to run with. Several times in the course of making our way across town

we found ourselves first at the light beside a mag-wheeled Super Car containing two or three young males. The reaction was always the same. All eyes instantly checked out the 396 emblem beside the side marker light on the front fender. Then back to the rear wheels to see if we were running slicks. Finally a quick glance at the Chevy II's driver just to see what kind of a guy would drive such a serious car. When the light turned green the procedure was also uniform. They would gently ease off in a fashion indicating "I pass." A Hemi Dodge followed for several miles but turned off because we couldn't catch a red light. Adolescent types in the pre-drivers license age bracket walking along the sidewalk would hear the authoritative exhaust rumble, turn and focus on front fender and shout "396, 396." That kind of recognition never happens in Fords of any kind and almost never in Plymouths or Dodges. It's the exact

same response you get in a Corvette, the most tuned-in car in the U.S. Boy, were we wrong. Bolt a 396 sign on a Chevy II and it's no longer innocuous, it's no sleeper and it's not a non-car. It's a tuned-in machine. Not just with the kids, either. We were stopped by the fuzz in a residential section of Royal Oak after leaving a friend's house about 10 o'clock at night. "You look suspicious," was the explanation. "Don't drive on these streets anymore," was the warning. They apparently have well-defined ideas about muscular Chevy IIs also.

The final test was Ted's Drive-In, the well-known teeny-bopper, car-culture hang-out on North Woodward Avenue. We rumbled down one row and after turning to go up the second the fuzz appeared and announced that if we didn't park immediately we'd have to leave.

It didn't make any difference that we were at least a generation removed from the regular customers. The car classified us. We noticed

and their standard Muncie linkage—which is quite the opposite of flawless. Since all the enthusiasts have been setting up a unified howl to protest the inadequacy of this linkage, Chevy engineers have been tinkering with the problem and with the help of one of Roger Penske's race mechanics have come up with a compromise solution. They've found that slightly mis-adjusting the linkage makes it more difficult to get caught in the reverse cross-bar on a 1-2 shift—our major complaint. On the other hand, it's harder to find reverse when you want it too, but still, no worse than a standard Volkswagen. Our test car had the benefit of this trick adjustment. It's an improvement but not the ultimate solution.

In only one area of the Chevy II's performance could we find fault, and that was braking. It was a dismal failure. Oddly enough, it isn't entirely a fault of the brakes. The leaf spring rear suspension has to share the blame. We're not categorically denouncing leaf springs—with proper development they can be made to do a more than satisfactory job. But the Chevy II needs help. During any braking test the rear axle sets up a violent hop/tramp mode which brings a certain verisimilitude to a panic stop. No matter how sophisticated the Chevy II's disc front/drum rear braking system is, controlled stops in an acceptable distance are simply out of the question. Our best stop was 267 feet at 0.80G and some stops took nearly 300 feet from 80 mph. Chevrolet is not the only manufacturer with this problem and we're sure that they're all aware that it exists. We can only shake our heads in disbelief that any responsible, government-fearing corporation would make a car with this problem available to the public.

Since our normal road course wasn't available for this test, our handling evaluation was done with the prudence required by public road driving. Once again, the leaf spring rear suspension proved to be skitterish on rough surfaces so that the need for help was obvious. However, on smooth surfaces the Chevy II is a genuinely controllable machine with none of the gross understeer found in 396 Camaros. The only suspension change for the 396 is in front spring rate which is increased to 347 pounds-per-inch from the 278 used with the

later that most other cars were allowed to drive through at least two rows before they were stopped. Now there's a clinical observation worthy of study by Chevrolet—not to mention that single working girl with her Saturday compulsion to wash cars.

Obviously, the sleeper we had expected was not only keeping us awake, but everybody else who saw it too. We were driving an easily recognized, big league super stocker and that's only slightly less fun. With that in mind, our scheduled test session at the drag strip was something to look forward to.

Understand that the Chevy II was a street car and not one set up for the strip. The 3.55 ratio rear gears are standard and quite a reasonable street set-up but you just get into fourth gear at the end of the quarter, which would never do for serious racers. Along with that are the hopelessly slippery UniRoyal E70-14 tires which squeal a lot but never seem to get a grip on the asphalt. You wouldn't expect a compact-sized car with an engine the size of Chevrolet's 396 to come anywhere near having acceptable weight distribution, but you're in for a surprise. Even with power steering and power brakes the Chevy II's front

wheels carried only 55.1% of the total car weight—better than almost any performance car we've tested. It's all in vain, though, because with the standard tires you have to get launched so gently to avoid going up in smoke that the quarter mile elapsed times are far less than they should be. We recorded a best run of 14.5 seconds at 101.1 mph. A very impressive terminal speed—within one mph of the 427 Corvette we tested (May) but 0.4 seconds slower in ET, which is almost entirely the result of poor traction. Also interesting, from a performance point of view, is that in a series of back-to-back runs starting with a cool car the terminal speed dropped from 101 to 99 mph in four runs. To combat exhaust emission Chevrolet is now operating their engines at higher coolant temperatures and is using an air pump to promote afterburning in the exhaust manifold, both of which contribute to higher underhood temperatures and an appropriate drop in the density of inlet air as the engine warms up to operating temperature. A fresh air package like that available on the Camaro would offer a significant improvement.

The test car was equipped with Chevrolet's flawless close-ratio 4-speed transmission

Above: One massive 4 bbl atop the 325-hp Chev 396.

ACCELERATION standing ¼ mile, seconds

375 hp CHEVY II	
400 hp CORVETTE	
DODGE HEMI-CHARGER	
325 hp CAMARO	

13 14 15 16 17 18 19 20

BRAKING 80-0 mph panic stop, feet

375 hp CHEVY II	
400 hp CORVETTE	
DODGE HEMI-CHARGER	
325 hp CAMARO	

210 220 230 240 250 260 270 280

FUEL ECONOMY RANGE mpg

375 hp CHEVY II	
400 hp CORVETTE	
DODGE HEMI-CHARGER	
325 hp CAMARO	

6 10 14 18 22 26 30 34

PRICE AS TESTED dollars x 1000

375 hp CHEVY II	
400 hp CORVETTE	
DODGE HEMI-CHARGER	
325 hp CAMARO	

1 2 3 4 5 6 7 8

CHEVY II NOVA SS

Manufacturer: Chevrolet Motor Division
General Motors Corporation
30003 Van Dyke
Warren, Michigan 48090

Vehicle type: Front-engine, rear-wheel-drive, 5-passenger coupe

Price as tested: $3687.95
(Manufacturer's suggested retail price, including all options listed below, Federal excise tax, dealer preparation and delivery charges; does not include state and local taxes, license or freight charges)

Options on test car:
375 hp engine ($500.30), close ratio 4-speed transmission ($184.35), limited-slip differential ($42.50), power assisted disc brakes ($100.10), fast ratio power steering ($84.30), custom interior ($221.00), AM pushbutton radio ($61.10), vinyl roof ($73.75), tinted glass ($30.55).

ENGINE
Type: V-8, water-cooled cast iron block and heads, 5 main bearings
Bore x stroke..4.094 x 3.76 in, 103.9 x 95.5 mm
Displacement...............396 cu in, 6500 cc
Compression ratio................11.0 to one
Carburetion.................1 x 4 bbl Holley
Valve gear.......Pushrod operated overhead valves, mechanical lifters
Power (SAE)..........375 bhp @ 5600 rpm
Torque (SAE)..........415 lbs/ft @ 3600 rpm
Specific power output..........0.95 bhp/cu in, 57.7 bhp/liter

DRIVE TRAIN
Transmission.............4-speed all-synchro
Final drive ratio......3.55 to one, limited slip

Gear	Ratio	Mph/1000 rpm	Max. test speed
I	2.20	8.6	55 mph (6400 rpm)
II	1.64	11.5	73 mph (6400 rpm)
III	1.27	14.9	95 mph (6400 rpm)
IV	1.00	18.9	121 mph (6400 rpm)

DIMENSIONS AND CAPACITIES
Wheelbase............................111.0 in
Track...................F: 59.0 in, R: 58.9 in
Length................................189.4 in
Width..................................72.4 in
Height.................................53.9 in
Ground clearance........................5.8 in
Curb weight..........................3470 lbs
Weight distribution, F/R............55.1/44.9%
Battery capacity..........12 volts, 61 amp/hr
Alternator cap...........444 watts, 37 amps
Fuel capacity...........................18 gal
Oil capacity.............................4 qts
Water capacity.........................23 qts

SUSPENSION
F: Ind., unequal length wishbones, coil springs, anti-sway bar
R: Rigid axle, semi-elliptic leaf springs

STEERING
Type........Recirculating ball, power assisted
Turns lock-to-lock.........................3.1
Turning circle curb to curb............41.5 ft

BRAKES
F:............11.0 in vented disc, power assist
R:....9.5 x 2.00 cast iron drum, power assist

WHEELS AND TIRES
Wheel size....................14 x 5.0-in
Wheel type...........Stamped steel, 5-bolt
Tire make and size.......UniRoyal Tiger Paw E70 x 14
Tire type................Tubeless, 4 PR
Test inflation pressures...F: 30 psi, R: 30 psi
Tire load rating......1190 lbs per tire @ 24 psi

PERFORMANCE
Zero to	Seconds
30 mph	2.2
40 mph	3.2
50 mph	4.3
60 mph	5.9
70 mph	7.5
80 mph	9.7
90 mph	11.7
100 mph	14.3

Standing ¼-mile........14.5 sec @ 101.1 mph
Top speed estimated................121 mph
80-0 mph..................267 ft (0.80 G)
Fuel mileage.......9-11 mpg on premium fuel
Cruising range....................162-198 mi

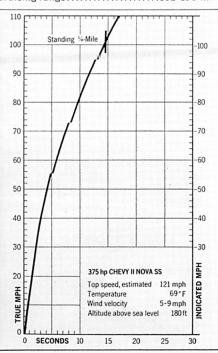

Standing ¼-Mile

375 hp CHEVY II NOVA SS

Top speed, estimated	121 mph
Temperature	69°F
Wind velocity	5-9 mph
Altitude above sea level	180 ft

TRUE MPH

INDICATED MPH

SECONDS 0 5 10 15 20 25 30

327 cube engine. You would expect this change to increase understeer but the result was in no way detrimental. Of course power induced oversteer is a readily available commodity—much like a Corvette. Chevrolet anticipated our handling evaluation by setting a noticeable amount of negative camber in the front suspension. We don't feel this is necessary for good handling in the Chevy II and even suspect that it may have been the cause of the poorer-than-normal directional stability over irregularly surfaced roads.

The optional fast ratio power steering in the test car definitely deserves mention. It provides a very quick ratio—just over three turns lock-to-lock—which would be almost unbearable in a manual steering car and at the same time has superb road feel and response. This power steering is a giant step ahead of the Ford and Chrysler competitors.

Most endearing of the Chevy II's qualities was its amazing ease of operation. Those who have envisaged the 375-hp engine to be an ill-at-ease refugee from the race track are only half right—it goes like a racer but otherwise behaves with prep school manners. It starts readily (although a little reluctantly when hot) and has no more than a pleasantly lumpy idle. The stumble we've grown to expect in big carburetor/manual transmission cars, when opening the throttle for acceleration from low engine speeds, is almost imperceptible and the properly-adjusted mechanical valve lifters are undetectable.

Driving, frequently a task in a high performance car, was nearly effortless. The difficulty with most big engine/manual

transmission cars is the disparity in effort between the clutch and all the rest of the driver controls. Chevrolet is normally the worst offender in this department, not because of clutch effort higher than competition but because the other controls are far lighter. Much to our surprise, all the controls—steering, brakes, shifter, accelerator, and clutch—were commensurate in effort on our test car. The entire credit for this startling bit of coordination goes to the experimental dual plate clutch which the Chevrolet engineers had installed into the test car to get the reaction of an unbiased critic. "Power assisted clutch," is the only suitable description from a driver's point of view. It's generally understood that dual plate clutches have increased capacity and life with a smaller diameter, and at the same time less pedal effort. It's just that Chevrolet is the first manufacturer to get the bugs worked out. Obviously the manufacturing cost is higher but it makes such an improvement in effort that we think it's worth nearly as much as power steering or power brakes. Unfortunately, you can't have it just yet. It's not scheduled for production until the '69 models, and then only with 350 cu. in. 4-bbl. engines and larger.

The Chevy II's instrument panel is a masterpiece in the great Chevrolet tradition. All the instruments; the speedometer, fuel gauge and optional clock, are grouped directly in front of the driver for quick, at-a-glance viewing. Sorry, but if you want to know anything else about what's happening inside your very special 375-hp 396 (made-of-all-very-exotic-pieces), you'll have to wait until one of the warning lights comes on—which simply serves notice that you should speak of your engine in the past tense. Not only is the panel hopelessly incomplete for a high performance car, but the heater controls must be operated by feel alone. They are unlighted and completely obscured by one of the fat steering wheel spokes anyway.

Padding on the instrument panel—free from decorative ridges and amply covering the most vulnerable area—was excellent. There are disadvantages to ample padding and these become obvious when trying to look around the rather far windshield pillars. Trying to see

out does present a problem in a Chevy II. The seating position is very high which gives a good view of the road but in effect clips off the world just above eye level. This is particularly noticeable in the front corners where the roof makes a blind spot as it dips down to blend into the windshield pillars. The same holds true in the rear quarters. Vision directly to the rear also suffers, because of the short vertical height of the sloping rear glass.

The ventilation in the Chevy II is so good it's almost a miracle. If Chevrolet was that smart, all of its cars would be this good. Apparently the shape of the body is such that the vent windows operate very effectively and yet almost totally without noise. The system is complimented by foot vents which are operated by conveniently located knobs in the side panels just below the dash. The result is ventilation way above the compact car state of the art.

Chevrolet shies away from calling the Chevy II a compact car. Rather, it's considered to be a smaller size Chevrolet that competes with Falcons and Valiants and Darts. That's about the only context in which a name like Chevy II makes any sense at all. All of this is meant, obviously, to categorize an everybody's junior Chevrolet. The junior Chevy with the senior engine, like our 375-hp Nova SS, competes with nobody's compact—it's an instantly recognized and feared street cleaner that pushes you well up the youthful car-culture respect poll. With the exception of the clumsy rear suspension the car is so well coordinated that we never once had the overpowered-car feeling. In fact, unless you just plain need the cargo capacity we think a performance car any bigger suffers too great a penalty in maneuverability and weight.

The 396 Chevy II sure wasn't the invisible sleeper we had expected but it was every bit as wild as we hoped.

MUSCLE MINI TESTS

In 1967, *Car And Driver* was out to blow everyone's mind—as usual. So in the last issue of that year, the magazine delivered a stupendously complete series of miniature, no-holds-barred tests comparing every new muscle car available in 1968. It was the Official Program for Cruise Night.

Mini-Tests, as the name implies, are something less than the full-scale road tests we do throughout the year as a matter of course.

On the other hand, we discovered that when we answer the innumerable queries for consumer-type information on a car our readers are thinking of buying, we can generally give them a pretty clear idea of what the car is all about in a few well-chosen words. That's what a Mini-Test is: a short, sharp vignette that reveals some basic truth about each car. The whole truth about the cars we're interested in will be laid out before you as the year unfolds in our full-length road tests.

Mini-Tests differ in another way from our standard format: they include a short check list, but no detailed graph with all the figures attached. That's because a good number of the cars we drove were pre-production prototypes whose performance sometimes varies significantly from the cars which will eventually see the showroom floor.

When we decided to write the Mini-Tests on every basic make and model for sale in this country, we realized that there are only about 50 U.S. and 50 imported cars—for a nice, round total of 100. We're taking the '68 American cars this month and the foreign cars next month.

A word of warning, don't be put off by some apparent duplication in the American car section. It doesn't take much to see that a fire-breathing Montego 427 is quite a different animal from an economical Comet 302, even though the two cars look nearly identical.

You'll find no difficulty in discovering our likes and dislikes. We're evaluating the cars from C/D's point of view. We're enthusiasts, so are you. The result is that, when we test a basic-transportation kind of car, we'll concentrate more on how it handles than on how many miles per gallon it gets.

These tests weren't intended to be our patented comparison tests, but we can't help noting that many of the American cars are alike. There may never have been a business as competitive as the automobile business, and, the way it is practiced in America, never one so imitative. If one auto-maker scores a success with a unique car (Mustang), it is axiomatic that the others will copy it (Barracuda, Camaro, Cougar, Firebird, Javelin). Moreover, there is probably more competition between divisions within the same corporation as between companies.

This intense competition—and the amazing technological similarity of most of these cars—has led to the most astonishing fact of all: there are no really bad cars made in America; some are just better than others.

Above, left to right: 1968 Buick Riviera Coupe; 1968 Pontiac Firebird.

Buick GS 400

The GS 400 was conceived to capture some of the youth market for the staid-image Buick.

Bulbous and styled something like a pre-war speed boat, the '68 GS 400 boasts a 400 cu. in. engine, which, in moderate state of tune, produces 340 horsepower. That may not make it a 100-mph car in the quarter, but does make it quick. All the more reason to order the optional front disc brakes that will snub the car down in a smoothly-controlled manner.

As in the case with most of the Buick line, handling is very good in spite of the suspension's soft feel, and the GS 400 isn't going to disabuse anyone about *that*. The ride is comfortable enough for the frailest of grandmothers, but the car manages to handle well enough to suit a grandson on his way to the local dragstrip.

Despite its 400 cu. in. engine (or for the tight-fisted, there's a GS 350 available as a sort of semi-Super Car), Buick's GS 400 lacks the hell-for-leather feel of, say, Pontiac's GTO. But for dusting off most cars, the GS 400 is plenty sufficient.

Its interior is more plush than most cars of this breed. All of which adds up to a Super Car for the middle-of-the-roader—the guy who wants dramatic performance when he calls for it, but who doesn't want to risk his license at every stoplight.

BUICK GS 400

Manufacturer: Buick Motor Division General Motors Corporation Flint, Michigan

CAR AS TESTED
Engine ....340-hp, 400 cu. in. V-8
Transmission ....3-speed automatic
Steering ....Power-assisted
Suspension ....Heavy-duty
Brakes ....Disc F, Drum R

CHECK LIST

ENGINE
Throttle Response ....Very Good
Noise Insulation ....Very Good

DRIVE TRAIN
Shift Linkage ....Excellent
Shift Smoothness ....Very Good

STEERING
Effort ....Very Good
Response ....Very Good

HANDLING
Predictability ....Very Good
Evasive Maneuverability ....Very Good

BRAKES
Directional Stability ....Very Good
Fade Resistance ....Good

INTERIOR
Ease of Entry/Exit ....Very Good
Driving Position ....Good
Front Seating Comfort..........Very Good
Rear Seating Comfort................Fair

GENERAL
Vision ....Good
Heater/Defroster ....Excellent
Weather Sealing ....Very Good
Trunk Space ....Good

Buick Riviera

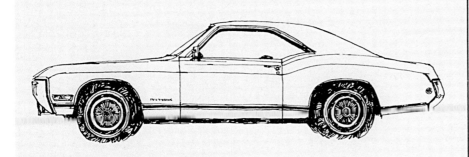

The Buick Riviera was an immediate hit when it was introduced in 1963. It's distinctive appearance and European-influenced 2+2 accommodations quickly established it as the car for the guy who had it made, yet was young enough not to worry about hardening of the arteries.

In the intervening years, the Riviera has vacillated in concept; seemingly destined to become an all-out GT car at one point (with the Gran Sport models) and then reversing course and becoming a floating, understeering, softly-sprung dreamboat. Finally, a well thought-out compromise has been reached. The 1968 Riviera boasts of both good handling and a smooth, quiet ride. When driven hard into a corner, the car displays an alarming amount of body lean, but don't let it worry you—until the limit of adhesion is reached, the Riviera remains quick, agile and predictable.

While handling improvements have been made to make the Riviera a much nicer car, and performance has been gradually increased, the guys in the styling department have dropped the ball. The Toronado-like new front grille/bumper gives what had been one of the most attractive cars on the road, a ponderous nose-heavy look completely out of keeping with the rest of the car. It's a shame seeing that, otherwise, the car has been so vastly improved.

BUICK RIVIERA

Manufacturer: Buick Motor Division General Motors Corporation Flint, Michigan

Engine ....360-hp, 430 cu. in. V-8
Transmission ....3-speed automatic
Steering ....Power-assisted
Suspension ....Standard
Brakes ....Disc F, Drum R

CHECK LIST

ENGINE
Throttle Response ....Very Good
Noise Insulation ....Very Good

DRIVE TRAIN
Shift Linkage ....Very Good
Shift Smoothness ....Very Good

STEERING
Effort ....Very Good
Response ....Good

HANDLING
Predictability ....Very Good
Evasive Maneuverability ....Good

BRAKES
Directional Stability ....Very Good
Fade Resistance ....Very Good

INTERIOR
Ease of Entry/Exit ....Very Good
Driving Position ....Good
Front Seating Comfort..........Very Good
Rear Seating Comfort...............Poor

GENERAL
Vision ....Fair
Heater/Defroster ....Excellent
Weather Sealing ....Excellent
Trunk Space ....Fair

Chevrolet Camaro Z-28

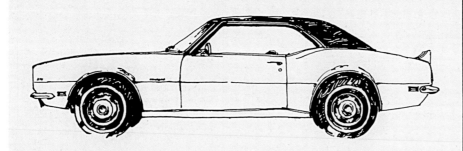

The Z-28 is the closest thing to a racing car you can buy from an American automaker. The Z-28 is a special option package that turns the Camaro into a Group 2 sedan; just add a rollbar and you've got all the pieces to go racing.

The heart of the Z-28 is a limited-production 302 cu. in. version of Chevy's small-block V-8, and it feels much stronger than the 327s and 350s that are sold in Chevy's Super Sport packages. The Z-28's 302 comes with a hot cam, a huge carburetor, solid lifters, and special rods and pistons. It's the most responsive production V-8 we've ever driven, and will whip the Z-28 through the quarter-mile at almost 100 mph. You also get a lot of other special stuff with the Z-28—like a handling package, heavy-duty suspension parts—and they won't sell it to you without power disc brakes and a close-ratio 4-speed gearbox. This year, multi-leaf rear springs have replaced the monoplate springs and single traction rod, and the shocks are bias-mounted fore and aft of the axle, and axle hop under acceleration is reduced. Some lack of positive axle location is apparent during a panic stop, but it's better than last year.

Related to ordinary Camaros, the Z-28 is what a Shelby GT-350 is to an ordinary Mustang—a lot tougher.

CHEVROLET CAMARO Z-28	
Manufacturer:	Chevrolet Division General Motors Corporation Detroit, Michigan

CAR AS TESTED

Engine ....290-hp, 302 cu. in. V-8
Transmission ....4-speed manual
Steering ....Power-assisted
Suspension ....Heavy-duty
Brakes ....Disc F, Drum R

CHECK LIST

ENGINE
Throttle Response ....Excellent
Noise Insulation ....Poor

DRIVE TRAIN
Shift Linkage ....Very Good
Synchro Action ....Excellent

STEERING
Effort ....Very Good
Response ....Very Good

HANDLING
Predictability ....Excellent
Evasive Maneuverability ....Very Good

BRAKES
Directional Stability ....Very Good
Fade Resistance ....Very Good

INTERIOR
Ease of Entry/Exit ....Fair
Driving Position ....Good
Front Seating Comfort ....Fair
Rear Seating Comfort...............Poor

GENERAL
Vision ....Good
Heater/Defroster ....Very Good
Weather Sealing ....Very Good
Trunk Space ....Fair

Chevrolet Chevelle SS 396

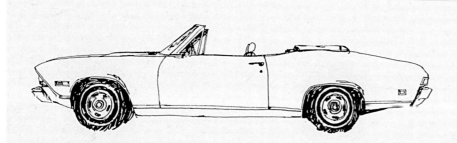

The Pontiac GTO was the original Super Car (an intermediate with a big V-8) back in '64. That same year, 100 Chevelles were built with the then-new 396 cu. in. V-8 (technically the most advanced high-performance V-8 in the world) and dubbed the SS 396. Chevy chief Pete Estes liked the car and its image, and ordered it into volume production in '65, and it has had support from the enthusiasts ever since.

For '68, all GM's Super Cars are built on the 112-in. (short) wheelbase version of GM's A-body—the one that is shared by all the divisions (except Cadillac) for the medium-small cars. Unfortunately, so much of this body is common to all the divisions that it seems to have caused some problems for the stylists and they have had to resort to some rather heavy-handed techniques, like weird grilles, to distinguish their car from those of sister divisions. The Chevelle's unenthusiastic appearance is a good example.

All the regular enthusiasts options are there, though: disc brakes, handling packages, etc., and the SS 396's over-the-road performance seems substantially improved over the '67's. In addition to being more nimble, the rear axle location has been revised to make cornering behavior more predictable. Be prepared, though, Chevy's cranked in more understeer.

CHEVROLET CHEVELLE SS 396	
Manufacturer:	Chevrolet Motor Division General Motors Corporation Detroit, Michigan

CAR AS TESTED

Engine ....325-hp, 396 cu. in. V-8
Transmission ....3-speed automatic
Steering ....Power-assisted
Suspension ....Heavy-duty
Brakes ....Disc F, Drum R

CHECK LIST

ENGINE
Throttle Response ....Very Good
Noise Insulation ....Good

DRIVE TRAIN
Shift Linkage ....Good
Shift Smoothness ....Very Good

STEERING
Effort ....Very Good
Response ....Good

HANDLING
Predictability ....Very Good
Evasive Maneuverability ....Good

BRAKES
Directional Stability ....Very Good
Fade Resistance ....Very Good

INTERIOR
Ease of Entry/Exit ....Very Good
Driving Position ....Good
Front Seating Comfort............Good
Rear Seating Comfort...............Fair

GENERAL
Vision ....Very Good
Heater/Defroster ....Excellent
Weather Sealing ....Good
Trunk Space ....Fair

Chevrolet Chevy II Nova SS 350

CHEVY II NOVA SS 350	
Manufacturer:	Chevrolet Division General Motors Corporation Detroit, Michigan

Engine ....295-hp, 350 cu. in. V-8
Transmission ....4-speed manual
Steering ....Power-assisted
Suspension ....Heavy-duty
Brakes ....Disc F, Drum R

CHECK LIST

ENGINE
Throttle Response ....Very Good
Noise Insulation ....Good

DRIVE TRAIN
Shift Linkage ....Fair
Synchro Action ....Good

STEERING
Effort ....Very Good
Response ....Good

HANDLING
Predictability ....Very Good
Evasive Maneuverability ....Good

BRAKES
Directional Stability ....Good
Fade Resistance ....Very Good

INTERIOR
Ease of Entry/Exit ....Good
Driving Position ....Fair
Front Seating Comfort.............Good
Rear Seating Comfort...............Fair

GENERAL
Vision ....Good
Heater/Defroster ....Very Good
Weather Sealing ....Very Good
Trunk Space ....Good

The '68 Nova SS 350 looks like a winner from every angle—and it will be, if the public can only forget all its ticky-tacky, cheaper-than-cheap predecessors. It is, in fact, a Camaro sedan, enjoying almost universal interchangeability of major mechanical components with Chevy's sporty car. In effect, this hot version comes off exactly like a Camaro with more room.

Although the 396 cu. in. V-8 and 3-speed Turbo HydraMatic transmission of the hottest Camaro may be lurking somewhere in the Chevy II's future, the top option currently available is the 295-hp 350 cu. in. V-8, with 3- or 4-speed manual box, or the prehistoric Powerglide. This engine delivers it performance as smooth torque, rather than screaming horsepower, which perfectly suits the overall concept of the car. Suspension performance is the same way—stiffer and better-controlled than on other Chevrolets, but still smooth and comfortable. With the optional discs come *two* advantages—great stopping power and better handling, believe it or not—because Chevy IIs with discs also have 6-inch rims instead of the 5-inchers that come standard.

The '68 Chevy II has grown an inch in wheelbase and six inches overall, but it's grown a mile in style, comfort, quality and performance.

Chevrolet Corvette

CHEVROLET CORVETTE	
Manufacturer:	Chevrolet Division General Motors Corp. Detroit, Michigan

CAR AS TESTED
Engine ....400-hp, 427 cu. in. V-8
Transmission ....3-speed automatic
Steering ....Power-assisted
Suspension ....Standard
Brakes ....Disc F, Disc R

CHECK LIST

ENGINE
Throttle Response ....Good
Noise Insulation ....Good

DRIVE TRAIN
Shift Linkage ....Good
Shift Smoothness ....Good

STEERING
Effort ....Fair
Response ....Very Good

HANDLING
Predictability ....Good
Evasive Maneuverability ....Very Good

BRAKES
Directional Stability ....Excellent
Fade Resistance ....Excellent

INTERIOR
Ease of Entry/Exit ....Fair
Driving Position ....Very Good
Front Seating Comfort.............Good
Rear Seating Comfort.............—

GENERAL
Vision ....Fair
Heater/Defroster ....Very Good
Weather Sealing ....Poor
Trunk Space ....Poor

The '68 Corvette is the wildest-looking production car Detroit has ever made, but underneath that radical "coke-bottle" styling, the mechanical components are much the same as the '67 models.

Modifications to the rear-suspension geometry, and the addition of wide-oval tires and wide (7-inch) rims have improved the handling characteristics above that of the highly-touted Sting Ray. There is some dispute about road feel and directional precision with the Corvette's optional power-assisted steering, but all agree that the car's cornering capabilities are first rate, with ride comfort about the same (which is definitely not "Jet Smooth").

The 3-speed Turbo HydraMatic finally replaces the 2-speed Powerglide on all models ordered with automatic transmission, and as far as we're concerned, it's the only way to go (short of anything but racing applications). The brakes, 4-wheel discs, are unchanged and still among the best in the world.

The new interior looks flashy, but isn't as practical as the old. The seats are more comfortable, but the stylishly-pinched waist has eliminated virtually all shoulder room and there's barely room between the steering wheel and the door panels. Also, quality control has been poor, at least on one of the early production models we tested.

Chevrolet Impala SS 427

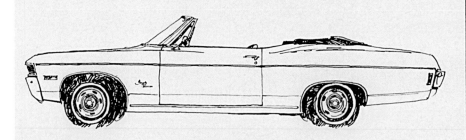

CHEVROLET IMPALA SS 427
Manufacturer: Chevrolet Division General Motors Corporation Detroit, Michigan

Engine ....385-hp, 427 cu. in. V-8
Transmission ....3-speed automatic
Steering ....Power-assisted
Suspension ....Heavy-duty
Brakes ....Disc F, Drum R

CHECK LIST

ENGINE
Throttle Response ....Excellent
Noise Insulation ....Good

DRIVE TRAIN
Shift Linkage ....Very Good
Shift Smoothness ....Very Good

STEERING
Effort ....Very Good
Response ....Good

HANDLING
Predictability ....Very Good
Evasive Maneuverability ....Good

BRAKES
Directional Stability ....Good
Fade Resistance ....Good

INTERIOR
Ease of Entry/Exit..............Very Good
Driving Position ....Good
Front Seating Comfort.........Very Good
Rear Seating Comfort ....Good

GENERAL
Vision ....Very Good
Heater/Defroster ....Excellent
Weather Sealing ....Very Good
Trunk Space ....Good

The Chevrolet Impala, in SS 427 guise, is what all of the king-size Chevrolets should be. Then they could bring out a genuine sports model that might more nearly deserve the SS appellation.

The "Super Sports" label, in Chevrolet parlance, has come to mean nothing more than a combination of trim options. Only when the "427" is added, along with a lot of other high-performance suspension goodies, does it really begin to mean what the enthusiast expects it to mean.

Our test car had a 385-hp, 427 cu. in. V-8, 3-speed automatic transmission, heavy-duty suspension, "rally" wheels with 6-in. rims, disc brakes and a limited-slip dif-ferential. Thus equipped, it came very close to being what we would like all American cars to be. It also had GM's well-organized Comfortron ventilation system, stereo tape, AM/FM radio, fiber-optic light monitoring system, electric windows and seats, and disappearing windshield wipers, which brought it close to being what *Chevrolet* would like all American cars to be.

It stopped and handled well, considering its great bulk, and it was smooth, dead-silent, and deceptively fast. It is the *only* full-sized Chevrolet that really gives its driver any feeling of security or well-being on a country road—and as nice as that is, isn't it too bad?

Dodge Charger

DODGE CHARGER
Manufacturer: Dodge Division Chrysler Corporation Detroit, Michigan

CAR AS TESTED
Engine ....425-hp, 426 cu. in. V-8
Transmission ....3-speed automatic
Steering ....Power-assisted
Suspension ....Heavy-duty
Brakes ....Disc F, Drum R

CHECK LIST

ENGINE
Throttle Response ....Very Good
Noise Insulation ....Fair

DRIVE TRAIN
Shift Linkage ....Poor
Shift Smoothness ....Good

STEERING
Effort ....Excellent
Response ....Very Good

HANDLING
Predictability ....Very Good
Evasive Maneuverability ....Very Good

BRAKES
Directional Stability ....Good
Fade Resistance ....Very Good

INTERIOR
Ease of Entry/Exit ....Very Good
Driving Position ....Good
Front Seating Comfort ....Poor
Rear Seating Comfort................Fair

GENERAL
Vision ....Good
Heater/Defroster ....Excellent
Weather Sealing ....Excellent
Trunk Space ....Very Good

Hey, this time the Dodge Brothers real-ly did it. After struggling along with the old Charger—a car that reminded veteran sales types at Chrysler of the Airflow disaster—this year they really bowled a strike with a new and completely revamped model—and it swings!

The 1968 Charger has to be one of the most visually exciting cars on the market, anywhere, and we are here to tell you that it's every bit as good as it looks. Naturally if you're going to swing for a machine like the Charger, you go for the super motor, right? And that has to be the optional 426 Hemi, right? And with the Hemi comes a really complete handling package, includ-ing stiffer shocks and springs, big front disc brakes, etc., right? So without ques-tion, that's the hot set-up for the Charger, right?

The interior of the Charger is every bit as nice as the outside—discreet, rich-looking and functional. Round instruments tell you what's going on, and the pleated, unruffled vinyl seats make you think of the Orsi Brothers or Pininfarina or somebody.

Packed with the Hemi, the Charger goes like its looks imply it should. Here is a genu-ine 150-mph car that does everything an au-tomobile should do, and well. Surely the Charger ranks among the best of this year's crop.

Dodge Coronet R/T

We might as well get it over with; R/T stands for Road and Track, and all of us dim-bulb sporty car types know what *that* means, don't we? Well, the Dodge R/T is not a dim-bulb sporty car in any sense of the word, but rather a well-balanced intermediate designed to make the same scene with cars like the GTO, 396 Chevelle, Road Runner, *et cetera* (and we know what that is, too, don't we?).

The Dodge R/T is a jazzed-up Coronet carrying some trim options, stiffer suspension and, if the buyer is wise, the gargantuan 440 Magnum engine. This monster is rated at 375 horsepower and will go around acting like a Hemi until some rather exotic speed ranges are obtained.

Like all of the Dodge/Plymouth intermediates built on this common Chrysler B-body, the R/T has a rather high, padded instrument panel lip that hampers forward visibility and detracts somewhat from an otherwise workmanlike, if somewhat pedestrian, interior design job.

The Chrysler Corporation has produced some really hot intermediates in 1968, and because of a wide overlap in engine, transmission and suspension applications, it is very difficult to state that one is better or worse than another. It can be said that they are collectively a good, solid bunch of performance machines.

DODGE CORONET R/T	
Manufacturer:	Dodge Division Chrysler Corporation Detroit, Michigan

CAR AS TESTED
Engine ....375-hp, 440 cu. in. V-8
Transmission ....3-speed automatic
Steering ....power-assisted
Suspension ....Heavy-duty
Brakes ....Disc F, Drum R

CHECK LIST

ENGINE
Throttle Response ....Very Good
Noise Insulation ....Good

DRIVE TRAIN
Shift Linkage ....Very Good
Shift Smoothness ....Good

STEERING
Effort ....Excellent
Response ....Very Good

HANDLING
Predictability ....Very Good
Evasive Maneuverability ....Very Good

BRAKES
Directional Stability ....Very Good
Fade Resistance ....Very Good

INTERIOR
Ease of Entry/Exit ....Good
Driving Position ....Good
Front Seating Comfort ....Very Good
Rear Seating Comfort ....Good

GENERAL
Vision ....Good
Heater/Defroster ....Excellent
Weather Sealing ....Very Good
Trunk Space ....Very Good

Ford Mustang GT/A

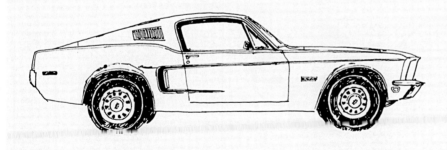

Last year, the 335-hp, 390 cu. in. Mustang was the hottest Mustang you could buy. This year it's only penultimate—the new top power-plant is a soaring, 390-hp, 427 cu. in. V-8; great for maximum performance, but a bit much for ordinary citizens.

By comparison, the 289 and 302 cu. in. V-8s are positively puny. The 390 is a good compromise, and wholly in keeping with the Mustang's image.

It's not for nothing that the Mustang has remained the most popular sporty car; it's fun to drive, well-built, reliable and inexpensive. It handles well, brakes firmly and accelerates nicely. It's a very comfort-able car to drive, although the seat rake adjustment feature has been eliminated for '68. (We used to unscrew the adjusting bolt altogether, and let the seat full back as far as it would go.)

Ford's high-compliance front suspension strut, pioneered last year by the Cougar, is now used on the Mustang. Harshness is better controlled at some penalty in steering precision.

The "Sport-Shift" 3-speed automatic is continued, and affords full manual control over upshifts and the 3-2 downshift.

Overall, the Mustang fully deserves its prominence in the sporty car field. After all, the Mustang created it.

FORD MUSTANG GT/A	
Manufacturer:	Ford Division Ford Motor Company Dearborn Michigan

CAR AS TESTED
Engine ....335-hp, 390 cu. in. V-8
Transmission ....3-speed automatic
Steering ....Power-assisted
Suspension ....Heavy-duty
Brakes ....Disc F, Drum R

CHECK LIST

ENGINE
Throttle Response ....Good
Noise Insulation ....Very Good

DRIVE TRAIN
Shift Linkage ....Very Good
Shift Smoothness ....Good

STEERING
Effort ....Very Good
Response ....Very Good

HANDLING
Predictability ....Very Good
Evasive Maneuverability ....Very Good

BRAKES
Directional Stability ....Very Good
Fade Resistance ....Very Good

INTERIOR
Ease of Entry/Exit.................Good
Driving Position ....Very Good
Front Seating Comfort..........Very Good
Rear Seating Comfort...............Poor

GENERAL
Vision ....Fair
Heater/Defroster ....Excellent
Weather Sealing ....Good
Trunk Space ....Poor

Clockwise from top left: 1968 Corvette;
1967 Camaro Z/28; 1968 Chevelle SS 396;
1968 Pontiac GTO; 1968 Plymouth GTX.

Ford Torino GT 427

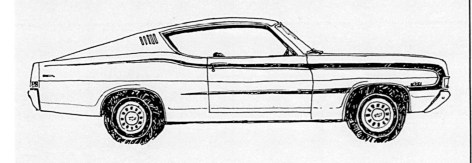

Ever since the Ford Motor Company gathered itself together and decided to go racing, its products have been steadily improved. The 427 Fairlane, featuring a racing-bred engine, handles well and stops superbly. You'd expect a 427 cu. in. engine to yank you down the road in no uncertain terms, and in the case of the Fairlane, you'd be right. In spite of its Thermactor exhaust emission control (fresh air injected into the exhaust stream as it leaves the combustion chambers) and a carburetor tuned so lean that it squeaks, the car is a right fair hauler for street or strip.

The engine, a street version of that which powered the Ford Le Mans cars and the NASCAR Grand National stockers, has been civilized (hydraulic lifters in place of mechanical tappets, etc.) but it hasn't been emasculated; it pumps out 390 hp. at 5600 rpm, and an impressive 460 ft-lbs. of torque at 3200 rpm.

Ford has seen fit to make its 3-speed automatic transmission mandatory with the 427 engine, and it's a sensible decision. The automatic is capable of handling all that torque, smoothly yet positively, and goes a long way towards cutting down the impact loadings on the rest of the driveline.

Designed to be a street racer, the 427 Fairlane does its job quietly but exceptionally well.

FORD TORINO GT 427

Manufacturer: Ford Motor Company
Ford Division
Dearborn, Michigan

CAR AS TESTED
Engine .... 390-hp, 427 cu. in. V-8
Transmission .... 3-speed automatic
Steering .... Power-assisted
Suspension .... Heavy-duty
Brakes .... Disc F, Drum R

CHECK LIST
ENGINE
Throttle Response .... Excellent
Noise Insulation .... Fair

DRIVE TRAIN
Shift Linkage .... Very Good
Shift Smoothness .... Fair

STEERING
Effort .... Very Good
Response .... Good

HANDLING
Predictability .... Very Good
Evasive Maneuverability .... Very Good

BRAKES
Directional Stability .... Good
Fade Resistance .... Very Good

INTERIOR
Ease of Entry/Exit .... Good
Driving Position .... Good
Front Seating Comfort .... Good
Rear Seating Comfort .... Fair

GENERAL
Vision .... Fair
Heater/Defroster .... Excellent
Weather Sealing .... Very Good
Trunk Space .... Good

Mercury Cyclone GT

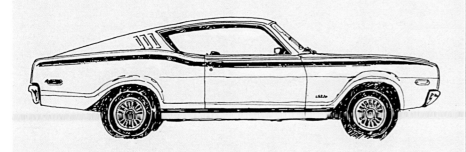

The Cyclone GT is Mercury's sporty intermediate—head to head with the Dodge Coronet R/T and Charger, Plymouth GTX, Pontiac GTO, Chevelle SS 396, Buick GS 350/400, Oldsmobile 4-4-2, and its own sibling, the Ford Torino GT. Available with either a formal or fastback roof, the Cyclone GT is designed to have an appeal broad enough to challenge all of them.

Like many of the industry's high-line cars, the Cyclone GT comes standard with much of the equipment that is optional on lesser models; bucket seats, heavy-duty suspension, wide-oval tires, V-8 engine, and Comfort Stream Ventilation are all part of the Cyclone GT package. Our test car was pretty well loaded; with 335 horsepower coupled to a 4-speed transmission, performance was spirited (but not breathtaking), and the special suspension and power disc brakes completed a well-matched package. Despite the firmer-than-standard suspension, ride comfort was very good, with at least part of the ride quality attributable to the seats.

Our only criticism of the Cyclone GT is of an abstract nature; it does not strike us as being special enough to compete on today's specialty car market. The fastback rage, for example, went out with the old Dodge Charger and the Marlin.

MERCURY CYCLONE GT

Manufacturer: Lincoln-Mercury Division
Ford Motor Company
Dearborn, Michigan

CAR AS TESTED
Engine .... 335-hp, 390 cu. in. V-8
Transmission .... 4-speed manual
Steering .... Power-assisted
Suspension .... Heavy-duty
Brakes .... Disc F, Drum R

CHECK LIST
ENGINE
Throttle Response .... Very Good
Noise Insulation .... Very Good

DRIVE TRAIN
Shift Linkage .... Good
Synchro Action .... Very Good

STEERING
Effort .... Very Good
Response .... Very Good

HANDLING
Predictability .... Very Good
Evasive Maneuverability .... Very Good

BRAKES
Directional Stability .... Good
Fade Resistance .... Very Good

INTERIOR
Ease of Entry/Exit .... Good
Driving Position .... Good
Front Seating Comfort .... Good
Rear Seating Comfort .... Fair

GENERAL
Vision .... Fair
Heater/Defroster .... Excellent
Weather Sealing .... Very Good
Trunk Space .... Good

Mercury Cougar GT·E

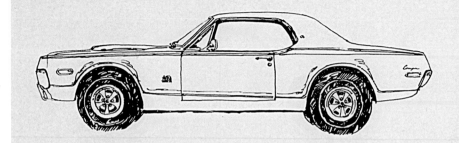

The Mercury Cougar is one of our favorite sporty cars. We like it because it embodies a combination of comfort, convenience and vice-free handling better than any of its competitors. In every sense of the word it's a premium car.

Particularly pleasant is the obvious emphasis that Mercury has placed upon creature comfort in the design of the Cougar's interior. The bucket seats are very comfortable (Detroit's best, we think). For those who want it, an adjustable steering wheel is available, permitting the owner to virtually put on his Cougar like a tailor-made suit. Controls are well placed (with the exception of the windshield wiper switch), and, equipped with the versatile 3-speed automatic transmission, the Cougar can be one of the most pleasantly effortless cars on the road.

But before you conjure an image as remote from a sports car as an ocean liner, Cougars are available with several different engines offering several different levels of performance—including the brute, tire-smoking, hell-bent-for-action GT·E package which comes with a detuned version of Ford's 427 NASCAR "Wedge." It's impressive all right, but for most types of driving we would be just as well satisfied with something tamer. But any way you build *your* Cougar, you'll love it.

Oldsmobile 4-4-2

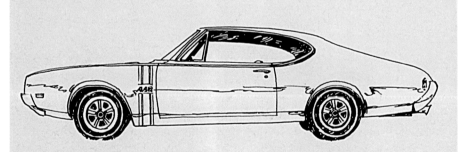

Oldsmobile's 4-4-2, never attaining the dedicated following of Pontiac's GTO, is still the best balanced Super Car around. Its handling is noticeably more predictable and more precise than the other light-bodied/big-engined street racers, performance is on a par with most, and for overall comfort and enjoyment, the 4-4-2 is a standout . . . in its own subtle way.

Not wanting to lose our driver's license, we tested the 4-4-2 with the standard 350-hp, 400 cu. in. engine. A "select-fit" version (presumably one step down from a blue-printed engine) comes with the optional Ram Air package, but this borders on being a strictly-for-the-strip combination that was a little too rich for our blood.

Rather than encountering the pronounced understeer that is present with most cars made in this country, we found the 4-4-2 to be a neutral handling car. This is mostly due to the use of a rear anti-sway bar (which also helps control axle hop under both heavy acceleration and hard braking).

Unless you are a dedicated drag racer committed to eliminating weight and drag at almost any cost, you'll be happier with the optional front disc brakes. The drums are adequate, but since the 4-4-2 can be driven like a sports car, we found the fade-free discs to be more in keeping with the car's capabilities.

Oldsmobile Toronado

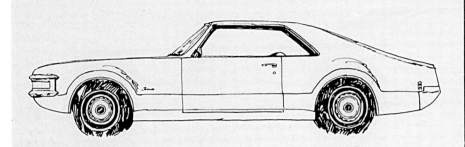

It's been two years since Oldsmobile introduced the Toronado and proved to a skeptical public that it is feasible to build a big, big-engined, front-wheel-drive specialty car. Last year Cadillac's Eldorado stole some of the Toronado's thunder, but Olds still has a good thing going.

For '68, engine displacement has been increased to 455 cu. in. on the standard Toronado. As in the past, the big car understeers, but no more so than most other Detroit full-size sedans, and it's a lot better than some. Trouble is, Toronado isn't *sold* as a full-size sedan, and somehow you expect more from it.

The brakes, a continuing sore point with road testers, are still not up to the job of hauling this behemoth down from high speeds without a lot of slewing, but there is a disc brake option that is a considerable improvement.

The strange thing about the Toronado is that it does not feel like a front-wheel-drive car. The only time you'll probably notice any difference is on wet roads. The advantages of fwd are negated by poor brake modulation; you become uncomfortably aware of the car's unconventional drive system when you find it pivoting around itself on the front wheels whenever you hit the brakes too hard and the wheels aren't aimed dead ahead.

Plymouth GTX

The GTX is Plymouth's jumbo street racer, complete with all the acceptable props—hood scoops, bucket seats, mag-type wheels, zoomie medallions and stripes—plus a very neat engine/chassis combo.

The standard GTX engine is the muscular Super Commando 440 cu. in. high-performance version. This massive, free-breathing powerplant is gutsy enough that it will make the GTX perform nearly as impressively as the optional, more expensive, slightly more temperamental Hemi. Coupled with the ultra-tough, ultra-flexible TorqueFlite 3-speed automatic (forget about 4-speed manual on a car like this unless you are a 32nd-degree drag racer), the 440 will do all the tricks and keep running forever.

The Chrysler Corporation B-body, from which the GTX is derived, features as neatly articulated yet as conventional a suspension system as there is in the USA. The heavy-duty shocks and springs that come on the GTX make it one of the most agile intermediates in the business. Add to this a set of 11-inch disc brakes at the front and you've got plenty of stopping power for a car that will come out of the gate with the best of 'em, and cruise for hours at 80 mph.

It looks good, the interior is tasteful, if slightly uninspired, and the GTX is a load of civilized performance for the money.

Plymouth Road Runner

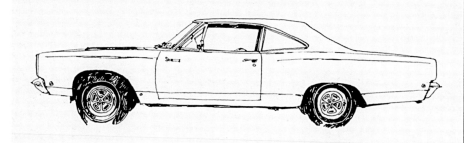

The Road Runner was originally conceived as a stripped Plymouth Belvedere, stuffed full of enough horsepower to make it a showroom version of the de-chromed, super-cool Q-ships that Young America presently drives on the street.

The project has, by-and-large, been completed without compromise, although the stylists and product planners couldn't resist overstating the non-functional hood scoops. Within the context of this market, the name is a stroke of genius, and Plymouth will doubtlessly exploit it for all it's worth.

The Road Runner is basically a Belvedere I, which is Plymouth's low-buck fleet special, equipped with a specially-tuned 383 cu. in., 4-bbl. V-8 and heavy-duty suspension. The result is the world's fastest club coupe. The interior trim is a bit sparse although improved upholstery is on the way. The car, like all Chrysler intermediates with heavy-duty suspension, handles very well, and the 383 gives it plenty of power for the street racing scene. However, if you are really serious about the whole thing, you'll spend the extra money for the fabled Hemi, which should put the Road Runner *right there* with the 427 Corvette.

This is the first car since the GTO to be aimed directly at American youth and it very probably is dead on target. But just wait till ol' Nader hears about it.

PLYMOUTH ROAD RUNNER

Manufacturer: Chrysler-Plymouth Division
Chrysler Corporation
Detroit, Michigan

CAR AS TESTED
Engine . . . . .335-hp, 383 cu. in. V-8
Transmission . . . . .4-speed manual
Steering . . . . .Standard
Suspension . . . . .Heavy-Duty
Brakes . . . . .Drum F, Drum R

CHECK LIST

ENGINE
Throttle Response . . . . .Excellent
Noise Insulation . . . . .Poor

DRIVE TRAIN
Shift Linkage . . . . .Poor
Synchro Action . . . . .Very Good

STEERING
Effort . . . . .Fair
Response . . . . .Good

HANDLING
Predictability . . . . .Very Good
Evasive Maneuverability . . . . .Good

BRAKES
Directional Stability . . . . .Very Good
Fade Resistance . . . . .Good

INTERIOR
Ease of Entry/Exit . . . . .Very Good
Driving Position . . . . .Good
Front Seating Comfort . . . . .Good
Rear Seating Comfort . . . . .Poor

GENERAL
Vision . . . . .Very Good
Heater/Defroster . . . . .Very Good
Weather Sealing . . . . .Very Good
Trunk Space . . . . .Very Good

Pontiac Firebird

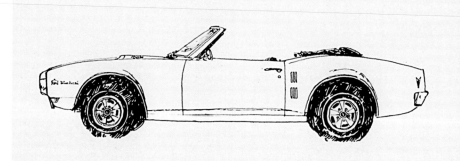

Did we hear you mention street racer? Would you prefer a European sports car? Pontiac offers both—in the same Firebird—through the magic of option lists. And something in between if you can't seem to make up your mind.

The biggest change in the '68 sporty car from the industry's most prolific innovator is a redesigned rear suspension intended to eliminate axle hop which plagued last year's model. The new multiple leaf springs and staggered shock absorbers help, but the axle still can't be called perfectly behaved. Handling, conversely, is excellent, lending confidence to even the most maniacal driving. Ride comfort, even with the optional heavy duty suspension, is very good.

The interior appointments of the Firebird are acceptable—but not exceptional. We were particularly disenchanted with the seats, apparently unchanged from last year. Another change due, but not made, is making the 3-speed automatic available with the 350 cu. in. engine, which needs all the help it can get. The 2-speed just isn't versatile enough.

The elimination of side vent windows might not have been such a good idea; the dash-mounted fresh-air vents don't pass much air, and there isn't adequate means for exhausting stale air.

PONTIAC FIREBIRD

Manufacturer: Pontiac Motor Division
General Motors Corporation
Pontiac, Michigan

CAR AS TESTED
Engine . . . . .320-hp, 350 cu. in. V-8
Transmission . . . . .2-speed automatic
Steering . . . . .Power-assisted
Suspension . . . . .Heavy-duty
Brakes . . . . .Disc F, Drum R

CHECK LIST

ENGINE
Throttle Response . . . . .Very Good
Noise Insulation . . . . .Good

DRIVE TRAIN
Shift Linkage . . . . .Good
Shift Smoothness . . . . .Very Good

STEERING
Effort . . . . .Very Good
Response . . . . .Very Good

HANDLING
Predictability . . . . .Very Good
Evasive Maneuverability . . . . .Very Good

BRAKES
Directional Stability . . . . .Good
Fade Resistance . . . . .Good

INTERIOR
Ease of Entry/Exit . . . . .Good
Driving Position . . . . .Good
Front Seating Comfort . . . . .Fair
Rear Seating Comfort . . . . .Poor

GENERAL
Vision . . . . .Good
Heater/Defroster . . . . .Very Good
Weather Sealing . . . . .Very Good
Trunk Space . . . . .Fair

Pontiac GTO

PONTIAC GTO

Manufacturer: Pontiac Division
General Motors Corporation
Pontiac, Michigan

CAR AS TESTED
Engine ....360-hp, 400 cu. in. V-8
Transmission ....3-speed automatic
Steering ....Power-assisted
Suspension ....Heavy-duty
Brakes ....Disc F, Drum R

CHECK LIST

ENGINE
Throttle Response ....Excellent
Noise Insulation ....Poor

DRIVE TRAIN
Shift Linkage ....Very Good
Shift Smoothness ....Good

STEERING
Effort ....Very Good
Response ....Very Good

HANDLING
Predictability ....Very Good
Evasive Maneuverability ....Good

BRAKES
Directional Stability ....Good
Fade Resistance ....Very Good

INTERIOR
Ease of Entry/Exit ....Very Good
Driving Position ....Good
Front Seating Comfort...............Good
Rear Seating Comfort.................Fair

GENERAL
Vision ....Good
Heater/Defroster ....Very Good
Weather Sealing ....Very Good
Trunk Space ....Good

Never a Division to rest on its laurels, Pontiac has had its stylists and engineers hard at work on the GTO ever since its introduction in 1964. There are few cars, domestic or foreign, that can boast better handling without an accompanying general deterioration in overall ride comfort. Our only complaint in the suspension department arose from severe rear axle hop encountered during hard braking from over 80 mph. The car still stops in a hurry, but the shaking and sudden noise scared the hell out of us. We were particularly surprised in view of the seemingly adequate number and strength of the links locating the coil-sprung rear axle; the severity and frequency of the judder caused us to check under the car to reassure ourselves that Pontiac hadn't gone back to leaf springs on the GTO. Otherwise, the suspension—together with the uncannily responsive engine—gives the GTO driver a feeling of supreme confidence.

Other manufacturers have built Super Cars with more brute acceleration, but when it comes to building a fully integrated package that combines ride comfort, handling, style and performance—all at a bearable price—the GTO is very tough to beat. Now, if they can only solve their production problems with the whiz-bang plastic bumper. . .

Shelby Cobra GT 350

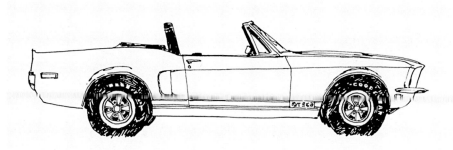

SHELBY COBRA GT 350

Shelby American, Inc.
Manufacturer: 4320 190th St.
Torrance, Calif.

CAR AS TESTED
Engine ....250 hp, 302 cu. in. V-8
Transmission ....4-speed manual
Steering ....Power-assisted
Suspension ....Standard
Brakes ....Disc F, Drum R

CHECK LIST

ENGINE
Throttle Response ....Excellent
Noise Insulation ....Poor

DRIVE TRAIN
Shift Linkage ....Excellent
Synchro Action ....Excellent

STEERING
Effort ....Very Good
Response ....Excellent

HANDLING
Predictability ....Excellent
Evasive Maneuverability ....Excellent

BRAKES
Directional Stability ....Very Good
Fade Resistance ....Very Good

INTERIOR
Ease of Entry/Exit ....Good
Driving Position ....Excellent
Front Seating Comfort ....Very Good
Rear Seating Comfort ....Poor

GENERAL
Vision ....Very Good
Heater/Defroster ....Excellent
Weather Sealing ....Good
Trunk Space ....Fair

The Shelby GT 350 is the Mustang that all Mustangs should be. When Carroll Shelby created the GT 350 in 1965, it was too much sports car and not enough *Gran Turismo*. It was a rough, tough, masculine brute, and you had to teach it who was boss. As a conversion of a sporty car, the GT 350 had more sheer guts than America's only genuine GT car, the Corvette, but it played sweet music to a fairly small audience of hard-core enthusiasts.

All that is changed now. The Shelby Mustangs aren't exactly emasculated, but they're toned down to the point where any little lady from Pasadena could drive one.

Most of the difference between the stock Mustangs and the Shelby versions is in the styling. The engines are a bit souped up, but they're perfectly tractable, the handling is more sure-footed, and the brakes are improved, but it's done largely with pieces that are optional on regular Mustangs.

One part that isn't optional on any other car in America is a roll-over bar, which ought to be mandatory in all convertibles. Shelby also offers racing-type inertia-reel shoulder harnesses.

Any Mustang driver who calls himself an enthusiast owes it to himself to try the GT 350 (or its bigger-engined brother, the GT 500); the styling and beneath-the-skin modifications are a real pay raise.

DAVID E. DAVIS, JR.

"Donna, if you read this, please tell the tall blonde in the tight pink pants who was making the spaghetti that I'm the guy who was driving the noisy black and white Z/28 camaro and I love her."

I was about to drive from GM's Arizona proving ground to Detroit in one of the first of Chevrolet's 1100 Z/28 (Trans-American sedan racing) Camaros. It was 2:30 on a Monday afternoon and I was hungry, so I stopped at Donna and Johnnie's Restaurant in beautiful downtown Norton's Corners, Ariz.

Donna, I spotted immediately. She was the cute little brunette, graying some, wearing a black bowling shirt that said "Donna" over her left breast. Johnnie, I think, was the terrific-looking blonde lady who had poured herself into a pair of pink pants and a matching poor-boy top, augmented by white Courrèges boots and an aluminum hair clip just in front of each ear. The hair clips were there to keep the steam from the spaghetti she stirred from straightening her ash-blonde curls. I had me a Coors beer and a plate of 35-cent spaghetti and—watching Johnnie flow smoothly back and forth from stove to counter—drifted into a wide-screen, Technicolor erotic fantasy wherein she accompanied me to Detroit and made me the happiest philanderer in the world.

I made it to a motel in Socorro, New Mexico, that first day, driving through Salt River Canyon and over the tops of the San Carlos Mountains. My racer was running like a train—it was geared to pull 90 mph at 4600 rpm—and I held it between 90 and 100 for hours on end, whistling down into the valleys and storming up through the hills on the other side, trying to pretend that this was the Mille Miglia and Old Pink Johnnie was playing Denis Jenkinson to my Stirling Moss. Moss should have been so lucky.

High on top of the mesa, crossing into New Mexico, it got dark, and the darkness was memorable. The sky was a black glass dome that curved right down to the edges of the earth in an unbroken hundred-mile circle around the Z/28. There were stars everywhere—not just overhead, but at eye level, not just through the windshield and side windows, but even in the rear-view mirror. Lights of cars coming at me from ten miles away shimmered and danced like ghostly magnesium flares.

Yowling along, I bored through the antic, straying beams of radio stations in far-off places like Shreveport and San Francisco. I knew how St. Exupéry must have felt about airplanes, and why he wrote "Wind, Sand, and Stars" and "The Little Prince." A man-made machine, very noisy and not too comfortable, had brought me closer to truth than Huntley and Brinkley and Time and my childhood's army of Anglo-Saxon holy men had ever been able to do. The radio tried to tell me about three burned astronauts and how they screamed, and about somebody's pathetic and groundless hopes for peace in Vietnam, but my machine had put me out of radio's reach.

On the second day, I drove 813 miles to Joplin, Missouri, and it wasn't the best thing I ever did. I had to foresake U.S. 60 for Route 66, and Route 66 is mainly ugly. I couldn't get anything on the radio except retarded local newscasters and disc jockeys, which I could turn off, but the only thing I couldn't escape was that Camaro seat. By Joplin, my tail was quite literally numb, I was in pain in several critical areas, and I often drove with one hand, hoisting myself clear of the seat with my left elbow on the armrest and my right hand braced on the center console. No, the second day was not fun.

Ah, but the third day made up for it. I was up at four in the morning, and on the road to Springfield, Missouri, where I again picked up my beloved U.S. 60, with its curves and hills and rough patches and reassuring loneliness. I got gas at a DX station in Springfield, and the old-timer attendant there told me that Route 60 was a very good road, and I'd be able to run 60-65 mph once I got out beyond the government land where it was very twisty. The Z/28 and I touched 60 once or twice when we were caught behind slower cars, but most of the way it was 4600 rpm and 90 mph and euphoria. We just flew low over that damp pavement toward a dawn that promised rain. I drove much too fast. I used too much road on most of the bends. The car stuck like glue on the pavement, but each time I crossed the painted center line, I'd lose adhesion on its shiny surface for an instant and I loved it.

By mid-afternoon I was in Berea, Kentucky, where I stayed at Boone Tavern and ate like a king and slept in a sensational four-poster bed—a bed made by Berea students as part of the college's very impressive crafts program.

On the last day the Z/28 still ran with brisk authority, and I'd come to love it so much in the mountains that I was almost willing to forgive the seat, but when I headed north to Detroit, the weather turned sour. It rained, snowed, got steadily colder, and I blew my chance for a big exit from a diner in Tipp City, Ohio. There was a lady there who looked just like Dan Gurney's wife—which is to say marvelous—accompanied by a short kid in a red cowboy suit. I finished my cheese-burger, picked up a container of coffee, and headed for my racer... pausing only to set the coffee on the roof of the car, remove my jacket, and make sure they were all watching. Then I blasted out of the parking lot at full chat, slithering madly in the snow, dumping my coffee off the roof and over the back window. I always do something like that.

And finally into Detroit. I left pink, voluptuous Johnnie in the car when I gave it back because I loved them both too much to choose between them. Somebody's going to buy that Z/28, and probably race it, and he'd damned well better be successful. He's got a first-class machine and the most wonderful co-driver in the whole world.

Goldilocks and the two Bears.

The Bear on the right is a stock Belvedere GTX.

That is to say it carries the standard 440 cu. in. V-8, which, aside from being the biggest GT engine in the world, generates 375 hp. and 480 lbs.-ft. of torque through a fast-shifting TorqueFlite automatic and the recommended 3.23-to-1 rear axle.

Said Bear also carries a heavy-duty suspension—including beefed-up torsion bars, ball joints, front stabilizer bar, shocks and rear springs—along with bigger brakes, low-restriction exhausts, a pit-stop gas filler, chromed valve covers, Red Streak tires, wide rims, hood scoops and bucket seats. And this is the *standard* Bear, mind you.

The Bear on the left is also a stock GTX—with a heavy-duty 4-speed gearbox—*and* a few extra-cost options, including the famed Hemi, with 426 cu. in. and 490 lbs.-ft. of torque. It also has our super-duty Sure-Grip differential; not to mention racing stripes and front disc brakes.

So what's the moral? Simply that GTX is one very tempting bowl of porridge. In one form, even Goldilocks can drive it (although you'll recall Goldilocks was a highly adventuresome kind of female). In another form, it's strictly for the "Move over, honey, and let a man drive" set. You know the story: there's bound to be one that's just right. After all, we're out to win you over. **'67 Belvedere GTX.**

BROCK YATES
STREET RACING

Organized drag racing was supposed to have turned hot rodding into something as respectable as apple pie and as legal as little-league baseball, but the truth is that drag racing on the public highways—street racing—is bigger than ever, and Detroit's Woodward Avenue is the street racing capitol of the world.

So here comes the Cheater, tooling his GTO down Woodward Avenue, looking for a little action. He eases away from the lights with the big engine rumbling ominously and the rear slicks making noisy whispers against the pavement. Very cool, the Cheater.

Across the mall, in the opposite lane, a Chevelle SS 396 and a Plymouth with the rear suspension jacked up maybe two feet in the air run side-by-side for a few seconds and then their drivers nail the wood and they spurt ahead like scalded dogs. They roar away into the night with the Cheater casually watching their progress in his rear-view mirror. Then a Mustang pulls alongside and a pair of high school kids—just strokes—gawk at the Cheater. He looks straight ahead, not bothering to acknowledge their presence.

In the pecking order of the Woodward Avenue racing scene, a guy driving a very strong street racer like Cheater's doesn't pay any attention to the strokes. Guys in other GTOs and 4-4-2s and Chevelles, yes, and guys in 427 'Vettes and Mopars, very definitely yes, but you want to watch it before you take a shot with them. A good 'Vette or a sharp Mopar will suck the doors off a GTO, so the Cheater has to be very cautious about what cars he chooses to race down Woodward.

The Cheater is operating in a very wild scene. By day, Woodward Avenue is a wide street that all the fat daddies from Royal Oak, Birmingham, and Bloomfield Hills use to drive into stolid old downtown Detroit—Motor City, by golly. But come sunset, Woodward Avenue becomes the street racing capitol of the world. Oh yes, there's some action around

L.A.—out in the Valley and in Downey and along the beach, and a lot of guys talk about Palm Beach and Miami and there's even a little street racing going on up in the Bronx and on the south shore of Long Island. But they don't cut it with the scene on Woodward, where maybe two thousand—really—cars are milling up and down the five-mile-long "strip" on any given night. Woodward is the Indianapolis of the street racers, and if you can make it there, baby, you will be very tough behind the wheel no matter where you go.

The Cheater is very tough. Mostly he sits in Ted's Drive In, one of three or four spots along the strip where real racers hang out. A lot of the high school strokes come in there too, revving their stock engines and showing off their mags and their uplift shocks, and guys like Cheater can tell them a mile off. But when some cat chugs through in a big Mopar with some wild grind that makes it idle rumpa-rumpa-rumpa, you know there is going to be some serious action. The Cheater wheels into Ted's and scans the scene. Like every night, it looks like the garage area at a big race. Lined up in the stalls are rows and rows of Super Cars with giant tires and hunched-up suspensions and hood scoops and fuel injection and blowers and mag wheels and smooth, cool looking paint jobs. In each car are a pair of guys—because you usually street race in pairs—and the scene, with all these stalls, reminds you of those Amsterdam prostitutes who sit in the windows, patiently awaiting the call to action.

Out in front, parked along the street, are some Corvettes and GTOs with nobody near them. They belong to very cool guys who hang out at nearby gas stations and bars and coffee shop counters, and if you want to take a shot with them, you have to know enough to be able to find them and ask something like, "Will that thing run?" and they answer, "You want to take a shot?" and then you'll go out to Interstate 75 and settle it. For cash.

As a matter of fact, it's not much of a secret that there are factory teams operating on Woodward. Not kids getting a mother's price on parts, mind you, but employees of the Detroit corporations that make and sell automobiles, right out there racing on Woodward Avenue like it was Daytona International Speedway. Call it "market research."

The factory guys don't have the blessing of the chairmen of the boards, mind you; nobody ever bothered to ask. And they race for kicks, to keep up with what's happening, not cash. One guy's favorite trick used to be to show up with a very stock automobile, arrange a rendezvous somewhere else for the race, then stop off along the way and switch cars. The second car was definitely not very stock. But hardly anyone falls for that gag anymore, and certainly not the Cheater.

The Cheater recognizes some of the regulars sitting in front of Ted's Drive In. The Shaker is out tonight, and so is Moses. He spots an open slot and backs in beside a rough looking GTO that belongs to a little guy wearing shades who they call Peanuts. Now Peanuts has a 430-inch engine in that wreck with the license plates wired on, and it is known to be a very tough machine to deal with.

Peanuts doesn't shift too well, so he has another guy at the wheel tonight, but neither of them pays much attention to Cheater as he backs in, cuts the engine and orders a cup of coffee over the squawk box. Pretty soon this haggard looking broad comes out of the drive-in with the coffee and the Cheater sits there scanning the action.

Out on Woodward, the strokes are roaring up and down, screeching their tires, and every once in awhile the fuzz will snap on their gum-ball revolving lights and pull some guy over and lay maybe a $200 fine on him. This is really a very good deal for the fuzz in Royal Oak and those other suburban towns, because the city fathers can make a lot of bucks off the racers in a given evening. Oh, they talk very big about the menace of the street racers, but they never make any really big push to shut down the action. After all, if you can make a few grand in fines every night, why spoil a good thing? But even then, pros like the Cheater watch it very closely when they run Woodward, and mostly they save their racing for the open spaces of I-75.

Pretty soon the Cheater looks over at Peanuts and says, "How's that thing running tonight?"

And the guy who is driving for Peanuts says, in a very cool tone, "Peanuts has the fastest '65 on the street."

So the Cheater says, "Is it worth twenty bucks?"

And then Peanuts turns his head and scans the Cheater from behind his shades so you can't tell whether he's bluffing or not and says, "Man, it ain't worth spinnin' the *key* for twenty bucks."

The Cheater lets that ride for a few seconds and then he looks Peanuts right square in the shades and says, "Like they say, man—money talks, but bulls- - t walks."

Now that is a very tough thing to say to a guy like Peanuts, but sometimes you have to be that way to deal with some cats, and sure enough, it is all that is needed for Peanuts to accept the challenge.

Because there was so much action around the drive-ins on Woodward, a law was recently passed that forbids car-hopping by the customers. Big signs proclaim that leaving a car on foot is illegal and most of the places have a rent-a-cop to enforce the regulation. This is kind of a drag, but it doesn't prevent the word from passing around the place that Cheater and Peanuts are about to take a shot.

There's a guy sitting in a red Mopar with American mags who calls over to the Cheater, "You better watch it man, you're dealin' with big heads and a Holley."

"Maybe," replies the Cheater, kind of under his breath, "but I've put the lunch to better equipment than that on the way to work. Peanuts never dealt with nothin' like this, so I wouldn't spend my money on him if I were you." The Cheater hunches forward in his seat and reaches for the ignition key. It is time to go.

Cheater is a guy in his early twenties, with a clean-cut Caucasian profile and short, athlete's blond hair. He is wearing a lightweight windbreaker and a pair of narrow-cut pants with the creases still in them, and Moms and Pops all over the country would take him into their arms and gladly call him one of their own. This is the way it is on Woodward; there are very few punks running equipment out there. The suburbs are rich, and the street racers are the products of fat-cat mid-western households who don't really care if their sons are out running $6,000 race cars up and down the public roads.

Sanctioned drag racing meets are supposed to have stopped all the illegal action on the streets and turned hot rodding into something as apple-pie sweet and legal as little-league baseball, but nobody really believes that. The drag strips have become so crowded that a guy is lucky if he can make three runs during an entire afternoon or evening, but on Woodward you might get fifty shots in a few hours. And they're all free, baby. Of course, pros like the Cheater can make a lot more coins on the street than on the track, where you get these 19-cent trophies with a phony gold car stuck on top of a cheap wood pedestal.

The word has passed around the drive-in and a couple of cars full of guys who want to watch ease out and head up Woodward toward I-75. Then Peanuts takes off, followed discreetly by the Cheater.

The Cheater takes it very slow up Woodward so the cops won't notice, then swings onto a deserted side street that heads toward the expressway. The engine seems to be running all right, but he lays it on the wood anyway, just to be sure. The exhaust noise swells inside the car as it leaps ahead in second gear, then reaches a frantic, instantaneous peak as he makes a lightning, full-throttle shift to third. The slicks yelp against the pavement and the GTO yaws sideways under power for a few feet before straightening out. The Cheater is ready.

He rolls onto the dark expanse of the expressway and heads west toward the rendezvous. Headlights pop into the rear-view mirror—one of the spectator cars. Then Peanuts shows up and eases into a

steady 60-mph formation in the center lane. A few more cars enter the convoy from the rear and they all roll down the expressway, waiting for the traffic ahead to clear.

Good street racers don't use the traditional wheel-spinning drag-type start from a standstill. First of all, you have to stop to do that sort of thing, and that means brake-lights flashing—a sure tip-off to the fuzz. Secondly, screeching tires get the neighbors up-tight, and finally, starts from a full stop are hard on clutches and rear ends. So a flying start is used, usually from about 30 mph, and the race goes up as high as necessary to determine the winner, which is sometimes 140 mph.

Peanuts pulls alongside the Cheater and rolls down his window. Cheater already has his down, so they rumble along, fender-to-fender for awhile, until they're in position. Then Peanuts yells, "Go!" and the race is on.

The sound of Peanuts' voice transforms the Cheater into a dervish on wheels. He throws his entire body against the gear lever as he rams the transmission from first to second. Wham! The Pontiac begins to moan in second and Wham! into third while Peanuts' ol' '65 hangs on maybe half a car length behind. Suddenly the GTO is running 100 mph and the Cheater flings it into fourth gear. Now he's beginning to get the advantage and Peanuts is falling farther back. He touches 120 mph and then eases off, letting Peanuts roll alongside once again.

"One more time," Peanuts shouts into the wind, and the two cars line up and scream into the night with their support vehicles trying to keep up. Once more the Cheater puts ol' Peanuts in paradise and it is all over.

They pull off at the next exit and stop at a deserted shopping center. They all talk quietly for awhile, and Peanuts tells the Cheater why he wasn't getting the kind of rpm he should have, and how it was leaking oil and how maybe he had 15 bent pushrods and how next time...

Old Peanuts hadn't really lost, because nobody ever really loses a street race. And by the same token, the Cheater hadn't really won, either, not really, except that he feels good enough to stuff his winnings into his wallet and head back toward Woodward for a couple more shots.

COMPARISON ROAD TEST
Z/28 CAMARO VS. "TUNNEL PORT" MUSTANG

The Lime Rock pit straight is a wavy, gray blur. Up front two roaring Holleys are trying to suck a hole in the atmosphere. "A 7000 rpm redline? Christ Almighty, it's gonna burst." But it doesn't, and Sam Posey snaps the shift lever into fourth at seven grand as the speedometer climbs past 110 in one of the absolute wildest street machines ever to come out of Detroit. No question about it; we're in the middle of one of the most beautiful goddam road tests in the annals of mankind.

Trans-Am sedans set up for the road. All right, the six sporty cars we tested (March) were exciting examples of the car builders' art—but they weren't mind blowers. They performed well, almost automatically, never making demands on the driver. But that was their shortcoming. A kind of polished lack of character.

An unsatisfied craving for total driver involvement prompted us to continue our search for that mystical machine. Not a near total fantasy of the Lamborghini Miura or Ferrari 275/GTB-4 sort, but something totally without pretense that might even outperform them. That's asking a lot. Ideally, it should be American. Should we—in the largest automobile producing country in the world—necessarily turn our lust-filled eyes to Europe?

What would it be then? There is always the Corvette, a truly sophisticated GT car, but the Corvette tends to be a glittering boulevard machine with little significant professional competition heritage. The more we thought about it the more we concluded the pure American GT concept is typified by the sporty cars and they are racers. Ask anyone who's seen Trans-Am sedans at 170 mph on the banks of Daytona. Now the plot: according to FIA those scrappy Trans-Am machines are Group 2 sedans and that means the manufacturer has to provide at least 1000 copies. We should be able to get one for a road

test. Right? While we're at it why just one? Why not get one of each kind and compare them? The Mustang and Camaro are obviously on even terms so it didn't seem quite fair to test a Javelin which has had less than a year of development time. We've gone pretty far in saying we're encouraged by the AMC effort, and the plain fact is that they deserve a little time to sort out their car.

What we wanted for this test were cars that any enthusiast could duplicate with factory parts and yet have performance and handling far beyond the sporty cars. Way, way beyond them. We wanted to wander info the office after the test dazed—surfeited. A night with Jane Fonda, a $1-million stake to blow at Monte Carlo, Saville Row to turn out an endless stream of 4-button brocaded double-breasted waistcoats. Velvet collars, Moet & Chandon, 320-foot steel-hulled diesel yachts. That's what we wanted. Trans-Am racers for the street.

FIA homologation papers were convincing evidence that each manufacturer had an abundance of high performance parts that would result, if everything was done just right, in a blindingly fast, exquisitely responsive street car. But the only way to be assured of the best combination of these delectations was to have the manufacturers supply the cars. That's where the footwork started.

C/D has been doing comparison tests for a while and in every test, when we find cars we like and cars we don't, we lay it on the line. In a 2-car test, the second place car is also the last-placed car and it didn't take Ford and Chevrolet awfully long to come to just that conclusion. Neither one wanted to play unless they could win. There would have to be rules or we'd end up with Mark Donahue's Camaro and Jerry Titus' Mustang—which would be a complete gas—but would miss the point entirely. It would all be pretty simple: any factory installed or dealer available part

would be acceptable if it was homologated. We suggested that the engines have the racing two 4-barrel intake system and tuned headers but mufflers would be used at all times. We wanted only factory-available street tires and we wanted the cars supplied with axle ratios as close to 4.10 as possible since both Ford and Chevrolet had homologated this ratio. Of course any homologated suspension parts would be acceptable and 4-wheel disc brakes would be a welcome addition. We warned that we would be on the look-out for cheaters so the engines had better not be bigger than the FIA 305 cubic inch limit and the cars had better not weigh less than the AMA registered curb weights, not the 2800-lb. Trans-Am minimum. Everybody agreed, shook hands and went back to neutral—and not so neutral—corners.

We had the beginning of a splendidly volatile mix, but we needed one thing more, and that would be Sam Posey. Nothing alive can withstand the magic, probing, X-ray eyes of Sam Posey. A fierce, brave racer who has startled his competitors by his absolute fearlessness—and his almost total understanding of how a car behaves under conditions of maximum stress, not to mention his endless pointed stream of talk about it. Yes, Sam Posey was perfect. In awe of nothing, living everything that separates cars from transportation modules, a driver with brio—and not aligned with any factory team. Everything was set. The very walls of the office quivered in anticipation.

In the succeeding days each manufacturer grew more and more up tight about second-place-being-last. Nervous telephone calls between Detroit and New York were unending. Each was afraid the other was going to build a trick car and put the hurt on his innocent, honest-as-it-can-be street car. They would supply an engineer with their car for adjustments, for keeping everyone honest,

and—to our howling disappointment—to return each car to its incubating shop in Detroit the very moment the tests were over.

The first day of testing would be at New York National Speedway where we would do the technical inspection to make sure that nobody had stuffed a 427 or half-thickness steel fenders or any other deceitful devices into our cars.

When we arrived the Camaro and Mustang were already parked, nose to tail, on the strip and much to our surprise, Ford Man and Chevy Man were talking to each other in civil tones.

What was going on here? The Camaro was dazzling. All squeaky clean, wearing its black Z/28 hood and deck stripes and front and rear spoilers. Not even any orange peel in its paint. Hell, it was beautiful, but we asked for a street racer, not a concours entry. Up front was the

Mustang, looking dusty from the trip, sporting a set of 7-inch-wide American Mag wheels and fat Goodyear donuts the likes of which we'd never seen before. A little rule ingenuity, and we hadn't even started examining the cars yet. Those mysterious tires put over 7.5-inches of rubber on the road and they said "Goodyear" on the sidewalls in great big white letters—just like a race tire. The size marking was F60-15 and the mystery deepened—nobody had ever heard of F60-15 but there they were, big as life. One thing for sure; they made the Camaro's standard E70-15s look like Suzuki tires and we weren't the only ones to notice it. "Uh, I don't know about those tires," said Chevy Man. He'd never heard of their like before. "No problem," said Ford Man leading with the old the-best-defense-is-still-a-good-offense trick. "You can get those real easy. How many do you want?" Along with "how many

do you want" he made it clear that, of course, there would be a bill, which slowed us down a bit. What would we do with a bunch of tires that were really too small to be real race tires and yet so big that they would probably rub on the fenders of every street car we could get our hands on? We had no quarrel with their choice of American Mags since the Shelby Mustangs come with 7-inch-wide wheels as standard equipment and the difference between magnesium and steel would never show up in the test. In fact, the Camaro could have used the 7-inch-wide Corvette wheel if they wanted to since it's available through their dealers, but they chose to stay with the standard wheels to emphasize what a good car the regular Z/28 is. "It's a difference in the basic philosophy of the people who built the cars," said Chevy Man later. "They're racers."

The simplest part of the tech inspection

1968 Camaros Z/28.

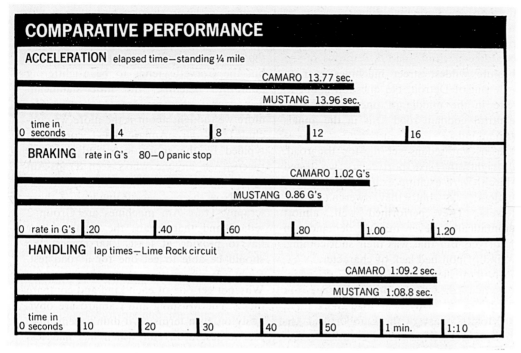

COMPARATIVE PERFORMANCE

ACCELERATION elapsed time—standing ¼ mile

CAMARO 13.77 sec.

MUSTANG 13.96 sec.

| time in seconds 0 | 4 | 8 | 12 | 16 |

BRAKING rate in G's 80—0 panic stop

CAMARO 1.02 G's

MUSTANG 0.86 G's

| 0 rate in G's | .20 | .40 | .60 | .80 | 1.00 | 1.20 |

HANDLING lap times—Lime Rock circuit

CAMARO 1:09.2 sec.

MUSTANG 1:08.8 sec.

| time in seconds 0 | 10 | 20 | 30 | 40 | 50 | 1 min. | 1:10 |

was determining weight—so that came first. Our worry about the Camaro being a concours entry was reinforced when the scale said 3480 lbs., 260 lbs. over the minimum.

"I was afraid of that," said Chevy Man. "With the power steering and power brakes and the custom interior it got a little heavy. We wanted to make a nice car but now I'm afraid we'll get drubbed."

On to the scale came the Mustang, watched by a half dozen very suspicious eyes. No reason for suspicion here, though, because the scale balanced out at 3282 lbs., 111 lbs. over its minimum.

O.K., both cars heavy; but with full street trim what do you expect? The Camaro even had a console, for Christ's sake. Underneath, both cars had a very ordinary looking suspension, neither with any sort of radius rods on the rear axle. In fact, the Camaro had the standard Z/28 front and rear springs and anti-sway bar, with the only change being the optional Koni adjustable shock absorbers. The Mustang used the heavy duty 390 GT front springs and anti-sway bar with export Mustang rear springs. Adjustable shock absorbers were used on the Mustang too, Konis in front and Gabriels in the rear.

To cheat in the engine department you'd have to go big; bigger than the allowable 305 cubic inches. Not that there'd be any particular

problem in doing that, especially with the Camaro, since the 327 and the 350 look the same on the outside as the 302. To catch cheaters, every drag strip worth its name has a device to measure cylinder displacement without removing the heads and New York National is no exception. We were pleased to find that both the Mustang and Camaro checked out at 302 cubes.

"It's really a pretty standard Z/28 engine," volunteered Chevy Man with some relief and no small pride. "It's got the standard camshaft and pistons so the compression ratio is 11.0 to one. About the only thing we've changed is the intake manifold and carbs, as you can see, and, of course, the dealer available headers."

He was being modest about the intake manifold; it was an arresting sight. It's a huge, single plenum chamber ram-tuned setup, very similar to the one used on Chrysler's NASCAR Hemis except that the Camaro had two 600 cubic-feet-per-minute Holleys mounted on top. "We don't recommend the two-by-four intake system for the street because the carburetors don't have chokes and there's no manifold heat. Really, it's just for racing. Works best in the 4800-7200 rpm range which you don't get to use much on the street. For normal driving the single 4-bbl. works better." The air cleaner for the Camaro was a masterpiece too. All black and chrome, it covered both carburetors and

was ducted into the cowl just at the base of the windshield where car speed packs high pressure air. The only other non-standard parts in the Camaro were the optional valve springs, transistor ignition with breakerless distributor, and the heavy duty L-88 clutch and flywheel.

Compared to the Camaro, the Mustang engine was all business. No chrome air cleaner or valve covers. Just plain old blue paint. Even the headers were kind of pale blue. Right on top was a super tall aluminum, two 4-bbl. inline intake manifold with a pair of 540 cfm Holleys and a paper element air cleaner. There it was, tunnel port fans, right in front of our very eyes. The real thing. "Well, yes, this is your regular 12.5 to one compression ratio, dry deck, tunnel port 302," allowed Ford Man still a bit defensive from the tire discussion. "How many do ya want?" Man, just the name tunnel port makes us stand at attention. It's really a simple idea but only Ford had the initiative to do it. Instead of trying to crowd the intake ports between the pushrods like everybody else, Ford just made the intake port as big as they pleased and then ran a little tube down through it for the pushrod to move inside of. A great idea. This particular 302 had a fairly tame (by race standards) camshaft and a dual-point distributor without the benefit of transistor ignition. An 8-quart road racing oil sump finished off the package.

Unfortunately, the Mustang had only a 3.91 axle ratio instead of the 4.10 we had asked for. It was the lesser of two evils. We've never considered Ford's locker rear suitable for the street, and they weren't overjoyed about it themselves, so they equipped the Mustang with their new limited-slip unit which is very similar in principle to what GM and Chrysler use. However, the highest numerical ratio available for that differential is 3.91. The difference between 3.91 and 4.10 is less than 5% and the Mustang's lower profile tires compensated for that difference.

The real testing was scheduled for Tuesday at Lime Rock. Posey had flown back from California on Monday, after finishing third in the Riverside USRRC in his Group 7 Caldwell, and we all arrived at the track almost simultaneously; Sam in his Gullwing Mercedes and us in the lumpy idling test cars. It was a little off-putting. There was Posey having traveled like 3000 miles and we were showing him a pair of what looked like showroom stock sporty cars. "Listen Sam, these are a pair of screaming muthas …" "Sam," "Sam?" It took some convincing but we got him out on the track. From then on he never stopped talking—and smiling.

The Camaro had been the quicker of the two the day before at the drag strip, turning standing start quarter miles in 13.77 seconds at 107.39 mph. The Mustang wasn't exactly a stone either, covering the same distance in 13.96 seconds at 106.13 mph. Just for comparison, the Ferrari 275/GTB-4 we tested (October, '67) was capable of 14.5 second quarters at 100 mph and the 400 hp, 427 Corvette (May, '68) was good for 14.1 seconds at 102 mph.

If there is such a thing as a home track for a race driver, Lime Rock would be that for Posey. Having grown up only five miles away, in Sharon, Connecticut, he spent a good deal of his spare time practicing there. He knows the way around. Since a road test was a whole new deal to Sam he was eager to get on with it, and was just as we suspected—he was ideal, all courage, willingness and technique—and no matter what he was doing, he talked about it. Flat out up the front chute, Sam was talking; through the right hander, wheels to the wall, Sam was talking; tail hung out and wailing, Sam was talking—and all in that same, even, cultivated tone. And all with that almost-uninvolved analytical approach. Posey the scientist at work. It was wild.

"You see, Lime Rock is a track that puts any big car with a fairly mushy suspension to the test right off. The first time you go through The Hook you suddenly realize you're going to have to do a lot of work to go really fast. It's actually a bumpy, hook-shaped turn that you drive with two apexes and it is, without a doubt, the toughest part of the course. There's just no way you can turn the steering wheel one time and expect it to go through."

We'd covered about half a lap in the Camaro when Posey came to the same conclusion about the steering that we had reached when driving up from New York.

"I like the power steering. I've never seen any reason why you should have to make a big effort to steer a racing car. In fact, it's a good case for as little effort as possible, particularly in a Trans-Am car. Some of these races you have to go 350 or 400 miles by yourself which is pretty formidable. I don't feel any less control because it's easy and it's got all the road feel I'd ever need. The thing is… all right, for one lap you might get fractionally more road feel from standard steering, but, ten laps later you're beginning to fight the wheel. You're getting tired and you're not getting so much road feel anymore. You're struggling with the car. This would definitely be the way to go in any prolonged, high speed situation. I like it a lot."

Posey's biggest surprise was the handling.

"It doesn't understeer near as much as I thought it would. You can hang the tail out quite nicely with a little throttle. Of course, it wallows in The Hook but other than that it's really delightful—terrific. Gawd, you could really get away from the cops in this thing."

The fuzz apparently sticks to Posey like it does to Brock Yates. Of course while he's saying these things we're zapping around Lime Rock in a roaring, tire squealing blur and Sam is hanging the inside tires on the edge of the track at every apex and kicking up a cloud of dust on the outside as we come out of every turn. The whole track seems to have changed shape since the first few laps. All the short straights seem shortened dramatically—in fact they look like they're about the length of the hood of the car—and Posey isn't turning in the corners anymore. No 3h, by now he's setting up way before them. Into the main straight. Shifts to fourth at 7000 rpm. The speedometer is past 110 mph. On the brakes at the 200-yard marker for The Hook. Down to third. Power on. Sam is sawing away at the wheel and the Camaro is bellowing and squealing and going around The Hook like it was on a tether. Posey feels that he has the Camaro pretty well sorted out so we pull into the pits to change to the Mustang.

Almost instantly the Mustang starts to an intense, deep-toned idle—the sound you'd expect from an engine that knew it could make over 400 hp from its modest 302 cubic inches

Order your Mustang as hot as you like

…even Shelby hot!

There's a GT package for every kind of Mustang. From the 289- to the 390-cu. in.V-8 and you choose pure stick shifting or SelectShift fully automatic/fully manual.

Every Mustang GT sits firmly on special wide oval tires, plus higher-rate springs, shocks, and stabilizer bar, GT stripes, natch, four-inch

fogs, and front power discs, too.

Want more? There's always Mr. Shelby's sizzling Mustang-based GT 350. Above, Mr. Shelby, with his GT 500—Le Mans developed 428-cu. in.,modified front suspension, four-leaf rear springs. And all the standard Mustang GT features. Order your Mustang as hot

as you like. Every Ford Dealer can get you a Mustang GT; many handle the Shelby cars. And you can add almost any extras, all the way to stereo tape. That way, even a hot Mustang can keep its cool.

THE ORIGINAL

MUSTANG

and wanted to get on with it. Posey puts on one of his enigmatic grins and pulls out onto the track, immediately commenting on the vastly different feel.

"This steering is something else—very heavy. Heavier by far than a Trans-Am car. It's even heavy in the straight. I think the chance of doing really well in this car may be fractionally jeopardized by the steering. The lap times will bear close scrutiny."

"Close scrutiny" for God's sake. He talks like that all the time, whether he's leaning on a fender or grooving through The Hook.

"This car has really excellent throttle response, better than the Camaro. The return spring is very stiff but something happens instantly whenever you push the pedal. The brake feels mushy. The free play seems to be three or four inches and then it doesn't want to stop the car."

Posey worried about the apparent lack of brakes so the approaches to the next few corners were devoted to brake testing.

"Christ Almighty, there's nothing there at all. It's just not braking, period. I'd be better off shifting down. That's a real disappointment."

The difference in the brakes was not coming as what you'd call a shocker of a surprise. The day before in tests the Camaro had performed brilliantly, stopping from 80 mph in only 209 feet at 1.02G, but try as we might, the best stop with the Mustang was 248 feet at 0.86G. Both cars had the racing 4-wheel disc system but Ford Man admitted that they were having trouble with caliper flex which gives a spongy pedal and that these brakes were the same as those on Trans-Am cars.

Posey's reaction to the Mustang's handling was more than just favorable.

"Except for the squealing of the tires, this car handles like a million bucks. The Hook just doesn't present the same problem in this car as it did in the Camaro. It understeers quite a bit but it's very stable. Although the steering effort is greater, it's compensated for by the race suspension, or at least it feels like race suspension, and the racing tires. In fact, I think the tires contribute a lot to my enjoyment of the car. I think we have a definite mismatch here. Ford has taken some considerable advantage with these tires and it would be quite intriguing to see what the Mustang could do with the Camaro's tires. I think this is proving that race tires are, in fact, better for going fast than street tires—and we needn't have come all the way to Lime Rock to see that."

Back into the pits and a discourse on driver environment in the two cars.

"Somehow, I feel more connected to the Mustang than I do to the Camaro. I think the seat has more lateral support. Either that or because it's covered with vinyl instead of cloth like the Camaro, the perspiration is making me stick to the damn thing. It's a shame the prime place in front of the driver in the Mustang instrument panel is reserved for the clock because the fuel and temperature gauges are hidden by the steering wheel rim. The Mustang has a nice big tach but it's difficult to read. The numbers are so close together it looks more like a speedometer and the speedometer has a redline and the tach doesn't—which is kind of a funny situation.

I might have gone up to 70 mph in first gear if I hadn't scoped it all out first. In neither car can I begin to see the instruments without taking my eyes off the road but it's hardest in the Camaro."

The instrumentation in the Camaro was almost nonexistent—a speedometer, fuel gauge, a few idiot lights and an accessory tach clamped to the steering column. Inadequate for a high performance car and only slightly worse than their optional instrument package which mounts all the small gauges on the console.

The test session in the Camaro was cut short by preignition in one of the cylinders which, fortunately, only melted part of the spark plug and distorted an intake valve rather than burning a hole in a piston as is normally the case. Had the Camaro been equipped with racing spark plugs it would have been a failure that probably could have been avoided. Even so, the Camaro was very quick while it lasted and Posey was surprised by his best lap time.

"Really? A 1:09.2? That would have put us somewhere in the middle of the Trans-Am grid here last year which is pretty intriguing since it's really a street car.

"There is a tendency for the rear wheels to lock up and the axle to tramp in braking and when I hit the bumps in The Hook it wants to plow straight off the road. The engine has all kinds of torque. I've been shifting at 6700 because there was no reason to go higher.

"The shift linkage is just absolutely terrible. I keep getting hung up in the reverse crossbar whenever I try to get into second. It's far too sensitive."

On the other hand, Posey was not at all surprised when we told him that he got the Mustang down to 1:08.8.

"I could have gone even faster if it wasn't for the brakes. I have to start braking about 100 yards earlier at the end of the straight than with the Camaro. It really sticks in the corners, though—goes through The Hook like a real racing car."

That only made us more badger-like in our curiosity about the tires. They were obviously wider than what Mustangs are made for since the paint was blistered on each side in front where the tire had been rubbing on the inside

of the fender. The first thing we did when we got back to the office was to call Goodyear in Akron. "An F60-15 does not exist," was the official answer. We explained they might not exist, but that we had five of them. And that, in turn, loosened up the Goodyears some. After a lot of mumbling it came out that the tires on the Mustang were experimental, super-low profile Polyglas jobs that had not been—and maybe never would be—released for production. They did say in a positive tone that they were pretty sore at Ford for letting us see their secret tires.

It's a damn shame to have to put either the Mustang or the Camaro in second, which is to say last, place. Both are easily the most exciting machines we've ever driven with price tags less than $10,000 and by far the best performing street cars ever. But there is a certain inevitability about the results of a comparison test so the Camaro gets the nod. In acceleration, both cars were nearly equal with the Camaro slightly, but consistently, faster. It wasn't much of a contest in the braking test with the Camaro stopping at a rate greater than one G. At Lime Rock the Mustang was a marginal winner but we suspect that with equal tires, the Camaro would have been pretty strong because of its better brakes. In defense of the Mustang, Posey says, "It would have a terrific advantage in a Le Mans start from the pizza parlor because you can't get the ignition key in upside down." And there's this to say about the Mustang too. Unlike the Camaro, we were allowed to keep the Mustang for several days after the test. It went rumbling and grunting by a Little League baseball game—and broke the whole thing up in the top of the third. The kids had to see what that fire-breathing monster was about. And when we passed a house with a GT350 in the driveway along about 7 p.m. the dining room erupted and people poured out windows, doors and chimneys. That's the effect it had. The Mustang even behaved impeccably in one of New York's patented traffic jams. Every kid on the block had to have a ride in it and wives stood around kind of hoping to fill their prom cards. Wild.

Trans-Amers, Mustang v. Camaro. Gawd!

TUNNEL PORT MUSTANG

Price as tested: N.A.

Price with factory options: $3719.69

(includes: GT package, radio, 4-speed transmission, limited-slip differential, tunnel port engine)

Price of dealer-installed parts: N.A.

(includes: intake manifold and carburetors, camshaft, distributor, special front disc brakes, special rear disc brakes, anti-sway bar, front springs, rear springs, exhaust headers)

ENGINE

Bore x stroke.....................4.00 x 3.00 in
Displacement.........................302 cu in
Compression ratio..................12.5 to one
Carburetion........2 x 4-bbl Holley, 540 cfm
Power (SAE).................................NA
Torque (SAE)................................NA

DRIVE TRAIN

Final drive ratio...................3.91 to one

Gear	Ratio	MPH/1000 rpm	Max. test speed
I	2.32	8.1	57 (7000)
II	1.54	12.1	85 (7000)
III	1.19	15.4	110 (7000)
IV	1.00	18.7	131 (7000)

DIMENSIONS AND CAPACITIES

Wheelbase...........................108.0 in
Track.....................F: 58.0 in, R: 58.0 in
Length..............................183.6 in
Width................................70.9 in
Height...............................51.6 in
Curb weight.........................3282 lbs
Weight distribution F/R..........55.2/44.8%
Fuel capacity........................16.0 gal
Oil capacity..........................8.0 qts
Water capacity.......................15.0 qts

SUSPENSION

F: Ind., upper wishbones, single lower arms with drag struts, 390 GT coil springs and anti-sway bar, Koni shock absorbers
R: Rigid axle, export rear springs, Gabriel Adjustomatic shock absorbers

STEERING

Type.........................Recirculating ball
Turns lock to lock.......................3.9

BRAKES

F:..........................11.4-in vented discs
R:..........................11.3-in vented discs
Swept area........................467.6 sq in

WHEELS AND TIRES

Wheel size and type.............15 x 7-in
  American magnesium, 5-bolt
Tire make and size..........Goodyear F60-15
Inflation pressures.......Drag strip F: 27 psi,
  R: 27 psi. Road course F: 36 psi, R: 26 psi

PERFORMANCE

Zero to	Seconds
30 mph	2.2
40 mph	3.1
50 mph	4.1
60 mph	5.4
70 mph	7.1
80 mph	8.6
90 mph	10.5
100 mph	12.5

Standing ¼-mile.....13.96 sec @ 106.13 mph
80–0 mph panic stop............248 ft (0.86G)
Road course lap time...............1:08.8 sec

CAMARO Z/28

Price as tested: $5440.38

Price with factory options: $3708.58

(includes: Z/28 option, 4-speed transmission, limited-slip differential, power disc brakes, air-spoiler equipment, power steering, radio, custom interior)

Price of dealer-installed parts: $1731.80

(includes: 2 x 4-bbl intake system, air cleaner and plenum assembly, rear axle assembly with disc brakes, special front disc brake assemblies, Koni shock absorbers, exhaust headers, HD valve springs, distributor, transistor ignition, HD clutch and flywheel)

ENGINE

Bore x stroke.....................4.00 x 3.00 in
Displacement.........................302 cu in
Compression ratio..................11.0 to one
Carburetion........2 x 4-bbl Holley, 600 cfm
Power (SAE).................................NA
Torque (SAE)................................NA

DRIVE TRAIN

Final drive ratio...................4.10 to one

Gear	Ratio	MPH/1000 rpm	Max. test speed
I	2.20	8.6	60 (7000)
II	1.64	11.5	81 (7000)
III	1.27	14.9	104 (7000)
IV	1.00	18.9	132 (7000)

DIMENSIONS AND CAPACITIES

Wheelbase...........................108.0 in
Track.....................F: 59.6 in, R: 59.5 in
Length..............................184.5 in
Width................................72.3 in
Height...............................50.9 in
Curb Weight.........................3480 lbs
Weight distribution F/R..........55.1/44.9%
Fuel capacity........................18.0 gal
Oil capacity..........................4.0 qts
Water capacity.......................16.0 qts

SUSPENSION

F: Ind., unequal-length wishbones, standard Z/28 coil springs and anti-sway bar, Koni shock absorbers
R: Rigid axle, standard Z/28 semi-elliptic leaf springs, Koni shock absorbers

STEERING

Type......Recirculating ball (power-assisted)
Turns lock-to-lock.......................3.0

BRAKES

F:......11.75-in vented discs (power-assisted)
R:......11.75-in vented discs (power-assisted)
Swept area........................461.2 sq in

WHEELS AND TIRES

Wheel size and type.............15 x 6.0-in
  stamped steel, 5-bolt
Tire make and size........Goodyear E70-15,
  tubeless
Inflation pressures......Drag strip F: 27 psi,
  R: 27 psi. Road course F: 47 psi, R: 38 psi.

PERFORMANCE

Zero to	Seconds
30 mph	2.2
40 mph	3.1
50 mph	4.1
60 mph	5.3
70 mph	7.0
80 mph	8.5
90 mph	10.3
100 mph	12.3

Standing ¼-mile.....13.77 sec @ 107.39 mph
80–0 mph panic stop............209 ft (1.02G)
Road course lap time...............1:09.2 sec

New Cyclone Spoiler. Passwor[d]
You'd better bring along a d[...]

Here's the muscle machine that puts wind to work for you. Tested out at 100 mph, front spoiler drops lift from 186 to 120.5 pounds. Rear spoiler cuts it down from 67.5 to a flat, fast 5.8. The Cyclone Spoiler comes equipped with all basic

competition hardware. CJ 429 V-8 (370 [...] Four-speed Hurst Shifter.* The works. G[...] from Mercury, password for action in the [...]

MERCURY CYCLONE Ford

FoMoCo's sleek Mercury Cyclone Spoiler joins the Muscle wars.

1969
Full Throttle

Pedal to the metal. Muscle Car sales are as high as Bob Dylan's eye.

Every Detroit carmaker has three or four muscle models. They come in every form, from big-engined pony cars to monster-block street-racers. Zero to 60 in five seconds is available to any hitchhiker worth her thumb.

And American Muscle is indisputably a "revolution." In mainline Detroit only a few years earlier, five seconds to 60 didn't exist. Now it's as expected and inevitable as underage drinking in Tijuana.

Motor racing, from quarter mile to super-speedway, is white-hot—and *Car and Driver* is all over it like chili on a Pink's hot dog. "Win on Sunday; sell on Monday," chants the choir—and Detroit hums along with racy shapes and big-blocks.

In NASCAR, an entire subdivision of American Muscle, seeking the 200-mph lap at Talladega, adopts the full fastback form. Even Richard Petty, "The King," forsakes MOPAR for Ford's fastback Torino 427 Cobra during the 1969 NASCAR season—achieving superlative results, but falling just short of David Pearson's Torino for the Grand National Championship.

Ford, Mercury, American Motors, Dodge, Plymouth, Pontiac and Chevrolet are all in racing up to their wallet. The muscle cars they sell to the enthusiast public come with everything except numbers on the door.

And the winner is...

COMPARISON ROAD TEST

SIX ECONO-RACERS

CHEVELLE SS 396 • COBRA • CYCLONE CJ • HEMI ROAD RUNNER • SUPER BEE • THE JUDGE

If you like the taste of whiskey you drink it on the rocks, right? Distilled. There's nothing very complicated about that. But what do you do if you really like the taste of automobiles? We'll tell you what. You pick one of Detroit's war-horses—the intermediates that carry the corporate banners as Grand National stock cars and drag racing super stocks. You order your car with every go, stop, and turn part available, but nothing else. You've got yourself an Econo-Racer.

Plymouth pioneered the idea when it introduced the Road Runner. Road Runner logic forthwith became impossible to argue with—as all of Detroit discovered—when, in the first year, 19.8% of the intermediate-size Plymouths were Road Runners. Dodge joined the movement with the Super Bee.

With the introduction of its 1969 models, the Ford Motor Company laid its Econo-Racer cards on the table—a Cobra for the Ford Division and a Cyclone CJ from Lincoln-Mercury. It wasn't bluffing either—no less than the 428 Cobra Jet engine as standard equipment in each.

But what about GM, which almost never admits a competitive urge? Chevrolet offers its SS 396 package on the 300 Deluxe 2-door coupe—which fits the Econo-Racer description regardless of what Chevrolet chooses to call it. Pontiac, too, was pushing The Judge over the horizon and couldn't be overlooked.

To make things simple in our test we asked for the base engine with the optional functional hood scoops on every car—with one exception, the Road Runner. Since the Super Bee and the Road Runner are mechanically identical it didn't make sense to have both of them with the standard 383, so we asked for the only other option—the 426 Hemi—in the Road Runner.

To keep everything even, each car was ordered with F70 tires, an axle ratio as close as possible to 3.50 with a limited-slip differential, disc brakes (which are available only with

power-assist), and power steering. Automatic transmissions were selected simply because, with street tires, they're the fastest way to go. Nobody can deny the importance of a tachometer in a performance car, so that part was in, and we specified styled wheels so our Econo-Racers wouldn't be confused with taxi cabs. That's all.

So you can imagine our surprise when only the Road Runner and the Super Bee arrived in fighting trim. The others had bucket seats and consoles—three of them even had trick steering wheels and electric windows. The Cobra and the Cyclone CJ were wearing their 1969 Econo-Racer name tags but they also had the same gadgets and glitter that have festooned Detroit performance cars for years. And the Chevelle, a Malibu 2-door hardtop, came complete with all of the gee-whiz trim, flashing light monitors and buzzing warning devices, not to mention an absolutely flawless metallic blue paint job. It was a veteran show car Chevrolet had sprung from its duties. Each of the cars had every piece of optional equipment we had asked for, but the manufacturers didn't have the restraint to stop there.

The extra equipment on the Cobra, Cyclone CJ and Chevelle are detrimental to the results of an Econo-Racer comparison test only in that they raise the price. The added weight may marginally reduce the performance, but should in no way change the basic feel which is of prime importance in this type of car. Unless you happen to live somewhere on the Great Plains, these cars are so quick you can seldom use wide-open throttle for more than a few seconds, and even then you use it with great respect or suddenly you're in American Samoa.

After two weeks, both on the track and on public roads, the staff knew which cars made the program, which didn't and why. Listed below—best first—are the Econo-Racers.

HEMI ROAD RUNNER

The Hemi Road Runner was an easy first choice, not so much because of the Road Runner as the Hemi engine and everything that goes with it. To say the Road Runner scored heavily in the performance part of the test is Anglo Saxon understatement in the best tradition. It was the quickest in acceleration, stopped in the shortest distance and ranked second in handling. That is a pretty tough record.

All the while the Hemi was proving itself to be the toughest car of the test, it was also proving to be the most exciting. Where the Chevelle, Cobra and Cyclone CJ give the impression of being hot sedans, the Road Runner comes in from the other direction—a tamed race car. And that impression isn't entirely wrong. Chrysler's 426 cu. in. hemispherical combustion chamber V-8 was never intended to quietly propel Imperials down the freeway/expressway/throughway/parkway. It was designed as a race engine, pure and simple. The whole idea was to put the hurt on Ford at Daytona because Ford was too far ahead for conventional weapons. Accordingly, the Road Runner's Hemi is the same basic engine used in Grand National stock cars and super stock drag machines.

What is it like on the street? Breath-taking. The Hemi Road Runner has more pure mechanical presence than any other American automobile—even more than the Z/28 Camaros we've grown to love. Of course the Hemi is noisy, although it's not an excessive amount of mechanical noise. After it's warmed up, the impact-extruded pistons no longer clunk around in their bores and the solid-lifter valve gear is almost totally silent. In fact in actual engine noise, the Hemi was quieter than the Cobra Jet. It's the power noise that sets the Hemi apart. It has an impatient, surging idle that causes the whole car to quiver. And there is that lump in the throttle travel. Stay on

the near side of the lump and you can drive at any speed you choose up to, say, 100 mph in relative calm. Go past the lump and you open everything in the two 4-bbl. Carters. The exhaust explodes like Krakatoa and the wailing howl of surprised air being sucked into the intakes turns heads for blocks. Baby, you know you're in the presence.

If you are on a drag strip, as we were, the standing quarter-miles can be covered in the 13.5 second range at just over 105 mph. For a 3,938-lb car, that is making it.

Of course the Road Runner's race car complexion is reinforced by its suspension. It is incredibly stiff—guaranteed to produce extreme discomfort for anyone but an enthusiast. All Hemi Road Runners are built with higher rate torsion bars and rear springs than their 383 counterparts. It has a strong under-steering nature that requires a heavy throttle foot to get the tail out, but it does corner very predictably with very little body roll.

In a car as fast as the Hemi, you'd better have brakes equal to the task—and they were.

The Road Runner stopped in a straight line from 80 mph in 245 feet (0.87 G), shorter than any of the other cars. However, brake fade was noticeably greater than in the Ford or GM cars. We normally make three stops from 80 mph. Since it was almost impossible to obtain impending lockup on the third stop we tried a fourth, just to see what would happen. Even though the pedal did bottom out and the required pedal pressure was very high, the Road Runner stopped in less distance than the first two tries—and with no swerving. We would consider the brakes very satisfactory for street operations.

In the driver's compartment the Road Runner was—as expected—stark. That is what Econo-Racers are all about. The instruments are arranged in a horizontal line on the dash, white-on-black and very easy to read. No oil pressure gauge was present or available, which registers as a true felony considering the $813 price of the Hemi. We weren't exactly turned on by the tachometer either—it had a circular face occupying a small rectangular spot in the instrument panel, half hidden by the steering

wheel rim. The Woolworth's Five and Dime appearance was combined with a 5000 rpm redline—about 800 rpm below where the transmission automatically upshifts.

The Road Runner's most conspicuous ornamentation change for 1969 is that the chicken decals are now in full color. No matter where you look—on the doors or the deck lid or the instrument panel or the steering wheel hub—there is that unfortunate beep-beep bird looking back at you. It's the only light touch on an otherwise totally serious car. That is, if you can have a light touch with a heavy hand.

In case you came in late, the Hemi-powered Road Runner is one hell of an Econo-Racer. It goes about its intended purpose with a sort of well prepared confidence not found in the others. It probably has zero appeal to the faint-hearted but that is the least of our worries—and it should be the least of yours. The only area in which it falls wide of the Econo-Racer goal is price. At $4,362.05, as tested, it wasn't the most expensive car of the group but it certainly would have been had they all been equipped as we suggested. With

Sunday afternoon at the drags, hood scoops snorting raw air…

just the options we asked for, the Road Runner still would have listed at almost $4,240. All we can say is that this kind of excitement doesn't come cheap, no matter what your hang-up is.

SUPER BEE

The issue was not nearly so clear in choosing a second-place car but, after polling the staff, the Super Bee was selected to fill that slot—with strong sentiment in favor of the Cobra nonetheless. The Super Bee was fourth in acceleration and third in both braking and handling, which add up to the same performance rating achieved by the Cobra. It was the exceptionally well-coordinated feel of the Dodge, combined with really outstanding instrumentation, that made the difference.

The test car was powered by the standard 335-hp 383 cu. in. V-8 breathing through the optional cold-air induction system that feeds fresh air to the carburetor through two hood scoops. Cloudbursts and storms will never see the inside of your engine because a red knob under the instrument panel (labeled "carb air") has been provided so that the driver can manually close the scoops. Of course, this little feature makes it very easy for us to see if Dodge is really giving you your money's worth in performance or if the scoops just add up to expensive decoration. Dodge does not speak with forked tongue. In a standing quarter-mile the open scoops are worth exactly one mile per hour and slightly more than one-tenth of a second in elapsed time.

Even though the Super Bee was the lightest car of the test, with a curb weight of 3,765 lbs, we were a little surprised when the average of our acceleration runs was 14.04 seconds at 99.55 mph. We know that a combination of the air scoops and the extra traction of the Polyglas tires is worth about 1.5 mph in the quarter but the car still seemed faster than other Super Bees we've driven. A careful scrutinizing session turned up two questionable pieces of hardware; a dual-point distributor and a large diameter exhaust system similar to that used on the Coronet R/T. A quick check of the AMA specifications—gospel throughout the industry—indicated the parts were standard equipment. Just on a hunch, we

checked further and discovered that the 383s coming off the assembly line, as we suspected, have single point distributors and smaller, 2.25-inch diameter exhaust pipes.

Knowing that, we can't consider our test car's performance to be representative of a 383 Super Bee you would buy. From our experience we would estimate a production car in good tune to run about 98.5 mph in the 14.20-second range.

In the braking tests, the Super Bee performed almost exactly like the Road Runner, which is not too surprising since they both use identical braking systems. The Dodge required an additional five feet to stop from 80 mph which is well within production variation.

Since the 383-engined cars have lower rate torsion bars and rear springs than the Hemi models, it is not surprising that they also have more body roll when cornering. In fact, the Dodge had more body roll than any other car in the test. Even so, the car handles well with moderate understeer and good directional control. The relatively quick power steering is an aid in maneuvering despite its light effort.

The Super Bee takes a giant step forward with its instrument panel—shared with its more expensive sibling, the Charger. This panel contains a complete set of easily readable gauges mounted directly in front of the driver—all marked in a no-nonsense style. Not so good was the column-mounted (automatic, remember) transmission shifter—also shared with the Road Runner. It was completely average in its operation with Jello-like detents that may be satisfactory for the unenlightened millions but not for a performance advocate.

Like the Road Runner, a high degree of excitement is engendered when you are driving the Super Bee. Somehow, it just feels like a racer.

COBRA

It's been a long time since we thought of a "Cobra" as a snake but we never expected to see the name attached to a car as big as Ford's new Fairlane-based Econo-Racer. Our test car was a fastback 2-door hardtop (there is also a formal roof hardtop available) with the standard 428 Cobra Jet (Ford is really hung up

on the Cobra name) engine and optional Ram-Air package.

The Cobra grabs the third spot in the test primarily because of its strong performance in the acceleration and braking tests. The Cobra Jet is known to be a tough performer on the dragstrip so the 14.04 second performances of the test car at 100.61 mph are well within its reputation. The special white-lettered F70 × 14 Polyglas tires used on the Cobra have a unique tread compound developed for dry traction, but even so, the torquey 428 could turn them with ease.

The hood scoop system, on both the Cobra and Cyclone CJ, has no manual control but, rather, is controlled by a vacuum motor that opens a trap door into the top of the air cleaner when the throttle approaches wide open. For that reason it was necessary to tape the door shut to simulate the non-Ram Air model. That little exercise paid off—we discovered the Cobra Jet has a definite appetite for fresh air because, without the scoop, it lost almost 0.2 seconds and 1.4 mph in the quarter. The Ram-Air package is expensive at $133.44, but it is very effective.

When you are trying for maximum performance—which is what these cars are all about—you become acutely aware of any shortcomings in the controls and instrumentation. The very large Cobra tachometer is mounted relatively close to the driver and aimed at his chest so that it is difficult to read. The panel contains four large, round dials but somehow everything but fuel level is left to warning lights—just what you would expect in a Falcon. The console shifter, too, was vague and Falcony in its operation. During the street driving part of the test, we noticed that the accelerator pedal assumed a low frequency up-and-down motion whenever we hit a bump. Apparently soft engine mounts are used and engine motion is translated back through the throttle linkage.

We haven't been able to fall in love with the power steering, either, which is of the high effort type—not to be confused with road feel. If we could use only one word to describe it, that word would be numb. If you turn the wheel two inches either direction from center, it just stays there, which demonstrates a certain degree of insensitivity. What we are trying to say is that the Cobra doesn't have controls in keeping with its performance.

But my goodness, Betsy—the Cobra does have good brakes. It could be stopped from 80 mph in 248 feet (0.86G) and did so three consecutive times with no serious fade and exceptional directional stability.

When it comes to handling we can only say that the Cobra performs in the current Ford pattern—strong understeer. Anyone who spins one of these cars has to be trying because it is as resistant to changing ends as anything we can remember.

Both the Cobra and the Cyclone CJ have a very comfortable and silent ride—exceeded only by the Chevelle. The ride harshness is more than acceptable for this kind of car and the high roll stiffness contributes to the comfort level when you get off that straight road. We would prefer more shock absorber control to damp out the low frequency floating motion that is most noticeable at high speed.

There were many very good qualities in the Cobra. Enough so that placing it third instead of second has started a kind of C/D civil war. Everywhere we looked we saw evidence of quality assembly. When you stand back and look at the Cobra with its competition-style hoodpins, bulging scoop and white-lettered tires you know it's a real racer. But when you drive it, it feels more like a family sedan with a big engine.

CYCLONE CJ

Differences between Mercury's Cyclone CJ and the Cobra are largely a matter of styling since both are mechanically similar. We ranked the Mercury below the Ford primarily because of its poorer braking performance—surely the result of production variation.

We found the Mercury's styling more to our liking even though both cars are nearly identical in silhouette. The Mercury seems cleaner—at least the hood scoop is. Ford, with its Better Ideas, decorated the rear of the Cobra's scoop with the turn signal indicators while Mercury was content to simply spray on some flat black paint. To us, a functional hood scoop is its own attraction so it doesn't have to

ECONO-RACER CHECK LIST						
(Cars rated numerically with 6 as maximum)	Chevelle SS396	Super Bee	Cobra	Cyclone CJ	The Judge	Road Runner
PRICE						
Price (basic econo-racer)	3409.10	3740.10	3792.78	3836.50	N/A	4239.45
Rating	6	5	4	3	2 est.	1
Price (as tested)	4048.25	3858.00	4043.23	4381.60	N/A	4362.05
Rating	4	6	5	1	3 est.	2
PERFORMANCE						
Acceleration	2	3	4	5	*	6
Braking	2	4	5	3	*	6
Handling	6	4	2	2	*	5
PERFORMANCE RATING	10	11	11	10	*	17
DRIVER CONTROLS						
Steering feel	6	4	2	2	5	4
Braking feel	1	5	4	2	3	6
Transmission shifter	1	3	4	4	6	3
Instrumentation	5	6	1	1	4	3
DRIVER CONTROLS RATING	13	18	11	9	18	16

Not representative

light up like a Christmas tree to prove its worth.

The Cyclone's basic equipment list was identical to all of the other test cars with one exception—the 3.91 axle ratio. We had expected the standard 3.50 ratio but a few minutes on the expressway was convincing evidence to the contrary. As you would calculate, the higher numerical axle ratio gave the Cyclone a slight edge in acceleration times. It was about a tenth of a second quicker in the standing start quarter; 13.94 seconds at 100.89 mph. A streetable car that will run a quarter in under 14 seconds is very quick indeed but the increase in engine noise at cruising speeds with the tall gear is not worth the performance gain.

We are also a little curious about the remarkable traction of the Cyclone's tires. Both the Cobra and Cyclone had special traction tires as standard equipment, but the Mercury would take full throttle off the line, which neither the Ford nor any of the other test cars could do.

The Cyclone's greatest shortcoming came to light in the braking tests. The rear brakes suffered from premature lock-up, resulting in poor directional stability and greatly increased stopping distances. Stopping from 80 mph required 283 feet (0.76G). This can be attributed to poor proportioning of the braking effort, a chronic problem with disc/drum combinations.

Everything said about the handling and

driver controls of the Cobra also pertains to the Cyclone. The Cyclone does have a slightly different instrument panel layout, however, which improves readability, particularly of the tachometer.

The Cyclone CJ can best be described as a gentleman's muscle car. Its competition-oriented external appearance is certainly in keeping with its wide-open throttle performance but the car has been carefully developed for minimum intrusion on the occupants' senses. At $40 more than the Cobra you can have a choice of styling.

CHEVELLE SS 396

If a committee of Detroit executives tested this same group of cars, the Chevelle would have been the overall winner—by miles. We ranked it fifth. There is a very fine line between endearing mechanical excellence and an automatic, remote-control automobile. Driving the Chevelle on any expressway is an uncomfortable hint of the future: sitting in an insulated capsule moving on a conveyer. Perfect for the 4-door sedan set but hard for the enthusiast to love.

The Chevelle was easily the quietest car of the test. Engine noise, including intake and exhaust, was almost undetectable with the

CHEVELLE SS 396

List price as tested: $4,048.25

Options on test car: 325-hp engine with SS package including styled wheels, power disc brakes and F70 x 14 tires, $347.60; automatic trans, $221.80; 3.55 limited-slip differential, $42.15; tachometer and instrumentation, $94.80; power steering, $105.35; AM/FM radio, $133.80; H.D. suspension, $5.30; rear window defroster, $22.15; power windows, $105.35; bucket seats and console, $174.90; tinted glass, $36.90; head restraints, $16.90; light monitoring system, $26.35; auxiliary lighting, $16.35; rear speakers, $13.20; all-vinyl interior, $12.65.

ENGINE
Bore x stroke.....................4.09 x 3.76 in
Displacement.........................396 cu in
Compression ratio.............10.25 to one
Carburetion...........1 x 4-bbl. Rochester
Power (SAE)...........325 bhp @ 4800 rpm
Torque (SAE).......410 lbs/ft @ 3200 rpm

DRIVE TRAIN
Final drive ratio......................3.55 to one

DIMENSIONS AND CAPACITIES
Wheelbase...............................112.0 in
Track.................F: 59.0 in, R: 59.0 in
Length..................................196.9 in
Width......................................76.0 in
Height.....................................52.8 in
Curb weight............................3895 lbs
Weight distribution, F/R.........57.0/43.0%
Fuel capacity...........................20.0 gal
Oil capacity...............................4.0 qts
Water capacity.........................23.0 qts

SUSPENSION
F: Ind., unequal length wishbones, coil springs, anti-sway bar.
R: Rigid axle, trailing arms, coil springs, anti-sway bar.

STEERING
Type........Recirculating ball, power-assisted
Turns lock-to-lock.....................4.25
Turning circle............................39.0 ft

BRAKES
F.....................11.0-in vented disc, power-assisted
R...9.5 x 2.0-in cast iron drum, power-assisted

WHEELS AND TIRES
Wheel size..........................14 x 7.0-in
Tire make and size.......F 70 x 14 Goodyear Polyester
Test inflation pressures...F: 26 psi, R: 26 psi

PERFORMANCE
Zero to	Seconds
40 mph	2.9
60 mph	5.8
80 mph	10.0
100 mph	15.2
Standing ¼-mile	14.41 sec @ 97.35 mph
80–0 mph panic stop	304 ft (0.70 G)

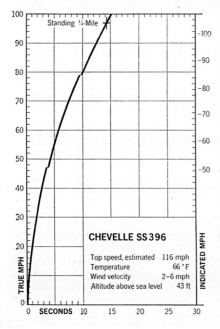

CHEVELLE SS396

Top speed, estimated	116 mph
Temperature	66 °F
Wind velocity	2–6 mph
Altitude above sea level	43 ft

SUPER BEE

List price as tested: $3858.00

Options on test car: 3.55 limited-slip differential, $102.15; power disc brakes, $93.10; head restraints, $26.50; foam seat, $8.60; automatic trans., $40.40; remote adjust mirror, $9.65; 3-speed wipers, $5.40; undercoating, $16.60; rear quarter air scoops, $35.80; rear bumper guards, $16.00; tachometer and clock, $50.15; cold air induction, $73.30; AM radio, $63.35; power steering $97.65; styled wheels, $88.55; F70 x 14 belted tires, $26.45.

ENGINE
Bore x stroke.......................4.25 x 3.38 in
Displacement...........................383 cu in
Compression ratio...............10.0 to one
Carburetion...........1 x 4 bbl Carter AVS
Power (SAE)............335 bhp @ 5200 rpm
Torque (SAE).......425 lbs/ft @ 3400 rpm

DRIVE TRAIN
Final drive ratio.....................3.55 to one

DIMENSIONS AND CAPACITIES
Wheelbase...............................117.0 in
Track.................F: 59.5 in, R: 59.2 in
Length..................................206.6 in
Width......................................76.7 in
Height.....................................54.1 in
Curb weight............................3765 lbs
Weight distribution, F/R.........55.7/44.3%
Fuel capacity...........................19.0 gal
Oil capacity...............................4.0 qts
Water capacity.........................17.0 qts

SUSPENSION
F: Ind., upper wishbones, single lower arms with struts, torsion bars, anti-sway bar
R: Rigid axle, semi-elliptic leaf springs

STEERING
Type........Recirculating ball, power assisted
Turns lock-to-lock.......................3.4
Turning circle............................44.0 ft

BRAKES
F.............11.0-in vented disc, power-assisted
R...10.0 x 2.5-in cast iron drum, power-assisted

WHEELS AND TIRES
Wheel size..........................14 x 5.5-in
Tire make and size.......F70 x 14, Goodyear
Test inflation pressures...F: 26 psi, R: 26 psi

PERFORMANCE
Zero to	Seconds
40 mph	2.8
60 mph	5.6
80 mph	9.1
100 mph	14.1
Standing ¼-mile	14.04 sec @ 99.55 mph
80–0 mph panic stop	250 ft (0.85 G)

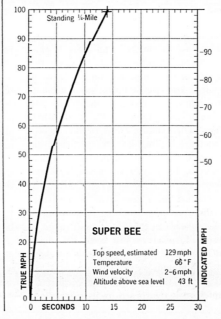

SUPER BEE

Top speed, estimated	129 mph
Temperature	66 °F
Wind velocity	2–6 mph
Altitude above sea level	43 ft

COBRA

List price as tested: $4043.23

Options on test car: Ram air engine, $133.44; bucket seats with console, $168.62; automatic transmission, $37.06; limited slip differential, $63.51; visibility group, $11.06; F70-14 belted tires, $77.73; rim-blow steering wheel, $35.70; power steering, $100.26; power disc brakes, $64.77; AM radio, $61.40; deluxe belt/warning light, $15.59; racing mirrors, $19.48; styled wheels, $17.69; tachometer, $47.92.

ENGINE
Bore x stroke.......................4.13 x 3.98 in
Displacement...........................428 cu in
Compression ratio...............10.6 to one
Carburetion...................1 x 4 bbl Holley
Power (SAE)............335 bhp @ 5200 rpm
Torque (SAE).......440 lbs/ft @ 3400 rpm

DRIVE TRAIN
Final drive ratio.....................3.50 to one

DIMENSIONS AND CAPACITIES
Wheelbase...............................116.0 in
Track.................F: 58.8 in, R: 58.5 in
Length..................................201.1 in
Width......................................74.6 in
Height.....................................52.6 in
Curb weight............................3890 lbs
Weight distribution, F/R.........57.7/42.3%
Fuel capacity...........................20.0 gal
Oil capacity...............................4.0 qts
Water capacity.........................19.6 qts

SUSPENSION
F: Ind., upper wishbones, single lower arms with struts, coil springs, anti-sway bar
R: Rigid axle, semi-elliptic leaf springs

STEERING
Type........Recirculating ball, power-assisted
Turns lock-to-lock.......................3.75
Turning circle.............................41 ft

BRAKES
F..................11.3-in vented disc, power-assisted
R...10.0 x 2.0-in cast iron drum, power-assisted

WHEELS AND TIRES
Wheel size..........................14 x 6.0-in
Tire make and size.......F70 x 14, Goodyear Polyglas
Test inflation pressures...F: 28 psi, R: 28 psi

PERFORMANCE
Zero to	Seconds
40 mph	2.8
60 mph	5.6
80 mph	9.1
100 mph	14.0
Standing ¼-mile	14.04 sec @ 100.61 mph
80–0 mph panic stop	248 ft (0.86 G)

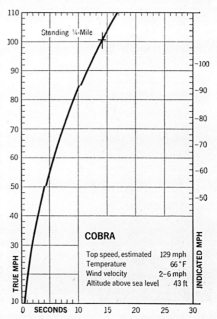

COBRA

Top speed, estimated	129 mph
Temperature	66 °F
Wind velocity	2–6 mph
Altitude above sea level	43 ft

CYCLONE CJ

List price as tested: $4381.60

Options on test car: Ram air engine, $138.60; bucket seats with console, $165.80; automatic trans, $42.00; 3.91 axle, $6.50; limited-slip differential, $63.50; light group, $19.50; rim-blow steering wheel, $35.00; power windows, $104.90; power steering, $94.60; power brakes, $64.50; AM/FM stereo radio, $185.30; rear speaker, $25.90; tinted glass, $35.00; deluxe seat belts, $15.60; racing mirror, $13.00; styled wheels, $116.60; tachometer, $48.00.

ENGINE
Bore x stroke.................4.13 x 3.98 in
Displacement....................428 cu in
Compression ratio..............10.6 to one
Carburetion.............1 x 4 bbl Holley
Power (SAE)........335 bhp @ 5200 rpm
Torque (SAE).........440 lbs/ft @ 3400 rpm

DRIVE TRAIN
Final drive ratio.................3.91 to one

DIMENSIONS AND CAPACITIES
Wheelbase.........................116.0 in
Track.............F: 58.8 in, R: 58.5 in
Length............................203.2 in
Width..............................76.0 in
Height.............................53.9 in
Curb weight.......................3860 lbs
Weight distribution, F/R........56.7/43.3%
Fuel capacity......................20.0 gal
Oil capacity.......................4.0 qts
Water capacity....................19.6 qts

SUSPENSION
F: Ind., upper wishbones, single lower arms with struts, coil springs, anti-sway bar
R: Rigid axle, semi-elliptic leaf springs

STEERING
Type........Recirculating ball, power-assisted
Turns lock-to-lock..................3.75
Turning circle.....................42.0 ft

BRAKES
F............11.3 in vented disc, power-assisted
R..10.0 x 2.0-in cast iron drum, power-assisted

WHEELS AND TIRES
Wheel size.....................14 x 6.0-in
Tire make and size.......F70 x 14, Goodyear Polyglas
Test inflation pressures....F: 28 psi, R: 28 psi

PERFORMANCE
Zero to	Seconds
40 mph	2.7
60 mph	5.5
80 mph	9.0
100 mph	13.9

Standing ¼-mile....13.94 sec @ 100.89 mph
80–0 mph panic stop..........283 ft (0.76 G)

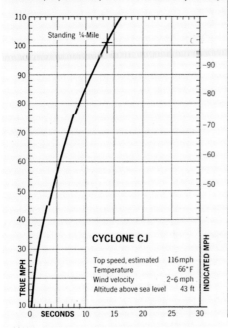

CYCLONE CJ

Top speed, estimated	116mph
Temperature	66°F
Wind velocity	2-6 mph
Altitude above sea level	43 ft

THE JUDGE

List price as tested: N.A.

Options on test car: Power disc brakes, $64.25; automatic transmission, $227.04; power steering, $105.32; AM/FM radio, $133.76; wood rim steering wheel, $34.76; tachometer, $63.19; instrument package, $50.55; power windows, $105.32; limited-slip differential, $63.19; rear seat speaker, $15.80; remote control mirror, $10.53.

ENGINE
Bore x stroke.................4.12 x 3.75 in
Displacement....................400 cu in
Compression ratio.............10.75 to one
Carburetion.......1 x 4-bbl Rochester
Power (SAE)........366 bhp @ 5100 rpm
Torque (SAE).......445 lbs/ft @ 3600 rpm

DRIVE TRAIN
Final drive ratio.................3.55 to one

DIMENSIONS AND CAPACITIES
Wheelbase.........................112.0 in
Track.............F: 60.0 in, R: 60.0 in
Length............................201.5 in
Width..............................75.8 in
Height.............................52.3 in
Curb weight.......................3898 lbs
Weight distribution, F/R........57.0/53.0%
Fuel capacity......................21.5 gal
Oil capacity.......................5.0 qts
Water capacity....................17.8 qts

SUSPENSION
F: Ind., unequal length wishbones, coil springs, anti-sway bar
R: Rigid axle, trailing arms, coil springs

STEERING
Type........Recirculating ball, power-assisted
Turns lock-to-lock..................4.0
Turning circle.....................38.0 ft

BRAKES
F............11.1 in vented disc, power-assisted
R............9.5 x 2.0-in, cast iron drum, power-assisted

WHEELS AND TIRES
Wheel size.....................14 x 6.0-in
Tire make and size........G70 x 14, Goodyear Polyglas
Test inflation pressures....F: 28 psi, R: 28 psi

PERFORMANCE
Zero to	Seconds
40 mph	see text
60 mph	see text
80 mph	see text
100 mph	see text

Standing ¼-mile....see text
80–0 mph panic stop..........see text

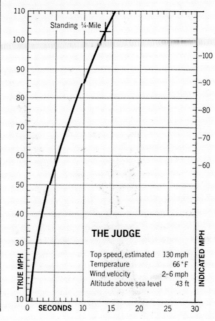

THE JUDGE

Top speed, estimated	130mph
Temperature	66°F
Wind velocity	2-6 mph
Altitude above sea level	43 ft

ROAD RUNNER

List price as tested: $4,362.05

Options on test car: 425-hp engine, $813.45; automatic transmission, $39.30; performance axle package with automatic transmission, $64.40; decor package, $81.50; remote control mirror, $10.45; power steering, $100.00; power disc brakes, $91.65; AM radio, $61.55; rear speaker, $14.05; tachometer, $50.15; undercoating, $16.60; F70 x 15 belted tires, $90.95.

ENGINE
Bore x stroke.................4.25 x 3.75 in
Displacement....................426 cu in
Compression ratio.............10.25 to one
Carburetion.......2 x 4-bbl Carter
Power (SAE)........425 bhp @ 5000 rpm
Torque (SAE).......490 lbs/ft @ 4000 rpm

DRIVE TRAIN
Final drive ratio.................3.54 to one

DIMENSIONS AND CAPACITIES
Wheelbase.........................116.0 in
Track.............F: 59.5 in, R: 59.2 in
Length............................202.7 in
Width..............................76.4 in
Height.............................54.1 in
Curb weight.......................3938 lbs
Weight distribution, F/R........56.4/43.6%
Fuel capacity......................19.0 gal
Oil capacity.......................5.0 qts
Water capacity....................18.0 qts

SUSPENSION
F: Ind., upper wishbones, single lower arms with struts, torsion bars, anti-sway bar.
R: Rigid axle, semi-elliptic leaf springs

STEERING
Type........Recirculating ball, power-assisted
Turns lock-to-lock..................3.5
Turning circle.....................41.3 ft

BRAKES
F............11.0-in vented disc, power-assisted
R..10.0 x 2.5-in cast iron drum, power-assisted

WHEELS AND TIRES
Wheel size.....................15 x 6.0-in
Tire make and size........F70 x 15, Goodyear Polyglas
Test inflation pressures....F: 26 psi, R: 26 psi

PERFORMANCE
Zero to	Seconds
40 mph	2.6
60 mph	5.1
80 mph	8.2
100 mph	12.3

Standing ¼-mile.....13.54 sec @ 105.14 mph
80–0 mph panic stop..........245 ft (0.87 G)

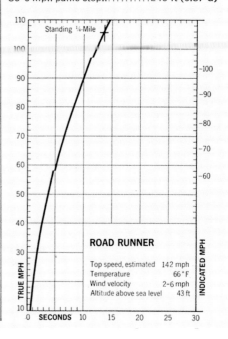

ROAD RUNNER

Top speed, estimated	142mph
Temperature	66°F
Wind velocity	2-6 mph
Altitude above sea level	43 ft

windows up. Road noise and ride harshness were at a minimum—partly a result of the polyester cord tires on the Chevelle instead of the fiberglass belted-construction tires used on the other test cars.

We picked the Chevelle for our Econo-Racer test because we knew it belonged there. Chevrolet, bound by the GM corporate tongue-in-cheek policy concerning competition, says very little about the high performance per-dollar value of the SS 396 but we know that it exists—and so do you. Since Chevrolet doesn't package an Econo-Racer in the manner of Chrysler Corporation, it was up to C/D to build one from the option list. This is a task easily done by ordering the base 325-hp SS 396 package (which also includes power front disc brakes, styled 7-inch wide wheels and F70 tires) on the 300 Deluxe 2-door coupe. With the other options, which we specified on all of our Econo-Racers, the Chevelle comes across the counter at $3,409—more than $300 under the Super Bee. That's an ECONO-racer.

As you can glean from the check list, the Chevelle was the slowest in acceleration, the most difficult to stop and the best in handling. That is quite a spread.

The Chevelle's acceleration potential was never fully realized because the polyester tires are far too slippery for dragstrip traction (fiberglass belted tires are not currently offered from the factory). An average of the two best runs gave us 14.41 seconds at 97.35 mph, but most of the test runs were clustered in the 14.60s at 96 mph.

Those familiar with the 325-hp 396 know it's not famous for rocket sled acceleration and may be surprised that the test car went as quickly as it did. So were we, considering that a similarly powered Camaro (March, '68) could not exceed 15.0 seconds at 93.9 mph. Some investigation indicates that the Chevelle exhaust system is far more efficient than that of Camaro and that the '69 exhaust emission control system, which does not use an air injection pump, improves output. The Chevelle also had the advantage of more break-in miles than any other car in the test.

The Chevelle's performance in the braking test is barely acceptable by our standards. Premature lock-up of the rear wheels caused poor directional stability and the required stopping distance from 80 mph was a very long 304 feet (0.70G.) If the Chevelle didn't fare at all well in the acceleration and braking portions of the test, it was unbeatable in handling—and good handling is a lovely thing to have around the house. The credit goes to the new heavy-duty suspension package that uses a rear sway bar to reduce understeer. We liked it a lot. The car corners flat and allows good directional control right up to the limit of adhesion. All this is complemented by Chevrolet's very accurate power steering; its only fault is a slow overall ratio of 4.25 turns lock-to-lock. An undesirable quirk of the rear suspension is a tendency for the axle to hop under acceleration when the tires are just barely slipping, and during hard cornering when there is some power application. No other car had this problem.

Our test Chevelle didn't do very well because it was neither econo nor racer. But don't lose heart, Chevy fans. It has the potential. We have already mentioned that the lower-priced coupe is a relative bargain—so if you throw in an extra $252.80 for the 375-hp 396 you will end up with the real thing. And we expect the real thing—Chevy Econo-Racer wise—is a good thing indeed.

THE JUDGE

We started the Econo Racer test with six cars and ended with five. The elusive sixth car was Pontiac's entry. The people at Pontiac in charge of supplying-cars-for-six-car-comparison-tests couldn't make up their minds whether our Pontiac was a prototype or a real car and the result was we couldn't get enough accurate test information about the car to put anywhere in the standings.

The Judge's purpose in life is to add some spice to Pontiac's GTO series. It's a variation of the GTO with the 366-hp 400 cu. in. Ram Air engine as standard equipment, along with G70 black wall fiberglass belted tires and styled wheels without the customary trim rings. The Judge stands out (leaps out, really) in a crowd because of its bright orange paint and a simulated aerodynamic wing attached to the deck lid. If there is any doubt, check for "The Judge" decals on the front fenders and deck lid.

A part of our normal road test procedure is a routine technical inspection. During this phase of the test we discovered that one of the vacuum hoses that controls ignition timing had been plugged internally so that the timing was no longer retarded at idle as is normally required to meet the exhaust emissions standards. We also noted that the coolant temperature was much lower than normal for a Pontiac since the change was made to a 190°F thermostat to aid emission control. Our suspicions were further aroused when The Judge wasn't happy even with the best fuel Sunoco has to offer.

A check of the identification numbers stamped on the block indicated the engine was actually a 1968 manual transmission Ram Air unit—which differs from the 1969 366-hp automatic transmission engine in several important areas including camshaft. "It belongs in the test," agreed Pontiac, "but it's kind of a prototype at the same time," they said. That's more-or-less mutually exclusive and our conclusion is that performance of The Judge would probably not be representative of a car a customer could buy.

To satisfy our curiosity about exhaust emissions we retained an independent testing laboratory (which also has government contracts for the same purpose) to test The Judge for compliance to the federal exhaust emission standards. The Judge did not pass. Federal standards allow an average of 1.5% carbon monoxide and 275 parts-per-million unburned hydrocarbons in the exhaust while the car is being driven through a predetermined cycle. Figures for The Judge were 2.65% CO and 549 ppm hydrocarbons. Pretty far off the mark.

With this evidence in mind we are convinced that Pontiac would not knowingly sell this car to a customer and, therefore, it is not suitable for a road test. A true picture of the handling or braking characteristics of The Judge was hard to get in focus because it came with seven-inch wheels—wider than the six inches which seemed to be the maximum available on The Judge at press time.

Clockwise from top left: 1969 Chevelle SS 396; 1969 Chevelle; massive, free-flowing Chevelle air cleaner; Super Bee logo; 1969 Dodge Super Bee; signature of The Judge; 1969 Pontiac GTO The Judge.

Top: 1969 Ford Torino Cobra. Below: 1969 Plymouth Road Runner.

PREVIEW TEST

MUSTANG BOSS 302

Ford's answer to the Z/28 rates an A.
It's easily the best Mustang yet—and that includes all the Shelbys and Mach 1s.

The test questions have all been asked and it's time for the Ford Motor Company to hand in its paper. Passing or failing will be determined, as much as anything, by the way the Mustang Boss 302 maintains its dignity on Ford's handling course, a serpentine stretch of asphalt in the middle of what could pass for one of Dearborn's golf courses. And right there it is, parked, or rather poised, at the entrance to the track—Ford's answer to the Z/28. The mood is tense. Matt Donner, principal engineer in charge of Mustang/Cougar ride and handling, waits, anxious to have the Cobra Jet Mach 1 blot removed from the record or at least superseded by something a bit more meritorious.

Two slightly worn crash helmets are produced from the back seat, one for Donner and one for our technical editor, doing nothing to dilute the battle-to-the-death atmosphere that strengthens as the moment for the shoot-out approaches. The Mustang doesn't help much either, sitting there like a cocked .357 Magnum ready to do its specialty with no

more than a nudge. Donner assumes his battle station behind the wheel. We will judge the first round from the passenger side. Seat belts; click. Shoulder belts; click. Key in the slot, turn … and the Boss 302 awakes with undisguised belligerence. Nose out on the track, first gear, second, third and a low anguished moan from the fat Goodyears as the Mustang threads into the first turn. Two necks strain to keep their heavy, helmeted heads balanced on their respective shoulders. Into the next turn, a tight 200-foot radius left hander, tail hung out and the inside front wheels clipping the grass at the apex. Left turn, right turn, lap after lap at exhilarating speeds—Donner is submitting his homework in a most convincing fashion.

Our turn. Easy at first, remembering the beak-heavy Mach 1 that plowed straight on with its front tires smoking if you tried to hurry. But the Boss 302 is another kind of Mustang. It simply drives around the turns with a kind of detachment never before experienced in a street car wearing Ford emblems. Faster and

faster, but its composure never slips. Adjust the line with the steering wheel or with the throttle or both. Hang the tail way out with a quick flick of the wheel and a legful of gas. Do whatever you like and the car complies with the accuracy of your shadow. Very simply, the Boss 302 is unshakable. Maneuvers that had been highly unsettling in previous Mustangs have a recreational air about them in the Boss 302. The car understeers, but not much—it has just exactly the right balance to allow you to drive instead of plow through a turn. The steering responds to corrections right up until you chicken out, and the car's attitude in a turn is extraordinarily sensitive to power. This is not to say that you spin out if you dip too deeply into the gas, but rather that you can order up and sustain any drift angle you like. Even better, the handling characteristics remain the same whether you're cornering at six- or nine-tenths of the car's ability. Without a doubt the Boss 302 is the best handling Ford ever to come out of Dearborn and may just be the new standard by which everything from Detroit must be judged.

While we're all reeling from this unexpected development perhaps we should retrace our steps back to the beginning and examine Ford's motives for such an advancement. You see, there is this thing called the youth market which appears to have an insatiable appetite for wildly trimmed performance cars and can summon up the cash, or at least the monthly payments, to indulge itself. Chevrolet has always been particularly sensitive to these youthful demands.

When Ford discovered that Chevy sold 7,000 Z/28 Camaros in 1968, and the marketing demographers predicted that up to 20,000 might be sold in 1969, there was no choice but hoist the bugle and blow the charge. Not only was Chevrolet selling cars to customers who might have bought an equivalent Mustang if it

was available, but Chevy was also achieving a fantastic reputation every time the David-like Z/28 dusted off somebody's, and maybe one of Ford's, Goliaths. It's not that Chevrolet had created a particularly conspicuous automobile, but the Z/28's combination of endearing mechanical presence and sparkling performance had made it the car for those in the know.

Ford needed the Boss 302 for one other reason. The SCCA says that for any trick part to be legal in the Trans-Am it has to appear on at least 1,000 street cars. That means that spoilers or aerodynamic improvements of any sort, and high performance engine parts like blocks and cylinder heads, will have to be at least limited production items. Building just a handful of parts like last year's 302 tunnel-ports is definitely verboten. So, since Ford has to build at least 1,000 of these pseudo-racers if it wants to play in the Trans-Am, it might just as well make them visible and attempt to chock the wheels of the fast selling Z/28.

Those are the reasons, but in Detroit's war of model proliferation to compete with, and get ahead of, everybody else's model proliferation,

Ford has treated itself to a healthy escalation. The Boss 302 is a hell of an enthusiast's car. It's what the Shelby GT 350s and 500s should have been but weren't. Ford stylists have done an admirable job in creating a visual performance image for the Mustang variants this year and the Boss 302 is no exception. It's clearly a Mustang but distinctly unique at the same time.

Matte black paint applied to the hood, rear deck and around the headlights is a standard part of the package, as is the tape "C" stripe with the Boss 302 insert on the side of the body. Since the shovel-shaped spoiler under the front bumper works, at least on the race track, it is standard equipment, too, because Ford wants to make sure 1,000 of them are sold before the first race. Something the less astute might not notice is that the scoop just below the rear quarter window has been filled in. As Jacque Passino said, "The purist car people expect scoops to scoop something, and since that one didn't it had to go." The real visual sauce—the venetian blind "sport slats" on the back window and the adjustable wing on the rear deck—is optional. The slats are actually a one-piece arrangement, hinged at the

top and latched at the bottom, so it can be tilted up before washing the rear window.

Styling is only a fraction of the Boss 302's story. The engine, since it is the basis for the Trans-Am racer, has not been neglected. Every spring it's time for the annual changing of the cylinder heads in Ford's performance department. Last year's tunnel-port racing setup is being replaced by a brand new design which has canted valves much like Ford's street 429 and Chevrolet's 396-427. Tunnel-ports are out but big valves are in. The intake valves, with a diameter of 2.23 inches, are only 0.02 smaller than those in a Chrysler 426 Hemi. Ports, too, are generous in size. The new heads are intended for racing as well as street use and will fit the 302 and 351 V-8s as well as all the 289s currently running around on the street. Other 1969 features include new pistons to conform to the new combustion chamber shape and 4-bolt main bearing caps for bottom end strength. An aluminum high rise intake manifold with a 780 cubic-feet-per-minute Holley 4-bbl. tops off the package. Ford rates the output at 290 hp (same as the Z/28) @ 5800 rpm, and no one will dispute that it makes at least that much. Standard with the engine is a wide ratio (2.78 first gear) transmission and a 3.50 axle, which strikes us as an ideal compromise for both low speed acceleration and comfortable expressway cruising.

New engine notwithstanding, it's the Boss 302's handling that makes the car outstanding and it was accomplished with relatively few changes. Most visible is the tires—Goodyear F60-15 polyglas balloons that put more than eight inches of rubber on the road—mounted on 7-inch wide wheels. The tires are so wide that special front and rear fenders, with revised wheel openings and reshaped rear wheel houses, had to be designed for the Boss 302. To clear the front suspension also required that the wheels be offset farther toward the outside of the car which, in turn, required new front spindles with larger wheel bearings. Fat tires have to really grip the pavement to be worth that much trouble—these do.

The Mustangs new-found handling ability demanded a greater revision of the engineering department's philosophy than it did of suspension parts. Kicking the understeering habit is no easier than giving up the weed or peyote nuts and Ford is to be commended on its rehabilitation. One thing was in its favor from the very start and that is weight distribution— 55.7% on the Boss 302's front wheels compared to 59.3% for the 428 Mach 1. But there is more yet. Front springs and anti-sway bar are softer on the Boss while the rear leaf springs are stiffer—all of which tends to reduce understeer. Shock absorbers and the suspension geometry is carried over with no modifications.

Whether you order manual or power steering, the gear ratio is the same, at 16-to-one. The test car, with its manual steering, never could be accused of a lack of road feel when we were flailing. Unfortunately, in this crowded world, you can't flail much and still keep a good grip on your driver's license, and power steering is far better suited to routine traffic situations. We've driven far worse manual steering cars but parking the Boss 302 is still equal to about six push-ups.

The Boss 302 we drove is an engineering prototype and the only one in existence at press time. In fact, it had been in Ford's wind tunnel to check the effect of the rear spoiler just

before our session at the test track. Normally we avoid doing a full road test on a prototype because it might not be typical of a production car, but in this case the weatherman didn't even give us a chance. The rain started between the handling course and Detroit Dragway, where the acceleration and braking parts of the test were to be conducted, and didn't stop for the rest of the day. For that reason the performance data on the specification page has been calculated from information supplied by Ford's engineering department—definitely not our normal procedure but better than nothing. We do have some very distinct driving impressions other than those on the handling course however, which should be passed along. Ride quality is toward the stiff side, particularly in the rear which crashes with vengeance over big irregularities in the road. Still, considering the handling, it's a good trade out.

When you speak of engines in this class of car the Z/28, with its nervous and jerky deportment and ultra-quick response in the 12-cylinder, dohc, Italian fashion, is the standard of comparison. The Boss 302 has a temperament completely unlike its competitor. It idles smoothly and quietly with almost no mechanical noise and has average response, neither quick nor slow. It could easily find a home in a Falcon and no one would be the wiser, at least until the Holley's secondaries snapped open. Ford claims that its new little motor actually makes more power than the Z/28 but, subjectively, the car doesn't feel quite as fast. Certainly it doesn't have the slightly tamed racing car personality which has won the Z/28 throngs of friends. Ford engineers even volunteered that the Boss can be readily launched in second gear and they're right—for whatever that's worth in your racer replica.

Roaring around Ford's test track and splashing through Detroit from suburb to suburb has made believers out of us. If the production cars are anywhere near as good as the prototype, the Boss 302 is easily the best Mustang yet, and that includes all of the Shelbys and Mach 1s. After receiving no recognition other than gold stars for attendance in our road tests for the last several years Ford has learned its lessons well. The Boss 302 Mustang earned itself an A for this semester.

MUSTANG BOSS 302

List Price as tested: $3958.43

Options on Test Car: Base 302 fastback Mustang, $2740.00; Boss 302 option, $676.15; rear spoiler, $19.48; sport slats, $128.28; radio, $61.40; styled wheels, $77.73; racing style mirrors, $19.48; limited slip differential, $63.51; decor group, $68.15; high-back bucket seats, $84.25; preparation and conditioning, $20.00

ENGINE
Bore x stroke....................4.00 x 3.00 in
Displacement........................302 cu in
Compression ratio...............10.5 to one
Carburetion.........1 x 4-bbl Holley T80 CFM
Power (SAE)..................290 @ 5800 rpm
Torque (SAE)................290 @ 4300 rpm

DRIVE TRAIN
Final drive ratio....................3.50 to one

DIMENSIONS AND CAPACITIES
Wheelbase..........................108.0 in
Track...................F:59.5 in, R:59.5 in
Length.............................187.4 in
Width...............................71.3 in
Height..............................49.2 in
Curb weight.......................3387 lbs
Weight distribution, F/R..........55.8/44.2%
Fuel capacity......................20.0 gal
Oil capacity........................5.0 qts
Water capacity....................15.5 qts

SUSPENSION
F: Ind., upper wishbones, single lower arms with drag struts, coil springs, anti-sway bar
R: Rigid axle, semi-elliptic leaf springs

STEERING
Type......................Recirculating ball
Turns lock-to-lock....................3.75
Turning circle.....................37.6 ft.

BRAKES
F:............11.3 in vented disc, power assist
R: 10.0 x 2.00 in cast iron drum, power assist

WHEELS AND TIRES
Wheel size......................15.0 x 7.0-in
Tire make and size. Goodyear F60 x 15 polyglas
Test inflation pressures...F: 26 psi, R: 26 psi

PERFORMANCE
Zero to	Seconds
40 mph	3.2*
60 mph	6.0*
80 mph	10.0*
100 mph	15.2*

Standing ¼-mile......14.57 sec @ 97.57 mph
*Speed time data calculated from information supplied by the Ford Motor Company

ROAD TEST

CHEVROLET CORVETTE COUPE

Its excellent engineering tends to be obscured by some rather garish styling gimmicks.

Another Corvette road test? One more plunge into the verbal thicket in an attempt to describe the exact sensation in the region of the fourth pelvic vertebrae when the throttle is punched on a 427-cu. in., 435-horsepower Stingray? More open combat with similes and metaphors for the sake of establishing the fact that the Corvette is a very rapid and exciting automobile—already an article of faith among the entire population, including pre-pubescent schoolgirls? Let's dispense with all that.

If we are going to discuss the Corvette at all, let's accept a dozen premises in its behalf and hopefully avoid traveling the same old paragraphs to the same old conclusions: (1) The Corvette is surely the most popular high-performance sports car ever built, with something in the neighborhood of 250,000 examples having been sold since it was introduced in September, 1963.

(2) It is available with a variety of power-train options, from the popular 350 cu. in., 300-hp "small engine" versions (which account for over 60% of sales) to the blockbuster 427 cu. in. units with outputs ranging from 390 to 435 horsepower, depending on which of the five optional setups is chosen.

(3) The small-engine Corvettes are marginally fast and extraordinarily civilized.

(4) The large-engine Corvettes are extraordinarily fast and marginally civilized.

(5) Corvette bodies are fiberglass, and rather heavy, somewhat noisy and tend to be expensive to repair. Corvette paintwork has a poor reputation for checking on the convex fiberglass surfaces, and the material will fracture and tear under impact. It is, however, difficult to dent and impervious to salt and other corrosive agents.

(6) Corvettes have never been totally accepted by the sports car purists, despite the fact that they will outperform—in a total sense—most of the sacred cows produced in Europe. In fact, if the Corvette was built by the dozens in a small factory in northern Italy, the same fetishists would acclaim it as one of the great automobiles of all time. However, it is dogma within this small but vocal claque that Detroit is incapable of producing automobiles that corner, brake and steer properly and the Corvette is doomed by its origins.

(7) The Corvette has an extremely loyal body of owners—probably the largest and most enthusiastic group of its type in the world. They are breathless supporters of their chosen car. Over 7,000 members belong to Corvette clubs and, shades of 1952, they wave at each other when meeting on the highway! The monthly Corvette News, published by Chevrolet, has a circulation of 102,000, more than a number of general interest automotive magazines.

(8) Corvettes are at the peak of the performance car pecking order. Among the vast underground of street racers that total millions across this land, the man in the 'Vette is king—especially the man with the number "427" displayed on his machine's hood. In fact, more "427" badges are sold than engines—as was the case with the legendary fuel-injection Corvette engines that were discontinued in 1965. In those days, the arcane little emblem that denoted a "fuelie" was the most popular bit in the Corvette parts bin. Within the subculture of drag racers and teenie throttle-stompers, the Corvette means instant status. In fact, sales surveys indicate that a growing majority of Corvette buyers are under 25, blue-collar types making less than $10,000 per year. Curiously, the next largest segment of buyers is over 50, white-collar men who earn over $15,000 per year.

(9) It being a mass-class sports car, the Corvette's excellent engineering tends to be obscured by some rather garish styling gimmicks that make the uninitiated wonder if the car is a fake—a lurid, bulging, silicone-filled, automotive Playboy Bunny. This confusing identity is the result of a confrontation on the part of Chevy engineer Zora Arkus-Duntov, who is well and truly the patron saint of all Corvettes, and the Chevrolet styling department. Duntov's primary aim in his professional life is to make the Corvette the finest sports car in the world. The styling department views his car as a unique opportunity to fool around with the swoopy shapes and flashing lights that somehow to them mean "sport." It is within this minor tempest that the Corvette encounters trouble: Duntov on the one hand viewing his automobile as a purposeful, well-balanced sports car, while his rivals see it as a Flash Gordon Thunderbird for the Hugh Hefner school of mass-cult glamor.

(10) Because of this identity dispute, habitability of the car has traditionally suffered. Only recently has the driving position and control placement become acceptable (forward visibility on the styling department's first version of the present Stingray was so bad that Duntov and his engineers had to delay its introduction for a full year), and the jazzy coke-bottle shape means limited passenger room and a deplorable absence of luggage space.

(11) Despite its hefty cost—approximately $5,000 to $8,000, depending on options—the Corvette is not a hallmark of quality. Components tend to come loose and detailed coachwork is generally below average for a car of this price (although no worse, it might be noted, than on some European exotica).

(12) Originally intended only as an image-builder and "loss leader." the Corvette has been a pleasant sales success for Chevrolet and produces a substantial annual profit. In 1969. sales should reach 30,000.

The particular subject of this test was something more than the average Corvette.

It was one of the aforementioned 435-hp monsters (the L-71. with three 2-barrels, cast iron heads and the optional transistor ignition), with a sprinkling of options, that ran the gamut between form and function. As an example of the identity problem that exists within the Corvette marketing structure, our test car was equipped with power windows and "off the road" (read "racing") external exhaust pipes. Within this framework of logic, Cadillac should be planning the Eldorado as a Grand National stocker.

Despite any efforts to soften its latent toughness with such niceties as power windows and an AM/FM radio, our Corvette came across as one thundering, hammering brute of an automobile. In bright red, the car had its share of scratches and rips in the fiberglass, giving it the appearance of a race-worn Ferrari (there is a Corvette cruising the streets of New York with Ferrari name plates affixed, as a matter of fact). Its giant exhaust pipes, its fat, black-wall tires and its disheveled surface gave it a fierce countenance indeed, but the incredible power of the beast didn't become apparent until its giant engine began to thump away and its wheels began to turn. Then it became a truly visceral experience to

motor along in the Corvette—at any speed. Tires whining, the awesome rumble of the exhaust sweeping through the cockpit, the emission pump pulley screeching, the fiberglass body creaking; sounds of a genuinely exciting vehicle. Enough sounds, incidentally, to render the radio useless and to severely limit conversation with the windows down, but worthy entertainment unto themselves. And after all, if the sensation of driving a potent machine like the Corvette isn't fun by itself, one is a fool to own it in the first place.

"It's a great machine," said one of the brightest young marketing and advertising types within the Chevrolet organization in an effort to describe the Corvette. "But it's not a terribly useful device. The present Corvette is more like a dune buggy than a conventional GT or sports car in that it can't do much that a functional automobile is expected to do." He is in many ways correct. The Corvette, with its giant engine and muscular drivetrain, packed into its space-age body, leaves precious little room for the human element. It is questionable, for example, that a couple could load aboard enough luggage for a civilized one-week journey without serious inconvenience. At the same time, the machine

has such an excess of power that prolonged driving on ice and snow would become a frustrating and worrisome task.

But on dry pavement, with no place to go except a carefree spin down some interesting roads, the Corvette is an ever-loving kick. The controls are nearly perfect, the throttle, clutch and brake pedals flawlessly placed, with smooth linkages that belie the potency of the car. The close-ratio manual transmission is a joy to operate, and the suspension—firm at low speeds, but perfect from 70 mph upward—is ideally suited for the automobile. In fact, one of the most extraordinary things about the Corvette is its overall smoothness. Most cars having an excess of 400 hp are jerky, neck-snapping, uncivilized and bull-like, but the Corvette's controls are so well designed that utter novices can jump aboard and drive like veterans—up to a point. It has been a long-standing Chevrolet policy to give their high-performance engines great smoothness, with none of the tricky carburetor gimmicks that bring on a great thrust of power whenever the throttle is opened. The throats of the three 2-barrel carbs are controlled by air flow rather than mechanical linkage, giving the engine a turbinelike smoothness. If power did

ACCELERATION standing ¼ mile, seconds

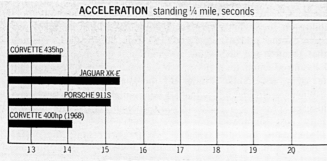

CORVETTE 435hp

JAGUAR XK-E

PORSCHE 911S

CORVETTE 400hp (1968)

13 14 15 16 17 18 19 20

BRAKING 80-0 mph panic stop, feet

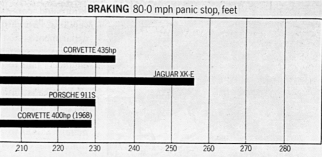

CORVETTE 435hp

JAGUAR XK-E

PORSCHE 911S

CORVETTE 400hp (1968)

210 220 230 240 250 260 270 280

FUEL ECONOMY RANGE mpg

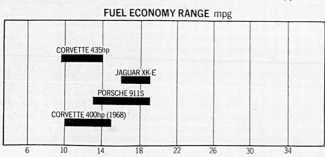

CORVETTE 435hp

JAGUAR XK-E

PORSCHE 911S

CORVETTE 400hp (1968)

6 10 14 18 22 26 30 34

PRICE AS TESTED dollars x 1000

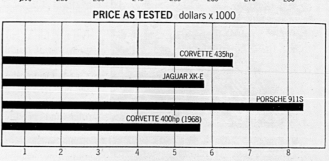

CORVETTE 435hp

JAGUAR XK-E

PORSCHE 911S

CORVETTE 400hp (1968)

1 2 3 4 5 6 7 8

CORVETTE 427 COUPE

Manufacturer: Chevrolet Motor Division
General Motors Corp.
30003 Van Dyke
Warren, Mich. 48090

Vehicle type: Front-engine, rear-wheel-drive, 2-passenger coupe

Price as tested: $6573.30
(Manufacturer's suggested retail price, including all options listed below, Federal excise tax, dealer preparation and delivery charges, does not include state and local taxes, license or freight charges)

Options on test car: Base car, $4895.00; softray tinted glass, $16.90; power windows, $63.20; rear window defroster, $32.65; positraction axle 370 ratio, $46.35; power brakes, $42.15; engine block heater, $10.55; full-transistor ignition syst., $81.10; 435-HP turbojet 427 V8 engine, $437.10; 4-speed close-ratio trans., $184.80; side-mounted exhaust system, $147.45; tilt-telescopic steering wheel, $84.30; power steering, $105.35; F70 x 15 red-stripe tires, $31.30; special wheel covers, $57.95; front fender louver trim, $21.10; audio alarm system, $26.35; speed warning indicator $11.60; AM/FM stereo radio, $278.10

ENGINE
Type: V-8 water-cooled, cast iron block and heads, 5 main bearings
Bore x stroke 4.25 x 3.76 in, 108.0 x 95.5 mm
Displacement.............427 cu in, 7000 cc

Compression ratio.............11.0 to one
Carburetion.................3 x 2-bbl. Holley
Valve gear.........Pushrod operated overhead valves, mechanical lifters
Power (SAE).............435 bhp @ 5800 rpm
Torque (SAE)..........460 lb-ft @ 4000 rpm
Specific power output........1.02 bhp/cu in, 62.2 bhp/liter

DRIVE TRAIN
Transmission.............4-speed, all-synchro
Final drive ratio.............3.70 to one

Gear	Ratio	Mph/1000 rpm	Max. test speed
I	2.20	9.5	62 mph (6500 rpm)
II	1.64	12.8	83 mph (6500 rpm)
III	1.27	16.5	107 mph (6500 rpm)
IV	1.00	21.2	138 mph (6500 rpm)

SUSPENSION
F: Ind., unequal length wishbones, coil springs, anti-sway bar
R: Ind., single trailing arms, fixed length half-shafts and lateral links, multi-leaf transverse spring, anti-sway bar.

DIMENSIONS AND CAPACITIES
Wheelbase........................98.0 in
Track, F/R...................58.7/59.4 in
Length.........................182.5 in
Width...........................69.0 in
Height..........................47.8 in
Ground clearance.................6.0 in
Curb weight.....................3450 lbs
Weight distribution, F/R......51.5/48.5%
Battery capacity..........12 volts, 62 amp/hr
Alternator capacity...........504 watts

Fuel capacity.................20.0 gal
Oil capacity..................5.0 qts
Water capacity...............22.0 qts

STEERING
Type......Recirculating ball gear with linkage booster
Turns lock-to-lock.................3.2
Turning circle curb-to-curb........35 ft

BRAKES
F:.........11.75-in vented disc, power assist
R:.........11.75-in vented disc, power assist

WHEELS AND TIRES
Wheel size.....................15 x 8.0-in
Wheel type...........Stamped steel, 5-bolt
Tire make and size.........Goodyear F70-15
Tire type.......................Tubeless
Test inflation pressures, F/R......24/24 psi
Tire load rating....1280 lbs per tire @ 24 psi

PERFORMANCE
Zero to   Seconds
30 mph........................2.2
40 mph........................3.2
50 mph........................4.2
60 mph........................5.3
70 mph........................7.0
80 mph........................8.6
90 mph........................10.7
100 mph.......................12.6
Standing ¼-mile......13.8 sec @ 106.8 mph
Top speed (estimated)..............138 mph
80-0 mph................235 ft (0.91 G)
Fuel mileage....9.5-14 mpg on premium fuel
Cruising range....................190-280 mi

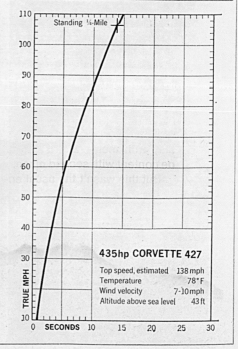

435hp CORVETTE 427

Top speed, estimated   138 mph
Temperature   78°F
Wind velocity   7-10mph
Altitude above sea level 43 ft

Standing ¼-Mile

come in with a bang, as on some other high-performance machines, the Corvette would be a fearsome racer, safe only in the hands of responsible professionals. As it is, only imprudent applications of power on wet or loose surfaces can be dangerous, for which most of those eager young customers should be thankful.

This overall élan of the Corvette makes its performance deceiving. In spite of all the sensory inputs, it never seems as if you're going that fast. Power comes so effortlessly that neither car nor driver is ever called upon to strain in the slightest. Almost anyone, for example, could run the car through the quarter-mile in excess of 100 mph. An interesting test of truly powerful cars is the 0-100-0 run, wherein the time to accelerate to 100 mph and brake to a full stop is recorded. The best clocking we know of for a street automobile is Ken Miles' 14 seconds in a 427 Cobra. A number of years ago Aston Martin advertised that its big Sixes would do the job in 25 seconds. We tried it once with the Corvette. On a bumpy pavement, with a less-than-perfect start, we made the trip in approximately 23 seconds. More practice and it is probable that the time could have been brought down near 21 seconds. With better tires another two seconds might have been shaved off. And therein lies the flabbiness in the Corvette's muscle . . . tires. The F70-type employed on the car are simply inadequate under heavy throttle and braking. They smoke, they screech, they lose adhesion, they are squirrelly in the rain. Duntov himself was hospitalized during the preparation of this test and we had no chance to discuss the problem with him, but he has said on past occasions that he is aware of the problem, but can find no other tires that work better. The owner's manual firmly warns that the car's suspension has been designed for these specific tires and no replacements should be tried. Nonetheless, it would be interesting to experiment.

Despite its tire weaknesses, the Corvette is a superior automobile in all departments of handling. Like the man said, the machine is excellent, but the car's functional applications are limited. In addition to the aforementioned storage deficiencies, it is full of minor irritants—many of them the responsibility of the stylists, not the engineers. To begin with, limited interior space makes things very hot indeed, the glories of "Astro-Ventilation" notwithstanding. With that great lump of hot iron mounted a few inches on the other side of the firewall, BTUs pour over the driver and passenger in unpleasant quantities, even at cruising speeds.

The windshield wipers are concealed beneath a moveable flap that looks as if it came from the wing of a Boeing 727. Before the wipers can become operable, this covering has to wind itself clear, a movement that takes several seconds. There are moments, especially in a car with the cruising potential of the Corvette, when several seconds with an opaque windshield would mean certain disaster, and peek-a-boo wipers become a grim bit of frivolity. The dash, while containing a lovely, large tachometer and speedometer, is cluttered with little lights that tell the driver what external illumination he has operating at any given time—in essence, gimmicks. And instead of a clock within the 5-dial instrument bank on the console, why not an oil-temperature gauge? The higher-performance 427s are known to be thirsty for oil (we used two quarts in 1500 miles) and the more that informs the driver about his expensive engine the better.

Fifteen years worth of Corvettes have been produced since 1953, using five body styles. The past two (1963-67 and the present design) have been esthetically delightful. A bit flamboyant, perhaps, but nonetheless pretty shapes that have few deficiencies in a purely artistic sense. But it is time for a change and the Chevrolet management knows it. Up to now, development has been evolutionary, with constant refinement of the basic front-engine, two-place roadster design. In 1956 came the first V-8, with its shocking acceleration, while 1963 brought the first Corvette coupe and along with it the masterfully articulated independent rear suspension. But at the same time the Corvettes have gotten heavier, and more complicated, departing in a sense from the original sparse, functional roadsters that first caused so much excitement.

It is known that Zora Arkus-Duntov is a great exponent of small-displacement, high-revving engines, and it would seem logical that he would be pushing for the manufacture of smaller, lighter Corvettes powered by the zappy. exciting, 302 cu. in. Z/28 engine. But here Duntov faces a difficult personal choice. Because he rightfully believes that his Corvette should represent the pinnacle of Chevrolet engineering, he cannot bring himself to accept producing his car with anything less than the biggest, most powerful engine in the Chevrolet line-up. He feels, with some justification, that it would be absurd to market a 305 or 350 cu. in. Corvette as the top performance car in the division when a customer could buy a Chevelle or Chevy II with a much larger and more powerful engine. Therefore he consents to his once-nimble machine being made bulkier and bulkier by the year.

The present Corvette will doubtlessly be the last front-engine model. It remains uncertain if the new rear-engine version will be introduced in 1971 or 1972 (a great deal depends on Ford and its rumored rear-engine sports car). Until then, the present Corvette will be marketed in essentially the same form as seen on these pages.

Although a number of prototypes have been tested, a certain amount of turmoil exists within Chevrolet as to exactly what form the new car will take. The present General Manager. John DeLorean, is as much an automotive purist as ever reached the top ranks of General Motors, and it is known that he is unhappy with the present Corvette. Rumors from deep inside the company indicate that DeLorean has pronounced that the mid-engine version must be a functional sports/GT car, weighing in the neighborhood of 2,600 lbs. and containing an engine of about 400 cu. in. This places a giant challenge before Duntov and his engineers. It means cutting the weight of the present car by 1,000 lbs. while keeping essentially the same size engine. Proper amounts of luggage space, etc. must also be included. If this can be accomplished with a fiberglass or steel body remains to be seen, but it can be assumed that DeLorean. who is an engineer himself, will drive hard to make the new Corvette lean and tough.

If he succeeds, it could mean goodbye to the jet-plane gimmickry. And for that, we'd all be thankful.

ROAD TEST

DODGE CHALLENGER R/T HEMI

Lavish execution with little or no thought toward practical application

Major truth: Since the first Mustang rolled out of a dealer's showroom in 1964 sales of that class of car have been as high as 13% of Detroit's total yearly volume—and Dodge has not enjoyed a single dollar of that business. Second major truth: It's bad enough to be late into the market place but to be late with the wrong kind of a car can be fatal (even if only crippling it is still an offense which requires all of the product planners to fall on their swords). Now let's talk about Dodge's new Challenger— easily three years too late to be a smashing success but something Dodge is counting on to make a few bucks with nonetheless.

To understand the Challenger you first better know a little bit about Chrysler Corporation and its strategies. Chrysler doesn't do anything first. Instead, it carefully watches what everybody else in Detroit is doing and when it sees an area of abnormal market activity it leaps exactly onto that spot. Because it always leaps late—which is inevitable if it doesn't begin to prepare its entry into the market until someone else already has one—it tries to make up for being late by jumping onto said spot harder than everybody else. That is why you didn't see a real Chrysler sporty car until 1970 (and that is why Chrysler's small car will be lucky to see light of day in 1971). There is another problem, too. Sometimes when you leap late you find that by the time you hit your target everybody else has gone somewhere else. This is painfully close to being the case with the Challenger/Barracuda because it is a bald-faced replica of the Camaro/Firebird which GM is planning to completely revamp in just a few months.

To further understand the Challenger you have to go beyond corporate stratagems and straight into the Dodge division. The Dodge boys fancy themselves as the only spark of vitality in the corporation, and right now they are flying high on the Charger, a model that does nothing more than a Coronet hardtop can do, except look better, and yet has outsold Plymouth's specialty car, the Barracuda, by two-to-one for the last couple of years. According to Robert McCurry, Dodge's general manager who has to be considered as a mild outlaw in such a conservative organization as Chrysler, this is to be the plan with the Challenger. Essentially a sporty car of the type everybody else is selling, it is meant to have more interior room (Dodge attributes a good part of the Charger's success to the 5-passenger capacity) and a comprehensive list of options. McCurry admits that the Challenger is not aimed at any specific type of buyer; not at the performance enthusiasts, not at the comfort seekers who might opt for a small Thunderbird, but rather at the entire sporty car market from Camaro to Cougar and hopefully anyone on the fringe as well. The Challenger's price target is directly between the Mustang and the Cougar—and to avoid competition from within the Dodge line the more expensive Dart models have been dropped.

That's what the Challenger is supposed to be. In the flesh it is a highly stylized Camaro with strongly sculptured lines, more tumble-home and a grille vaguely in the Charger tradition. There's no doubt it is a handsome car but it also has a massive feeling which is totally unwelcome in a sporty car—a massive feeling which results from a full five inches more width than a Mustang and a need to sign up with Weight Watchers. The Hemi-powered test car weighed 3,890 lbs and if any normally equipped V-8 Challenger with a full gas tank weighs less than 3,550 lbs we would be surprised. Dodge is quick to point out that the Challenger's 110-inch wheelbase is two inches longer than that of the Barracuda and, in fact, longer than any other sporty car except for the 111-inch Cougar. The extra two inches are intended to provide relief for the acute shortage of rear leg room common to sporty cars. To check out this claim we parked the Challenger next to C/D's Blue Maxi Camaro for a little side-by-side comparison. After crawling around in both interiors it is clear that the inside of the Challenger is up to two inches wider, particularly in front seat shoulder room. But face it, width isn't that important in a 4-passenger car when there is already enough room for two people side-by-side. A far more important dimension is rear seat leg room and there the Challenger has, at very best, an inconsequential half-inch advantage over the Camaro. Sitting back there, you still have no choice but to spread-eagle your legs around the front seat backs when they are in their full rearward position—it's uncomfortable and damn near impossible to sustain for a trip of any duration. In addition, the Challenger has noticeably less headroom in the rear—enough less to make that seat unsuitable for anyone over six feet tall. It is true that the Challenger's front bucket seats have a longer range of adjustment which means that when the seats can be pushed farther forward there is definitely more useful room in back than in the Camaro. One of the managers in Dodge's product planning section summed up the situation this way, "In the other sporty cars the rear seat is worthless about 95% of the time. That area in the Challenger is worthless only about 75% of the time."

You can see that the Challenger isn't a family car. The sad part is that Chrysler also passed up a splendid opportunity to make an exceptional performance car. It's simply too heavy. The idea of a "sporty" car weighing within 100 lbs of a comparably equipped Road Runner or Super Bee is ridiculous. Along with all of the weight comes a weight distribution problem—58.9% on the front wheels of the Hemi-powered test car. What has happened is that Chrysler has built itself a "performance" car that is 300 lbs heavier than a Cobra Jet Mustang and almost as nose-heavy. Nice going, you guys.

And the Challenger is so wide that it has none of the compact agility normally associated with this class of car. Before we go any further we should make it clear that the test car is perfectly satisfactory for normal maneuvers like going to church and fetching grandma but you don't buy Hemis for that kind of duty. Strong understeer is apparent in places where you might try to hurry, like expressway entrances, and really flogging on a twisting road or a tight road course is a waste of time. The car just won't cooperate. The front wheels begin to lose steering response and to keep from nosing off into the woods you have to use a fantastic amount of power—a fairly risky operation when sometimes the power brings the tail around like a swinging gate and sometimes it just pushes your nose into the woods faster. Just like everybody else in Detroit, Chrysler is afraid to build its powerful cars with anything resembling neutral steering because they are afraid that some clown will tap the throttle in a corner and spin himself into somebody's petunia patch. But we think they should worry just as much about someone finding himself moving too fast in a corner and having no steering response—the car continuing along its path regardless of which way you point the wheels—which is exactly what happens with excessive understeer.

The Hemi's road course performance was hamstrung by two distinct difficulties. First, the carburetors cut out so badly in turns that the whole operation is deprived of the power necessary to negate the understeer and you end up moving very slowly on a very erratic line. The other problem concerns the 24/28 psi tire pressure recommendation—a curious recommendation indeed for such a nose-heavy car. It turns out that this backwards bias is a palliative for tricky transient handling in the small engine Challengers, but the decal with that recommendation appears throughout the model line because whatever department is in charge of affixing the decal can't be bothered to distinguish between Hemis and Sixes. We did try the Challenger with equal pressure in the tires but even that doesn't cure all of

6,000 RPM
FOR LESS THAN $3,000
DART SWINGER 340

Play your cards right, and three G's can put you in a whole lot of car this year, Dart Swinger 340. Newest member of the Dodge Scat Pack. You don't make it on looks alone. 340 cubes of high-winding, 4-barrel V8. A 4-speed Hurst on the floor to keep things moving. All the other credentials are in order. Just check at right. Then check with your Dodge Dealer. Especially about the price.

STANDARD DART SWINGER 340 EQUIPMENT
- 340-cubic-inch 4-bbl. V8
- 4-speed full synchromesh with Hurst shifter
- Heavy-duty suspension
- Dual exhausts
- D70x14 wide-tread tires
- Dart Swinger bumblebee stripes
- Performance hood with die-cast louvers
- 3.23 axle ratio. 3.55 and 3.91 are optional ratios, with Sure Grip differential.

Dodge CHRYSLER MOTORS CORPORATION

Dodge Scat Pack ... the cars with the Bumblebee stripes

the evils. Curiously enough considering the unfavorable weight distribution, traction is not a problem. The fat F60-15 Polyglas tires and Chrysler's biased rear suspension (all 440 and Hemi Challengers have rear springs which tend to equalize loading on the rear wheels during acceleration) combine to do a good job of putting the power on the road.

The engineers who develop the ride and handling of Chrysler cars admit that the big engine Challengers (Hemis and 440s have the same suspension) were never a high priority project. Most of the effort was directed instead at the 340 and 383 4-bbl. models—which have a different suspension package that includes a rear anti-sway bar to reduce understeer—and the engineers claim that those models are every bit as agile as Z/28 Camaros and Boss 302 Mustangs. Unfortunately, the smaller engines are completely overshadowed by the two 440s—4-bbl. and 6-bbl.—and the Hemi. Moreover, the Challenger is so heavy that the smaller engines are unable to provide competitive performance so the engineers'

handling efforts might better have been applied somewhere else.

There are probably a number of you out there in readerland mumbling to yourselves that anybody with a brain knows the Hemi is by far the heaviest engine Chrysler builds and if we were looking for a well-balanced car we should have picked something else. That's true, and yet the Hemi is also the only real racing engine in all of Detroit that you can dial up from your corner dealer with relative ease. You can't just tick off a Boss 429 on a Ford order form and expect to get it, and aluminum 427 Chevys certainly don't grow on trees. We try to test a Hemi every year just to stay in touch with Chrysler's big gun and to see how that hyper-active horsepower generator is fairing in the less forgiving world of exhaust emissions. Of course it makes for a fast Challenger—14.1 seconds in the quarter at 103.2 mph—but this Hemi was contrary to our past experience in that it didn't offer more pleasure than grief. It was very ill at ease in traffic with a torturous idle when held in drive

While *Car and Driver* was testing the top-of-the-line Challenger R/T Hemi, Dodge advertised a new mini-blaster—the well-muscled, $3,000 Dart Swinger 340.

ACCELERATION standing ¼ mile, seconds

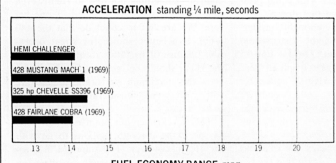

HEMI CHALLENGER
428 MUSTANG MACH 1 (1969)
325 hp CHEVELLE SS396 (1969)
428 FAIRLANE COBRA (1969)

13 14 15 16 17 18 19 20

BRAKING 80-0 mph panic stop, feet

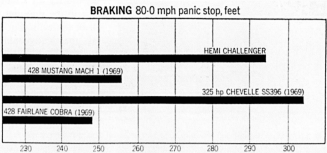

HEMI CHALLENGER
428 MUSTANG MACH 1 (1969)
325 hp CHEVELLE SS396 (1969)
428 FAIRLANE COBRA (1969)

230 240 250 260 270 280 290 300

FUEL ECONOMY RANGE mpg

HEMI CHALLENGER
428 MUSTANG MACH 1 (1969) N/A
325 hp CHEVELLE SS396 (1969)
428 FAIRLANE COBRA (1969)

6 10 14 18 22 26 30 34

PRICE AS TESTED dollars x 1000

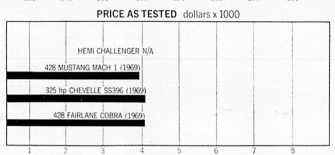

HEMI CHALLENGER N/A
428 MUSTANG MACH 1 (1969)
325 hp CHEVELLE SS396 (1969)
428 FAIRLANE COBRA (1969)

1 2 3 4 5 6 7 8

DODGE CHALLENGER R/T

Manufacturer: Dodge Division
Chrysler Corporation
P.O. Box 1259
Detroit, Michigan 48231

Vehicle type: Front engine, rear-wheel-drive, 4-passenger coupe

Price as tested: $ N.A.
(Manufacturer's suggested retail price, including all options listed below, Federal excise tax, dealer preparation and delivery charges, does not include state and local taxes, license or freight charges)

Options on test car: 425-hp Hemi engine, styled wheels, F60-15 tires, automatic transmission, limited-slip differential, power steering, power brakes, Special Edition trim package

ENGINE
Type: V-8, water-cooled, cast iron block and heads, 5 main bearings
Bore x stroke..4.25 x 3.75 in, 108.0 x 95.2mm
Displacement.....................426 cu in, 6990cc
Compression ratio.................10.3 to one
Carburetion..................2 x 4-bbl Carter AFB
Valve gear........Pushrod operated overhead valves, hydraulic lifters
Power (SAE)............425 bhp @ 5000 rpm
Torque (SAE)..........490 lbs-ft @ 4000 rpm
Specific power output.........1.00 bhp/cu in, 60.9 bhp/liter
Max recommended engine speed...6500 rpm

DRIVE TRAIN
Transmission.............3-speed, automatic
Max. torque converter..............2.1 to one
Final drive ratio.................3.23 to one
Gear Ratio Mph/1000rpm Max. test speed
 I   2.45   9.6   58 mph (6000 rpm)
 II 1.45 16.2   97 mph (6000 rpm)
 III 1.00 23.6 111 mph (4700 rpm)

DIMENSIONS AND CAPACITIES
Wheelbase...........................110.0 in
Track, F/R...................59.7/60.7 in
Length............................191.3 in
Width..............................76.4 in
Height.............................51.4 in
Ground clearance....................N.A. in
Curb weight.......................3890 lbs
Weight distribution, F/R..........58.9/41.1%
Battery capacity..........12 volts, 70 amp/hr
Alternator capacity.................444 watts
Fuel capacity........................18.0 gal
Oil capacity..........................5.0 qts
Water capacity.......................16.0 qts

SUSPENSION
F: Ind., unequal length control arms, torsion bars, anti-sway bar
R: Rigid axle, semi-elliptic leaf springs

STEERING
Type........Recirculating ball, power assisted
Turns lock-to-lock.........................3.5
Turning circle curb-to-curb............42.0 ft

BRAKES
F:..11.0 x 3.0-in cast iron drum, power assisted
R:..11.0 x 2.5-in cast iron drum, power assisted

WHEELS AND TIRES
Wheel size.........................15 x 7.0-in
Wheel type.............Stamped steel, 5-bolt
Tire make and size..........Goodyear F60-15
Tire type..............Polyglas, tubeless
Test inflation pressures, F/R.......24/28 psi
Tire load rating.....1500 lbs per tire @ 32 psi

PERFORMANCE
Zero to   Seconds
  30 mph..............................2.3
  40 mph..............................3.3
  50 mph..............................4.3
  60 mph..............................5.8
  70 mph..............................7.3
  80 mph..............................8.0
  90 mph.............................10.9
 100 mph.............................13.4
Standing ¼-mile.......14.1 sec @ 103.2 mph
Top speed (estimated)..............146 mph
80-0 mph...................294 ft (0.72G)
Fuel mileage.......7-12 mpg on premium fuel
Cruising range...................126-216 mi

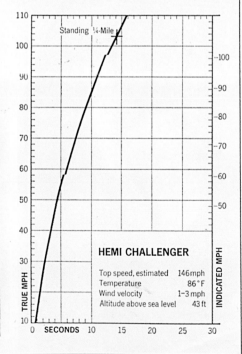

HEMI CHALLENGER
Top speed, estimated   146mph
Temperature   86°F
Wind velocity   1-3 mph
Altitude above sea level 43 ft

Standing ¼-Mile

TRUE MPH / INDICATED MPH

against the brake and very poor low speed throttle response. Not infrequently it would backfire through the carburetor when coming off idle and, occasionally, after a backfire, die right in the middle of the street leaving us to wonder how much impertinence one should put up with just to go 103 mph in the quarter. At first we blamed the tighter 1970 emission regulations but a conversation with the manager of Chrysler's engine development laboratory dispelled that idea. The 1970 Hemis have hydraulic lifters, higher idle speeds and a solenoid valve on the primary carburetor to close the throttles completely when the ignition is shut off (to prevent after-running), but none of those things should impair driveability. We are left to conclude that this Hemi is a victim of poor quality control—something not new to Hemis even though we have never had a bad one before. We are left to conclude that the 440 6-bbl. is a better choice for street operation because of its fatter torque curve and the Hemi should be reserved for those who want the maximum performance and are willing to spend considerable time tuning to get it.

This Challenger did point out the value of specifying the right options to go with the Hemi, however. The standard 3.23-to-one axle ratio is not enough to offset the Hemi's soft low speed performance and the cold air induction hood is essential because, without it, the test car lost 2 mph in the quarter when the underhood temperature reached its normal operating level.

This Challenger, equipped with the standard drum brakes, also pointed out the need for ordering the optional discs if you value good braking performance. The self-energizing drums are difficult to modulate and more inclined to fade. Even so, the test car's poor braking performance— 294 feet (0.72-G) from 80 mph—is far more a result of poor braking distribution than of poor brakes. As seems to be normal for Chrysler products, the rears locked up well before the fronts which dramatically reduced the efficiency of the system.

As there are optional brakes and optional engines so are there a multitude of appearance options—all of which are

calculated to give the Challenger that broad-based appeal which Dodge is counting upon. For example, take something as seemingly mundane as a hood: there is the standard no-frills simply-cover-the-engine hood, the bulging R/T hood (all performance models are called R/T), and the high performance hood with a big hole in it for the shaker-type scoop. Inside the car all of the R/Ts have a special instrument cluster with four round dials: one each for the tach, speedometer, clock, and the remaining one reserved for all of the small gauges. Then, for those who aren't satisfied with less than the best room in the house, there is the Special Edition trim option which can happen on either the standard Challenger or the R/T. The most straightforward part of the SE package is the seats—either cloth or leather covering. The cloth ones on the test car merit our approval even though they aren't very buckety. But the rest of the package is of dubious value. You get an overhead console with warning lights for the following offenses; door ajar, low fuel and seat belts. "Low fuel" may be helpful even though the ceiling is a strange place for that warning to appear and "seat belts," which operates on a time delay so that it stays on about 30 seconds after you close the door, may actually remind someone to buckle up. But nothing could be more worthless than "door ajar" which operates on the same time delay as "seat belts." It simply means that you have to wait that 30 seconds after you shut the door for the light to confirm that it is really closed—If you take the warning at face value and keep slamming the door the light will never go out. All this overhead console amounts to is an excuse for the product planners to hang a piece of bright work on the headliner and thereby "create the impression of greater value" when in reality it is next to useless (the Mustang and Cougar at least had a pair of map reading lights in their overhead console which worked very well). The final goodie in the SE package is a vinyl roof with a tiny back window—meant to recreate the visual ecstasy of a Carson padded top from the early Fifties. Unfortunately the normal rear window

opening has been made smaller by blocking off a band several inches wide across its bottom, which means that you can no longer see any of the rear deck from the driver's seat and the Challenger consequently becomes a park-by-ear car. In all, the SE package serves to exemplify the entire Challenger approach—lavish execution with no thought to practical application.

Dodge figures it has to offer more in the Challenger because it will sell at a higher price than the Mustang/Camaro/Javelin class of sporty cars. We do find the Challenger's interior to be visually very dramatic. The inner door panels, pebble-grained one-piece molded plastic affairs, are deeply sculptured but unfortunately are as hard as a plastered wall. The door lock button has been replaced by a lever in the armrest—a lever which is cleverly positioned exactly where your elbow wants to go. Armrests are also molded into the flimsy panels that flank the rear seats but they are so high that anyone tall enough to use them comfortably won't fit into the back seat in the first place.

But never mind all of these details. If Dodge's sporty car is like everyone else's its success will depend entirely upon public acceptance of its looks. We've never accused the Mustang of being a wizard car but it sells like one and we think the Challenger has got it covered in the looks category. Still, we are disappointed that looks are awarded such a high priority over function and we think Dodge has had enough time to build a more purposeful car. It's our humble suggestion that, to avoid similar ineptitude in the future, all of the Challenger product planners fall on their swords immediately.

JOE WHITLOCK
A SIX PACK FULL OF 'SHINE

An independent survey to determine the supercar's potential in certain regional economies of the South.

"Young fella, if you'uns telling the truth about not working for the federal gov'ment and you'uns work for one of them New York magazines like you'uns is saying and you'uns want to ask me some questions about making likker, then I'm gon' ask you to git off my property in a big hurry. Folks in these parts knows about New Yorkers. Now git!"

Scratch the white two-story house just beyond the Goodwill Freedom Baptist Church.

"My friend, you're asking questions that I ain't 'bout to answer. Now if you got business on my front porch, state it. If you don't, then I'm gon' say you look a lot like that salesman from Raleigh that got my little Ema pregnant. And I'm gitting my shotgun!"

Exit left. Hastily. Scratch the house behind the store with the Sun-Drop Cola sign.

"Young man, you look just like that college boy what came here to take the census and I ain't gon' tell you what my husband did to him. Now git on, afore I have to wake him up."

Scratch the store with the Sun-Drop Cola sign.

"Don't nobody 'round here wear funny breeches like that and don't nobody ask stupid questions neither. We ain't got nothing to talk about, so go on someplace else."

Scratch the house trailer just beyond the big white chicken barn.

"Sonny, my Jeb has been out of Atlanta almost five years and he don't drink, make ner haul anything stronger 'n coffee. If he owes you some money, then say so. If he don't even know you like you saying, then you'uns better be moving on . . . 'cause he'll be coming home from work to'rectly."

Scratch the whole damn county.

Finding a bona fide liquor runner to road test a car when you're wearing funny breeches and little Ema's pregnant is a pain.

"Frankly, Preacher Morris, I don't know

what to do. Thought maybe you could offer a suggestion. Nobody'll get into any trouble. We are even willing to pay them and sign a contract saying we won't use their names. We will (stroke of genius) even give some money to your fine church."

"How much money do you think that magazine of your's would be giving the church? It's deductible, you know."

"Fifty?"

"How about a hundred?"

"Fine. Meet me at the church after morning service next Sunday. About 1:00. I'll have some fine young men to drive that car of yours . . . and God bless you, son."

You can always count on a man of the cloth.

Dawn breaks on Mash Sunday and you have to skirt town to pick up the photographer. It's a long drive to the foothills of the Appalachians and the good Rev's already figuring on how to spend the C note.

"Christ, man, I wasn't speeding! What'd you stop me for? I just left the house."

"Now young man, I never said you were speeding, did I?"

"Well? What the hell's going on?"

"Now you just relax and watch your tongue. I didn't say you were speeding but I didn't say you weren't driving too fast for conditions, either."

"What conditions? I couldn't have been going over twenty when that blue light started flashing!"

"I could say all that dew on your rear window made that car a hazard to traffic . . . but there isn't any traffic at 6:00 in the morning. You did see the blue light through the window, too. What I really want to know is what's a car like that, with out-of-state plates, doing on an out-of-way North Carolina back road at 6:00 on a Sunday morning? It looks out of place... and you don't look

like the type that'd be going to early mass."

Magazine. Driver's license. Photographer. Road test. Mountain scenery. Press cards. Insurance papers. Business card. Address. Phone number. Fishing license. Next of kin. Geneva Convention card.

"Aw, come on, huh?"

"You still gotta admit it looks funny. Sounds funny, too. Who ever heard of a car called a Six-Pack? Six-pack of what? Looks like something somebody'd haul liquor in the way it's sticking up in the back. Go on, son. I'm sorry to have held you up. You be careful with that thing, you heah? ... You still have to admit it looks out of place."

Maybe I should have gone to early mass. Spiritual assistance can be helpful when you have to face a waiting photographer with eight cups of coffee churning in his morning-after belly.

The good Reverend Morris was waiting, idly pulling patches of crabgrass from around a few tombstones in the small graveyard adjacent to his church.

"Good day, gentlemen. The deacons are through counting the collections for today, but I'll be happy to put your donations in tonight's plate. And bless you.

"I want you young gentlemen to go down this road about two miles and take the first paved road to the right after you pass a couple of big white chicken barns on the left. About a mile down that road is a little white store with a Sun-Drop Cola sign out front.

"Ol' J.B. Smith don't do business on Sunday, but he'll be sitting out front with a couple of his nephews and they know what to do. Incidentally, I thought it might help so I told ol' J.B. that you went to school with my son Larry.

"J. B. says he'll have them two boys drive that car for you and he said they'd all tell you what you want to know. Course, I told him you'd pay 'em good and about them legal papers, too."

Nothing slack about the preacher.

Down the road, past the chicken barns again, and back to the Sun-Drop sign. There he was, big as life, ol' J.B., faded bib overalls, see-thru nylon short-sleeved shirt, spotted straw hat with a prominent sweat ring and $40 loafers sporting a spit shine. And sipping an honest-to-goodness Sun-Drop Cola.

"You fellas want a Sun-Drop? Strongest thing we got in these parts." Ol' J.B. chuckled and smiled through teeth that looked like rusty railroad spikes.

"Wife said you'uns was by here last week," he said.

I was enjoying my first-ever Sun-Drop.

"Can't pay no mind to women. She thought you worked for the federal gov'ment. Them two nephews of mine'll be along to'rectly to drive that car for you. Both of 'em used to race cars over at Harris on Saturday nights 'til one went in the Army and the other got in trouble and had to go to jail for a spell."

It became obvious that ol' J.B. was a talker, so we settled down on a bench while he sucked on his Sun-Drop and wiped his chin with a railroad bandana.

"Preacher Morris said you wanted to know about making 'shine? Course, that paper you got says you can't use my name. I guess I can answer most questions you'uns got on the subject. I went to court fourteen times for making the stuff. Wasn't convicted by four, though, and that was when they caught me red-handed a'cooking at the still.

"When I got out of Atlanta in '54 I come back home here and bought this store. Ain't messed with the stuff since. Too troublesome. 'Bout the only time you see it anymore is just to drink a drop or two on special occasions.

"Federal gov'ment got more agents in this county nowadays than I got chickens in them barns over yonder. Taxes and agents. That's all the gov'ment is. This country's in a hell of a mess. You can't grow no tobacco unless they say so, and then they put a tax on smoking. You sure can't make no likker no more, and when you buy it you have to pay more in taxes than you do for the stuff in the jug. It won't be long a'fore they figure out how to put a tax on

going to bed with the ol' lady. It's damn shame what Yankees and city folks have done to this country.

"I told ol' jedge whatshisname, War-lick, I believe, when they sent me to Atlanta that last time, that the reason I was making likker was because it was a man's God-given right to make likker. Hell, I was making it to drink. I wasn't making it to sell! He knew it, too. Know what he said? Said the federal gov'ment passed a law a long time ago saying you couldn't make likker. The FEDERAL GOVER'MENT! What a goddam bunch of hipercrits. Wouldn't no use to arguin', though, 'cause the federal gov'ment was paying him to judge.

"Ain't made a drop since that last time … but I believe I'd go back to cooking if ol' Judge Hill was still alive. He believed it was a man's God-given right, too, and he didn't care nothing about the federal gov'ment, neither."

Ol' J.B. didn't leave any doubts about his feeling for the folks in Washington.

He polished off the last swig of his Sun-Drop and glanced up the road where a white '67 Ford and a perfect specimen of a black '55 Chevrolet—mags and Sears' seat covers included—were rounding the curve.

"Here come them boys, now," J.B. smiled.

Lamar Gene ("I don't care if you use my first name") and Bubba ("me neither") exchanged greetings, accepted a cool Sun-Drop from "Uncle J.B." and plopped down on the initial-scarred bench in front of the official "Smith's Crossroads General Store" (the sign was inside over the drink box).

Bubba's Ford was a spotless 2-door Custom with a 427 Highway Interceptor crammed under the hood ("she goes pretty good"). Lamar Gene's Chevy was a collector's item, handmade almost, from the 396 engine ("I rebuilt it myself") to the twin polished pipes. Nothing gaudy. Something a guy has to stop and look at. He flicked on the stereo tape unit ("I just got this and I want you to listen to them speakers") and Glen Campbell unloaded with a little "Galveston" on everybody in Smith's Crossroads.

Both nephews had an abundance of black hair, complete with healthy sideburns. Both had short-sleeved sport shirts with sleeves rolled up a couple of turns. Both had on

starchy-looking "wheat jeans" and both had on $40 loafers with spit shines.

Hot-dog loafers and hot-dog cars are commonplace with virile mountain males. They all share a fierce pride in their abilities to drive an automobile, too, and they all hold an amazing interest in what's under a hood.

The brothers finished their Sun-Drops at precisely the same instant.

"Uncle J.B. says you want us to drive that car you got there and tell you whether or not it would make a good liquor car," Bubba said. "Tell you right now, it won't make no liquor car.

"Ain't never been but one good 'jump car' ever made and that was a '40 Ford. Runners still swear by '40 Fords. I once got 35 cases of half-gallon jars in a '40 Ford. Took the back seat out and covered it up with a bedspread so it'd look like a seat. Runners around here was the last ones to let them '40 Fords go. Saw one the other day that a man wanted $2,200 for... and I bet he'll get it, too.

"I can look at that car you got there and tell you that no runner ain't never gon' buy one. It's too purty for a jump car. Ain't nobody gon' leave nothing like that on the side of the road. Besides, speed don't do you too much good no more, now that them agents are all using radios. You just need an old car with a pretty good engine in it. Don't use overload springs no more, either. Too easy to spot. Usually just put an extra leaf or two in the springs. Besides, folks around here don't make much liquor no more. Ain't that right, Uncle J.B.?"

"Bubba's right, son." J. B. had been carving over a minor obscenity on his bench.

"Federal gov'ment agents is just too thick. Making likker used to be the only industry we had and it kept the grocery stores and the car dealers and the gas stations in business. Hell, if I ordered an extra ten pounds of sugar off the truck now they'd come a'running. Folks just don't make the stuff much no more. Why, them agents blew up 27 stills in this county last month. Man's a fool to make 'shine nowadays.

"They fly them little planes all over the woods and every time they see a puff of smoke a bunch of 'em come rolling up in a brand new car to see what's causing the fire. Hell, the other day they spotted an old rusty still up yonder on the hill near the apple orchard and drove up there in a brand new Ford and blew the damn thing up. An old colored farmer down the road built that still a long time ago and ain't nobody worked it in over two years. The federal gov'ment 'most tears up a brand new Ford just to get up there and blow it sky high. One of my cows lost a calf just 'cause of the noise. That's the gov'ment for you."

J.B. muttered something about Strom Thurmond and how he should have made it on the Dixiecrat ticket back in the Fifties. He went back carving over another four-letter word.

"I bet that thing would be a 'hoss' down at Shuffletown drag strip," Lamar Gene finally said. He had been giving the Dodge a thorough going over.

"I bet it'll haul ass. They say them 440 engines that Dodge is making is going in a lot of police cars now. That 'Six-Pack' means it's got them three 2-barrels in it, huh? Ought not write it on the hood like that, though. Every high school kid in town's gon' gawk all over it.

"How 'bout if I drive it?"

Bubba was allowing how he went to Atlanta and why and it wasn't so bad, but he didn't want to go back when Lamar Gene stoked up the 'Six-Pack' and roared off down through the country.

Seems that Bubba's sabbatical in Atlanta was the result of a master plan that didn't work.

"Oh, I never even come close to getting caught when I was haulin' the stuff over to Winston and down to Charlotte," he said. "Know them roads too good. I got a little greedy and that's what got me in trouble.

"I 'bout had to whip my ol' lady, but one day she finally let me put a 280-gallon still in the basement of the house. I had the smoke coming out of our regular chimney. I thought I had a good idea but I didn't. Wasn't much point in running when they found me working it, either... being right there in my basement. That got me two good years in Atlanta.

"Wasn't so bad. I made enough money to build the house I got now. I figured I might as well make my time useful over there and I got

pretty friendly with a guard in the motor pool. Found out he'd sell me a case of pints for $100."

Bubba was telling war stories and ol' J.B. was carving and listening.

"That guard, he'd pay $60 a case for that good stuff and we was hiding it in the garage. We'd drink a little and sell the rest for $10 a pint to all them Hoffa boys that was in Atlanta back in them days. Business was good and them two years went by fast. But I don't ever want to go back to jail. Once is one time too many."

You could hear Lamar Gene coming a long time before the Dodge came into sight. Two cars were following him; a Ford Torino and a Dodge Charger.

"I had to let Ludie and Spratt and Burr and Sam here drive this thing," Lamar Gene smiled. "Hope you don't mind. That thing's a running piece."

The photographer and the "test crew" (Bubba and Lamar Gene with two new assistants, Spratt and Sam) rolled off down the road for some "testing" and picture taking while ol' J.B. (now on his third Sun-Drop), Ludie, Burr and I stayed at the store. I had no choice. The car was full.

"Y'all doing a story for a New York magazine on haulin' liquor?" Burr asked. "You come to the wrong place. All the big-money liquor outfits are out in Mississippi and Alabama now. ATU man told me the other day that they found a 400-barrel operation out there someplace and two agents got killed when they went to blow it up. A couple more agents was with 'em and they just had a little trial. Tried, convicted and shot them bootleggers right on the spot."

"Ain't like it used to be right after the war," Ludie offered. "I used to make two runs a week down to Charlotte and they'd put it in 'stash' houses until they could sell it to 'shot' houses. They'd cut it with water and sell a shot for a quarter and everybody was happy.

"When them Yankee syndicates found out they could haul a load of sugar down here in a tractor-trailer rig and take a load of 'shine back the whole place went crazy. They was selling it for six-bits a shot in New York."

Ludie was a student of the industry.

"Back before the war all the people making

liquor was highly respected folks. It started changing right after I got out of the Army. The demand kind of ruined everything. The makers was setting up cheap stills that didn't cost too much. Just wasn't no craftsmanship anymore.

"Man'd be a fool to drink that stuff. It got so'd you couldn't find a place where they made liquor to drink. Some cookers was even putting in chicken drops to speed up the process. They was making it to sell and it wasn't long before the agents was thick as flies."

"Besides, all them Interstate Highways took all the fun out of haulin' a load," Burr added. "Anybody can drive on them things... and the police is always 'round."

"My brother'n-law builds race cars and he was bringing back a truckful of rear-ends from Holman-Moody the other day up the Interstate and the radar got him twice for speeding," Ludie said. "When he pulled off the Interstate to come over the crossroads here he got stopped three times by agents. They all saw his trunk loaded down and thought he was haulin' again.

"Hell, a man's a fool to haul nowadays."

"I never did get involved with those syndicate people," J.B. interrupted. "Didn't trust 'em. You could tell they come from up North by the way they talked. That bunch turned the local likker industry into an export thing. Ruined it. Man can't make 'shine around here no more. Them 27 stills they Mowed up wasn't making no good stuff. Just stuff for the Yankee haulers."

The "crew" came limping back to the store after an hour or so. The Six-Pack was covered with dust and mud and it looked like it had been eating chickens.

"Don't worry about the chicken feathers," the photographer said. "We stopped and paid the farmer five bucks apiece for the ones we killed."

The big car, obviously triumphant, rested alongside J.B.'s place of business. The only signs of fatigue it rendered were occasional 'cracks' from the cooling radiator.

When it became time for a final round of Sun-Drops, 'ol' Uncle J.B.' was in such a good mood he forgot to collect for the drinks.

"Bubba tried to tear your damned car up,"

Lamar Gene said through a laugh. "Run it off the mountain by the orchard and through the creek. Slung mud all over Spratt and that camera fella. That thing ain't missed a lick. It'll run like hell.

"Uncle J.B.? You remember that old bridge down by the Kinard place? The one they just put new pavement on? That car hit ninety before it got to the ol' graveyard. Bubba's Ford won't do that."

The boys ooohed and aaahed a little bit about the 440 and sipped Sun-Drop and talked about shooting ground hogs and about the good old days when Ludie's brother was working for the sheriff because he had been an M.P. in the Army, and how they had to fire him because he'd race police cars and wouldn't give nobody a ticket.

Bubba was in a more serious mood.

"It's a man's right to drive a good car and that's a good 'un," he said slowly. "It'd be crazy enough to work, too. I could haul a bunch of loads with that thing before the feds got around to figuring out what I was doing.

"How much do you reckon one of them Six-Packs cost?"

Dodge CHRYSLER

Our Plum Crazy Challenger R/T Is No Shrinking Violet.

No way is 1970's all-new, high-performance car going to go unnoticed. Not with a mean 383 Magnum V8. Nor with an optional choice of engines, all the way up to the "Haulin' Hemi." Nor with that super-purple paint job—one of the new high-impact colors* for the Dodge Scat Pack. Challenger R/T comes with all the other going goodies, too: 3-on-the-floor full-synchro manual transmission • Rallye Suspension (includes front sion bars for extra-stable handling) • Rallye Instrument Cluster • HD drum-type brakes • Wide-ad tires • New longitudinal stripe or popular bumblebee stripe. 1970 Plum Crazy Challenger R/T. the first in your crowd to drive the Dodge Super Grape.

*Optional, at extra cost.

the cars with the Bumblebee *stripes*

1970–1972 Muscle Car High Summer and Requiem

Soon as you've got it ... they change it.

Just when every American-performance buyer was happy, American Muscle began to change. There were stylistic excesses, certainly—like Pontiac GTO's pricey, hefty, clumsy The Judge, plastered with "psychedelic" decals from prow to stern.

Just the same, 1970 also saw some of the most concise, satisfying shapes of the entire era—Pontiac Firebird Trans Am, Chevrolet Camaro Z/28 and the voluptuous Plymouth Road Runner—peak stylistic expressions of American Muscle.

Yet *Car and Driver*, the muscle car's staunchest supporter in its first years, saw problems. By now, the suits in the Detroit boardroom had gotten involved: was American Muscle veering off into self-satire? Would the minimalist, hot-rod inspired young muscle buyer take one look at ornate new mainstream muscle cars and walk away shaking his head?

More ominously, the automobile-insurance industry, scandalized by American Muscle's "unsafe" performance, was determined to price young muscle-car buyers out of the market. Air pollution, too, was a growing national concern—and dirty, huge 455-CID muscle-car powerplants were no friend to clean air.

Sales began to dwindle in the early 1970s. But with the anti-muscle fuel-mileage hysteria created by the OPEC Fuel Embargo in 1973, for all practical purposes, American Muscle was over.

Purple Prose: The Dodge Challenger R/T Convertible is one of the high-water marks of gorgeous Muscle.

ROAD TEST

PONTIAC GTO 455

You have to give the stylists the most credit for making this GTO attractive.

The guys in charge of keeping Pontiac's GTO pumped up have been hard at it. To keep the original super car vital in a market that is all but turning cartwheels to attract the newly affluent youth, they've dressed it in a highly fashionable new suit, tweaked the suspension a bit and dialed up an optional 455 cubic inch V-8. We like the result. We think you will too. In fact, we even think that your father and mother and the guy down the street who is a florist will like it. That should tell you something about the GTO, particularly about the GTO as a nervous, goose-pimple-raising performance car.

You have to give the stylists the most credit for making the GTO desirable—they've pumped the hardest. They've managed to mold a car that looks good to almost everyone—no easy task in a world rapidly approaching standing room only with automotive styling critics. The GTO's beauty lies in a strong basic shape—voluptuous yet tasteful—and it needs no tack-on trim to make it work. It is a car that people will buy for the styling alone, whether or not they like performance cars, and fortunately for those who don't, the GTO has a reserved personality that will wear well over the long run.

For the street-prowling youths whose social standing depends upon having the meanest tire burner on The Avenue, however, the GTO may have lost its luster. It's not that the Pontiac guys in charge pumping in the propellent have completely neglected their job—they did come up with the 455 you will remember—but they seem to have been pumping against a slow leak. The GTO isn't very fast. Don't misunderstand. By ticking off the proper options on the dealer's order form you can build a brisk GTO, but it won't be equal to the heavy-handed street cleaners that are setting the pace these days. This deficiency, if that is the way you see it, can be traced to

the Pontiac high-level management's view of performance. With the exception of a kind of half-hearted dabble in the Trans-Am, Pontiac has remained aloof from the racing scene for what is fast approaching a decade. The GTO, despite its highly touted reputation as a performance car, has never been involved in anything tougher than the grass roots level of drag racing. It is still coasting on the inertia it built up when it was first introduced in 1964 as the first visible big-engine intermediate. The result of all of this is that even though the GTO progressed in areas of handling, comfort and appearance with the best of the Detroit crop, its acceleration—which is the foundation upon which super cars are built—has hardly changed in the past three or four years.

Pontiac is just now starting to worry. The handwriting is unmistakably on the wall in the form of declining sales figures. Last year Plymouth's Road Runner outsold the GTO and the point is really driven home with vigor when you remember that Plymouth has another car in that market segment, the GTX, which when added in, makes the gap even wider. And then this year, despite its brilliant styling, the GTO didn't take off on introduction day like it was supposed to. It seems that the showroom charm of a performance image which worked so well for the GTO early in its career is now working for somebody else.

If performance was purely a function of engine displacement the GTO would never be more than a blur on your retinas. But it doesn't work that way. In fact, Pontiac is in the curious predicament of having two 400 cubic inch engines that make more horsepower than the 455. If you ask Pontiac engineers to explain this unseeming arrangement they kind of look at the floor, shift their weight from one foot to the other, and mumble something about not being quite prepared when the General

Motors hierarchy lifted the longstanding ban on engines larger than 400 cubic inches in intermediate-size cars. They were working on a big engine at the time, a 455 for the Bonnevilles and such, but it wasn't intended to be a high performance engine. They had taken last year's 428, whittled the bore out 0.030 and made up the rest with more stroke. So the 455 is a long-armed chuffer if there ever was one.

Still, there wasn't any choice. If Oldsmobile, Buick and Chevrolet were going to have engines over 450 cubes in their A-body cars, then the GTO had to have one too. So in went the 455. They could have screwed on the big port heads and plugged in the long duration camshaft from the Ram Air IV; that stuff will all fit. It probably would have made the GTO go like a nickel rocket too, but they knew better than to do that. The business of collecting up the spent GTOs that would have fallen along the wayside after a short, dazzling flash and reloading them on warranty was out of the question. Consequently, the 455 is a torquey, low-revving device that makes very little ruckus and works great with an air conditioner—which is the way the test car was set up. Pontiac very definitely wants you to keep the revs down so the tach has a 5100 rpm redline and a 3.31-to-one axle ratio is standard (3.07 with an automatic). You can have a 3.55 by special order but nothing more drastic than that. The test car used a close ratio 4-speed manual transmission and the standard 3.31 rear, unfortunately without a limited-slip. Although the engine is obviously very tame, with a full, flat torque curve, the GTO wasn't quite as drivable as it might have been—a fact that can be largely blamed on GM's method of meeting the 1970 emission specifications. The GTO has what is known in Detroit as Transmission Controlled Spark. This system has a switch mounted on the transmission that senses which gear is engaged and, in the

first and second gear, sends a signal to the distributor that kills the vacuum advance. It should have no effect on all-out performance because there is no vacuum advance at wide-open throttle but it does make response a bit sluggish, particularly at low speeds.

We all know, of course, that low speeds aren't what most people buy GTOs for. This one set no records for acceleration—15.0 seconds at 96.5 mph in the quarter. It was a decidedly non-racer kind of car. Despite all the things you've heard about GTOs being meant to burn away from traffic lights, this one was far better suited to cross-country touring or sporty commuting. It was too heavy to be a racer because of all the convenience devices; air conditioning, electric windows, power

steering, power disc brakes and an arm's length list of other less weighty options. So equipped, the GTO is a very pleasant, self-assured automobile—the kind of car that will never disappoint someone who bought it because he was smitten by the styling.

The GTO is a driver's car but this is not to say that you have to be an enthusiast to appreciate it. Pontiac has done a good job of positioning the controls and making them work accurately. The variable-ratio power steering has good road feel, the clutch has a short travel and yet requires delightfully low pedal effort and the Hurst-shifted gearbox is magnificent. Almost every manufacturer in Detroit buys the Hurst shift mechanism for their 4-speeds but most of them connect it to

the transmission with their own rubbery levers and rods which negates half the precision of the Hurst. There is apparently somebody at Pontiac who likes to throw a good shift and we're with him. We wonder if he is also the one responsible for the optional $5.27 shift knob, a black plastic sphere about the size of a tennis ball that really gives you something to grab. And while we're talking about controls let's not forget the quick-ratio accelerator—a subtle piece of Pontiac psychology intended to create the impression of a hyper-active steed.

Psychology can be used for handling too. About half the drivers in the world (none of them C/D readers) are convinced that handling excellence is inversely proportional to body roll. With a new rear anti-sway bar this year in

addition to a stiffer front bar, the GTO should zoom right to the top of this group's list. Even with the rear bar the car very definitely understeers, particularly with the extra weight of the air conditioner on the front wheels, but it is a very satisfactory compromise for almost any situation you will ever encounter on public roads. Also to its credit the GTO manages to handle well without having a teeth-chattering ride. It is on the stiff side but it lacks the sharp harshness that characterizes other, particularly non-GM, performance cars. This is just one of the many factors that tends to make the GTO a satisfying car for a broad range of buyers.

But even though it is normally mild and mannerly it does tend to lose its aplomb when it has to stop in a hurry. The rear wheels tend to lock up prematurely resulting in poor directional stability, fade resistance is moderate and the axle occasionally hops. The phenomenon of brake hop, while disconcerting, is not uncommon in performance cars, particularly those with manual transmissions. It is not so violent in the GTO that you have to lift your foot off the brake pedal to avoid what feels like self-destruction—it's that bad in some cars—but it is high time Detroit discovered a way to do away with it all together. Even with all of these minor ineptitudes being brought into play at the touch of the brake pedal the GTO still managed to stop in 284 feet (0.75G) which puts it somewhere in the third quarter of its class.

If you continue this process of assigning rank, you will find that the interior scores

much higher—well into the top quartile in fact. The battle for broad appeal is at least half won by strong, innovative styling, both exterior and interior, and this is where the GTO seizes its advantage. The instrument panel is simple and well laid out; three round dials set into a wood-like background directly in front of the driver. The only deficiency is that the tachometer is recessed too deeply to be readily visible. A feature that stands unique among all Detroit cars is the GTO's optional console—a smoothly-molded, vinyl-covered shape containing a deep glove box and defying every

known Motor City styling principle by being completely barren of chrome trim. In a day when building to the state of the art is to bolt something resembling a nickelodian between the seats, we're all in favor of the GTO console.

When you combine all of the many impressions of the GTO into one overall view the car assumes a quietly satisfying glow. It is reserved rather than mechanically inspirational and best suited to the fashion conscious automotive enthusiast. Down at The Club it will look great, but on the way home mind your own business if you don't want to get snuffed by almost any one of the patrolling guerrillas. That's really a bit unjust. The GTO isn't that kind of car. It's kind and friendly—almost anyone would like it. But in a GTO you're typecast. If you don't believe it just lay your 455 cubic inch, 360-horsepower Pontiac GTO on your family insurance agent. He and the fuzz are the only ones who can find anything threatening about it.

Above: Ads for the new Pontiac Firebird showed styling that was as sensuous as the new GTO.

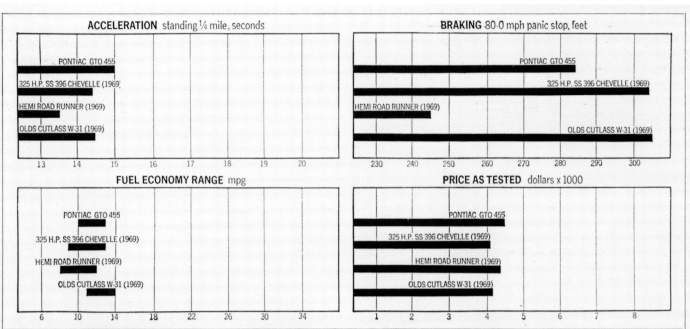

ACCELERATION standing ¼ mile, seconds

- PONTIAC GTO 455
- 325 H.P. SS 396 CHEVELLE (1969)
- HEMI ROAD RUNNER (1969)
- OLDS CUTLASS W-31 (1969)

13 14 15 16 17 18 19 20

BRAKING 80-0 mph panic stop, feet

- PONTIAC GTO 455
- 325 H.P. SS 396 CHEVELLE (1969)
- HEMI ROAD RUNNER (1969)
- OLDS CUTLASS W-31 (1969)

230 240 250 260 270 280 290 300

FUEL ECONOMY RANGE mpg

- PONTIAC GTO 455
- 325 H.P. SS 396 CHEVELLE (1969)
- HEMI ROAD RUNNER (1969)
- OLDS CUTLASS W-31 (1969)

6 10 14 18 22 26 30 34

PRICE AS TESTED dollars x 1000

- PONTIAC GTO 455
- 325 H.P. SS 396 CHEVELLE (1969)
- HEMI ROAD RUNNER (1969)
- OLDS CUTLASS W-31 (1969)

1 2 3 4 5 6 7 8

PONTIAC GTO

Manufacturer: Pontiac Motor Division
General Motors Corp.
Pontiac, Michigan 48053

Vehicle type: Front engine, rear-wheel-drive, 5-passenger hardtop coupe

Price as tested: $4481.84
(Manufacturer's suggested retail price, including all options listed below, Federal excise tax, dealer preparation and delivery charges, does not include state and local taxes, license or freight charges)

Options on test car: Base GTO coupe, $3267.00; 360-hp V-8, $57.93; 4-speed transmission, $184.80; G70-14 white letter tires, $66.35; power steering, $105.32; power disc brakes, $64.25; styled wheels, $63.19; tachometer and gauge cluster, $50.55; air-conditioning, $375.99; power windows, $105.32; power door locks, $45.29; console, $55.82; optional shift knob, $5.27; sport steering wheel, $34.76.

ENGINE

Type: V-8, water-cooled, cast iron block and heads, 5 main bearings
Bore x stroke.4.15 x 4.21 in, 105.3 x 107.0 mm
Displacement............ 455 cu in, 7450 cc
Compression ratio................10.25 to one
Carburetion.....1 x 4-bbl Rochester Quadrajet
Valve gear........Pushrod operated overhead valves, hydraulic lifters

Power (SAE)............ 360 bhp @ 4600 rpm
Torque (SAE)........... 500 lbs-ft @ 3100 rpm
Specific power output........0.79 bhp/cu in, 48.3 bhp/liter
Max recommended engine speed....5100 rpm

DRIVE TRAIN

Transmission............4-speed, all-synchro
Final drive ratio..................3.31 to one

Gear	Ratio	Mph/1000 rpm	Max. test speed
I	2.20	10.6	54 mph (5100 rpm)
II	1.64	14.2	72 mph (5100 rpm)
III	1.28	18.2	93 mph (5100 rpm)
IV	1.00	23.3	110 mph (4750 rpm)

DIMENSIONS AND CAPACITIES

Wheelbase...........................112.0 in
Track, F/R....................61.0/60.0 in
Length.............................202.9 in
Width...............................76.7 in
Height..............................52.0 in
Ground clearance......................4.1 in
Curb weight.........................4209 lbs
Weight distribution, F/R........57.3/42.7%
Battery capacity........12 volts, 61 amp/hr
Alternator capacity................444 watts
Fuel capacity.....................20.0 gal
Oil capacity........................5.0 qts
Water capacity.....................17.5 qts

SUSPENSION

F: Ind., unequal length control arms, coil springs, anti-sway bar
R: Rigid axle, trailing arms, coil springs, anti-sway bar

STEERING

Type.........Recirculating ball, power assist
Turns lock-to-lock....................3.25
Turning circle curb-to-curb...........37.4 ft

BRAKES

F:..........10.9-in vented disc, power assist
R:....9.5 x 1.9-in cast iron drum, power assist

WHEELS AND TIRES

Wheel size....................14 x 7.0-in
Wheel type............stamped steel, 5-bolt
Tire make and size..........Firestone G70-14
Tire type........fiberglass belted, tubeless
Test inflation pressures, F/R......24/24 psi
Tire load rating.....1620 lbs per tire @ 32 psi

PERFORMANCE

Zero to	Seconds
30 mph	2.4
40 mph	3.5
50 mph	4.9
60 mph	6.6
70 mph	8.5
80 mph	10.8
90 mph	13.3
100 mph	16.0

Standing ¼-mile..........15.0 sec @ 96.5 mph
Top speed (estimated)................120 mph
80-0 mph...................284 ft (0.75 G)
Fuel mileage........10-13 mpg on premium fuel
Cruising range.....................200-260 mi

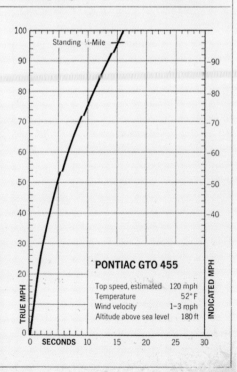

PONTIAC GTO 455

Top speed, estimated	120 mph
Temperature	52°F
Wind velocity	1-3 mph
Altitude above sea level	180 ft

Standing ¼-Mile

ROAD TEST
CHEVROLET CAMARO

The Z/28 version would be every bit as much at home on the narrow, twisting streets of Monte Carlo as it is on Interstate 80.

The world's menu of powerful GT cars contains a few selections of uncommon merit. Almost invariably they are European, frequently Italian in descent, few in numbers and high in price—the precious gems of the car builder's art. There is nothing precious about the Camaro Z/28, Chevrolet will stamp them out like the government does cupro-nickel quarters, but it is an automobile of uncommon merit. It would be every bit as much at home on the narrow, twisting streets of Monte Carlo or in the courtyard of a villa overlooking the Mediterranean as it is on Interstate 80. It's a Camaro like none before.

As everyone knows by this time the 1970 Firebird and Camaro were introduced late in February rather than during Detroit's annual fall festivities. Several weeks before Camaros were due in the showrooms, Chevrolet turned loose a half-dozen Z/28s to various members of the automotive press for whatever kind of evaluation pressmen make. We had requested one with an automatic transmission—the Blue Maxi, with its 350 cu. in. Z/28, had already convinced us that the manual transmission combination was more than satisfactory—and such a car was waiting. It was an early production model that had been carefully inspected and the result was an automobile of commendably high quality.

Almost all car flakes dream of driving some new car before it's available to the public and it can be a completely unique experience. It can also give you an insight not otherwise possible. One young man summed it up best. "I know it's a Z/28, but a Z/28 what?" Only the hard core car underworld knew that it was a Camaro. The rest had to ask. And although we think it's a stunning machine from almost any vantage point, it generally went unnoticed—even in Los Angeles where the car reigns supreme. It's a hard situation to explain. We can only theorize that the Camaro's finely drawn shape, free of Detroit's customary visual trickery, is somewhat removed from the mainstream of public taste. Indeed, if the world approves of Monte Carlos and Rivieras, the Camaro must be an eyesore. We can only hope that is not the case. In fact, there is good reason to believe that the Camaro and Firebird are the leading edge of a new trend in Detroit styling. The Europeans, particularly Giugiaro, have popularized the concept of a strong, simple shape with extreme tumblehome and tuckunder that doesn't need stick-on ornamentation to make it work. The Camaro is certainly of this school. Only the high, pointy grille seems inconsistent with the rest of the car.

And as the styling is restrained in comparison to past Camaros so seems to be the performance image. The cold air induction hood is gone now and so is the Z/28's front spoiler. A change in the Trans-Am rules allows the racers to use a front spoiler whether or not one is available from the factory, and Chevrolet figured it was no longer worth the trouble to bolt them on at the production line since customers just knocked them off on curbs and snow banks anyway. But the cold air hood is another matter and the racers need that. Actually, it's not so much performance as performance image that's been dulled. The engines, which have most of the say about performance, are stronger than ever. The Z/28 is richer by 48 cubic inches and 70 rated horsepower (tough break for those with insurance worries), 350- and 375-hp 396s (now actually 402 cubic inches) are still on the list

Camaro Sport Coupe with Rally Sport equipment.

and a 454 lies hidden in the fine print. No discrimination against thrill seekers there.

Somehow, though, the Z/28 is not as thrilling as it once was. It's more tolerant to driving techniques now, more mature in its behavior. All things considered, it's a better engine now but the loss of a carefree and irrepressible adolescent spirit can never be witnessed without some regret. And although the Z/28 seems much tamer now than it once did, the transformation is more a function of the car than of the increase in displacement. The mechanical lifter valve gear still makes its busy clatter and the exhaust pulses still cascade and reverberate through the pipes with the same abandon they always did, but the sound engineers have so diligently sealed off the passenger compartment that all of those endearing vibrations are filtered out somewhere before they reach your ears. It's a whole different kind of car now. Better, but not unilaterally. In their zeal, those persecutors of noise have even gone so far as to clamp a silenced air cleaner down on top of the Holley 4-bbl. (automatic transmission versions only). The result is a car of brilliant performance

for its displacement and with prep school manners—not the combination that brought the Z/28 to pre-eminence within the car culture.

But it does deliver the performance. The automatic transmission test car had a little help from a 4.10-to-one axle ratio, not exactly what we would have dialed up of our own free will. The surprising part is that the high-winding gear is relatively tolerable in this speed-limited United States, provided you're not short of gas money. The interior noise level is so modest that, had we not known about the ratio, we might have suspected some affliction of the tachometer. If you're interested in acceleration, however, the 4.10 is no more than strategic excess. The Z/28, despite its increase in muscle, is still soft on the low end and with the automatic it would probably bog with a lesser gear. The test car suffered no such infirmities: 14.2 seconds at 100.3 mph in the quarter is as good a measure as any of its physical fitness. Because of the high coolant temperatures required for emission control the power drops off as the engine reaches operating temperature. When fully warmed up the Z/28 is 1–2 mph slower—a situation avoidable when

outside air is ducted into the carburetor.

Predictably, the automatic is a great pain reliever when you're beset with a traffic jam. And with the console shifter you are better off leaving the shifting to whatever makes it automatic. If you try to do it yourself you will probably, unless you sandpaper your fingers, lose your way through the shifting maze. Because the detent for the 1–2 shift is indiscernible the result is too often 1–3. Chevrolet promised a motorcycle-type ratcheting shifter several years ago but as soon as our backs were turned it reneged.

Or perhaps the engineers became involved in something else, steering and suspension for example. The new Camaro has completely redesigned steering linkage, now located forward of a line through the ball joints rather than behind as in most other cars. To reduce noise and ride harshness all suspensions have a certain compliance, or ability to deflect, built in. With the linkage mounted forward, the compliance toes the wheels in an understeering direction which contributes to more manageable transient handling. Along with this, all power-steering Z/28 and SS

Camaros have a special high-effort steering gear. High effort is not to be confused with increased road feel but it does reduce the tendency to overcorrect. The result of these two developments is a car of exceptional road handling—probably the best Detroit has ever produced. The transition as you enter a curve or change is extremely predictable and this, combined with a low body roll angle, is the essence of good road handling. In more demanding situations, those which you would encounter on a race track or perhaps on a road you had all to yourself, the Camaro is disappointing. It understeers heavily; sometimes you can trick it and get the tail out, sometimes you just have to slow down until the front tires regain their hold on the pavement. Never does it offer the driver very much road feel and never does it give him any confidence. The engineers admit being faced with a compromise, ultimate cornering ability or transients, and they chose the latter. And the driver's lot is made even more difficult by the seat which is just the inverse of a bucket—a seat that is easier to fall out of than in to.

Another thorn which the engineers had to consider was the limited-slip differential which increases understeer in direct proportion to its limited-slip qualities. Since it's not standard equipment—and over-steer is considered to be dangerous—the base car must have built-in understeer. It follows, then, that the limited-slip car will have even more understeer. The logical solution would be to make the limited-slip a mandatory option since, on a performance car, most buyers order it anyhow and then tune the front and rear anti-sway bar rates for that situation. But for now you'll have to take the Camaro for what it is, a highly developed touring car, and don't expect too much in more demanding situations.

Certainly the brakes are up to any touring demands. Front discs are standard and the test car had the optional power assist. This car represents something new for Chevrolet in that high pedal pressure was required to produce impending lock-up rather than the normal touch on the pedal. The stopping performance was very good, slowing from 80 to 0 mph in 228 feet (0.93G). Directional stability was extremely good because the front wheels locked up first

and, while fade was made apparent by an increase in pedal pressure, the three test stops were nearly identical in length.

The mechanical Camaro is obviously successful in its performance and the engineers responsible for that have also come up with a few more subtle technical innovations. One is the Delco battery which secures its cables to the posts with threaded fasteners rather than the traditional clamping method that not infrequently works loose or corrodes into ineffectiveness. Another is the styled wheels which, while they look very much like cast alloy wheels, are actually welded together from a conventional steel rim and a deeply drawn steel center. Although they are no doubt heavier than the standard wheels, and far heavier than the real magnesium wheels they imitate, they should not be subject to the normal problems (corrosion, low impact strength and lug nuts working loose) that plague the general run of cast wheels. And the last bit of technical wizardry that caught our eye is the glove box door hinge which has no moving parts. It's a strip of plastic—one side bonded to the dash, the other to the door—and the strip bends when the door is opened. It's one hinge that will never need oiling.

One of the most conspicuous features of the Camaro's layout, and not necessarily an improvement, is the new long doors. No more is there a rear quarter window, it's all in the door. And not only are the doors longer but they are also moved rearward in the body. Entrance to the rear seat is decidedly easier, but to the front is harder. In a narrow parking slot the exit space for a front seat passenger is inconveniently small and the process is made more difficult by the door's excessive weight, partly attributable to its length and partly to the side impact beams enclosed within.

Of course, the elimination of a window on each side should reduce the chance of wind noise but no such luck on the test car. Chevrolet is trying a new type of window seal on the Camaro and the assembly line workers obviously haven't figured out how to fit it on the car yet. The result was a chorus of wind whistles—the only objectionable noises to be heard in an otherwise sound quarantined car.

The spirit of compromise so apparent in

the Camaro's handling and door arrangement carries over strongly into the interior design. The dash now groups all of the instruments directly in front of the driver—a fantastic improvement from the optional gauge cluster that looked up at you from the console in past Camaros—but the small gauges now are very small and no matter what your height, some of them are likely to be blocked by the steering wheel. And while we are on the subject, the optional gauges of the past are still optional. Only the speedometer and fuel gauge are standard.

Another of the more obvious compromises is the optional console. It sticks up somewhat higher than the seat cushions and has two recesses in each side in which to stow seat belt buckles. The problem is that the recesses, which are not very handy for their intended purpose, tunnel so deeply into the console that the bin inside isn't big enough even for road maps.

Generally, the Camaro's interior is quite hospitable. Visibility forward is very good because of the narrow, curving windshield pillars, and the wide C-pillars to the rear are less obstructive than they would appear from the outside. The seats in the test car were more upright than those of the early press preview cars (C/D, March) and the driving position suffered slightly. We particularly like the Camaro's inner door panels which are molded of a soft material that gives the sensation of deep padding. It is far more appealing than the hard panels used on Chrysler's sporty cars.

The Camaro, like all cars from Detroit, is a series of compromises, one upon another. At least in the Camaro they've all been made in pretty much the same direction, that of a stylish, quick grand touring car. And yet, even though the Z/28 is not at all race car-like, some of the strongest suggestions of its competition potential are right on the surface. Those to whom power bulges and love mounds are the only readable evidences probably wouldn't notice, but check the way the glass is nearly flush with its surrounding sheetmetal. That wasn't done for gas mileage. After two years of being Trans-Am champion things are expected of Camaro, and if John Delorean and Jim Hall both like this one it has to have something going for it besides nice manners and a pretty fender.

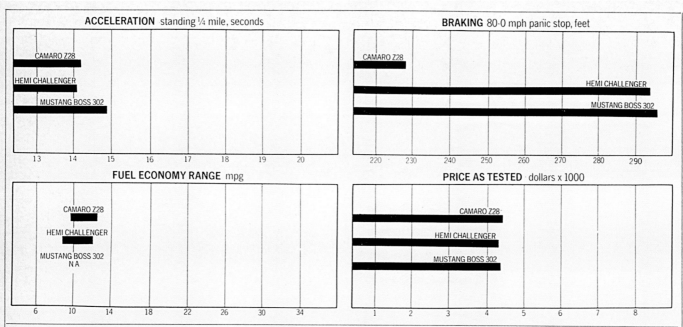

ACCELERATION standing ¼ mile, seconds

| | 13 | 14 | 15 | 16 | 17 | 18 | 19 | 20 |
CAMARO Z28
HEMI CHALLENGER
MUSTANG BOSS 302

BRAKING 80-0 mph panic stop, feet

| | 220 | 230 | 240 | 250 | 260 | 270 | 280 | 290 |
CAMARO Z28
HEMI CHALLENGER
MUSTANG BOSS 302

FUEL ECONOMY RANGE mpg

| | 6 | 10 | 14 | 18 | 22 | 26 | 30 | 34 |
CAMARO Z28
HEMI CHALLENGER
MUSTANG BOSS 302 N A

PRICE AS TESTED · dollars x 1000

| | 1 | 2 | 3 | 4 | 5 | 6 | 7 | 8 |
CAMARO Z28
HEMI CHALLENGER
MUSTANG BOSS 302

Camaro Z/28

Manufacturer: Chevrolet Motor Division
General Motors Corporation
Detroit, Mich. 48202

Vehicle type: front engine, rear-wheel-drive, 4-passenger coupe

Price as tested: $4475.70
(Manufacturer's suggested retail price, including all options listed below, Federal excise tax, dealer preparation and delivery charges, does not include state and local taxes, license or freight charges)

Options on test car: Base V-8 Camaro, $2839; rally sport, $168.55; custom interior, $115.90; door edge guards, $5.30; visor mirror, $3.20; Z/28 package, $572.95; automatic trans., $221.80; limited slip diff., $44.25; power steering, $105.35; power brakes, $47.40; custom seat belts, $12.15; console, $59.00; tinted glass, $37.95; special instrumentation, $84.30; auxiliary lighting, $11.10; sport mirrors, $26.35; AM radio, $61.10; rear speaker, $14.75; tilt wheel, $45.30

ENGINE
Type: V-8, water-cooled, cast iron block and heads, 5 main bearings
Bore x stroke 4.00 x 3.48 in, 101.6 x 88.4 mm
Displacement................350 cu in, 5740 cc
Compression ratio................11.0 to one
Carburetion................1 x 4-bbl Holley
Valve gear.........pushrod operated overhead valves, mechanical lifters

Power (SAE)............360 bhp @ 5600 rpm
Torque (SAE)............370 lbs-ft @ 4000 rpm
Specific power output........1.03 bhp/cu in, 62.9 bhp/liter
Max recommended engine speed...6500 rpm

DRIVE TRAIN
Transmission................3-speed, automatic
Max. torque converter...................2.1
Final drive ratio..................4.10 to one

Gear	Ratio	Mph/1000 rpm	Max. test speed
I	2.48	7.4	48 mph (6500 rpm)
II	1.48	12.3	80 mph (6500 rpm)
III	1.00	18.2	118 mph (6500 rpm)

DIMENSIONS AND CAPACITIES
Wheelbase................................108.0 in
Track, F/R.....................61.3/60.0 in
Length....................................188.0 in
Width......................................74.4 in
Height....................................50.1 in
Ground clearance........................4.5 in
Curb weight.............................3640 lbs
Weight distribution, F/R........56.7/43.3%
Battery capacity..........12 volts, 61 amp/hr
Alternator capacity...................444 watts
Fuel capacity.........................20.5 gal
Oil capacity.............................4.0 qts
Water capacity..........................16.0 qts

SUSPENSION
F: Ind., unequal length control arms, coil springs, anti-sway bar
R: Ind., rigid axle, semi-elliptic leaf-springs, anti-sway bar

STEERING
Type..........Variable-ratio recirculating ball, power assist
Turns lock-to-lock.........................2.6
Turning circle curb-to-curb............37.5 ft

BRAKES
F:...........11.0-in vented disc, power assist
R:...........9.5 x 2.0-in drum, power assist

WHEELS AND TIRES
Wheel size............................15 x 7.0-in
Wheel type......styled, stamped steel, 5-bolt
Tire make and size..........Goodyear F60-15
Tire type.........Fiberglass belted, tubeless
Test inflation pressures, F/R........24/24 psi
Tire load rating.....1500 lbs per tire @ 32 psi

PERFORMANCE
Zero to	Seconds
30 mph	2.1
40 mph	3.1
50 mph	4.4
60 mph	5.8
70 mph	7.3
80 mph	9.2
90 mph	11.6
100 mph	14.2

Standing ¼-mile........14.2 sec @ 100.3 mph
Top speed (observed)..................118 mph
80-0 mph..................228 ft (0.93 G)
Fuel mileage...9.5-12.5 mpg on premium fuel
Cruising range....................195-265 mi

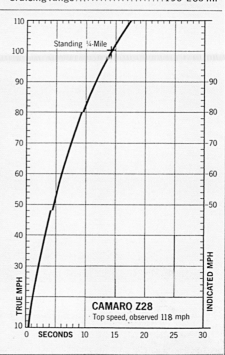

CAMARO Z28
Top speed, observed 118 mph

ROAD TEST
PLYMOUTH ROAD RUNNER

They're going to be eating their livers, those other car company guys, when they see the new Road Runner. It has a look born of purpose and muscles where the others have flab. While the government-fearing opposition has been putting antimacassars on their street racers, Chrysler has been standing on the gas, and the car kids are going to be driving Road Runners just because last year's hot set-up now looks 10 years old.

What we're telling you is that the Road Runner and the other Plymouth intermediates are all new. Well, they aren't all new but the part that you see is. Underneath they're pretty much the same as what Plymouth has been serving up for the last handful of years— with strategic improvements, of course. All of the standard engines will have lower compression ratios so that they can live on 91 octane fuel.

New sound deadening devices are scheduled to kill off some of the din associated with Plymouth's unit body, and company officials have promised to ream out those guys down in the plant who are in charge of quality control. All of this will hopefully bump Pontiac out of third place once and for all and, right now, that's Plymouth's biggest project.

Some years ago, in anticipation of this struggle, Plymouth summoned its elite corps of product planners from their long winter's naps for some sort of invincible marketing plan. The planners responded with an idea that has come to fruit in the 1971 intermediates—now called Satellites rather than Belvederes—the scheme is curious enough to merit discussion.

The cornerstone of the plan is the observation that a large volume of customers will part with an extra lump of cash for a uniquely styled 2-door hardtop. The Monte Carlo is based on the Chevelle; the Charger springs forth from the Coronet; the Grand Prix is little more than a stretched and re-skinned Tempest—yet the folks are willing to pay upwards of $150 more for the special hardtop, just for its styling. So Plymouth reasoned that if the customers want the unique coupe that much, why not drop the standard hardtop altogether and just offer the special one? And to make it more attractive, sell the new coupe at the price they would have charged for the standard model. Everybody will think they are getting something for nothing and the assembly will have to run double speed.

The result of all this circuitous logic is two separate lines of Plymouth intermediates— Satellites (4-doors) and Sebrings (2-door hardtops). The sedans have 117-inch wheelbases; the hardtops are 115 inches. And each has a unique skin, right down to the bumpers so that each looks entirely different.

Plymouth readily admits that two suits of sheetmetal cost more than one and since they will be selling the new hardtops for about the same increment over the sedans as they did before, there will be a squeeze on the per-car profit. "Have to make it up by selling more cars," they say. On hearing that, it is pretty hard to keep a straight face. How does that old car salesman's line go? "Lose a little bit on each one but make it up in volume."

Assuming that it is possible, there are still a few questions. Will the customers recognize this as a special hardtop when there is no standard one to compare it to? Since the scheme obviously relies on establishing the 4-doors as the "basic" models, it was decided to make their styling very conservative. The stylists outdid themselves—its possible the hardtops look so good in comparison, that no one will want the sedans.

Whether or not the whole thing works, good has come from the idea. The Road Runner and its Sebring companions have a lap on everybody in styling.

Dimensions	1970	1971
Wheelbase	116.0 in.	115.0 in.
Track, F/R	59.7/59.2 in.	60.1/62.0 in.
Length	204.0 in.	203.2 in.
Width	76.4 in.	79.1 in.
Engine		
Standard engine	383 cu. in., 335 hp. V-8	383 cu. in., 300 hp. V-8
Compression ratio	9.5 to one	8.7 to one
Max. option	426 cu. in., 425 hp. V-8	426 cu. in., 425 hp. V-8
Compression ratio	10.2 to one	10.2 to one
Tires		
Standard	F70-14	F70-14
Max. option	F60-15	G60-15

ROAD TEST
PLYMOUTH GTX

In an era when the term "Super Car" is being whispered rather than shouted through the halls of Detroit, Plymouth bucks the trend by proudly announcing the birth of its all-new GTX

As it crouches in its parking space under a coat of Curious Yellow paint and a white vinyl top, the 1971 Plymouth GTX seems neither malignant nor odious. Its tires, incredibly fat, black Goodyears, with raised white letters on the sidewalls, and its stripes, issuing forth from nostrils on each side of the hood and streaming down the front fenders, suggest "sport" in much the same visual language as stainless steel tennis rackets, exotic metal skis or even those "competition-striped" sneakers. But the difference is that the Plymouth GTX is a "performance car"—it has a 440 cubic-inch, high compression engine—and that is enough to provoke a measure of public wrath. Many—disciples of Ralph Nader, Sierra Club-inspired conservationists, and urban planners—are proclaiming the death of performance cars. And the insurance companies, with their "horse-power surcharges," are doing their best to nail shut the coffin.

All of this has not gone unnoticed within the insulated walls of Detroit. The car manufacturers are apprehensive and, with the exception of Chrysler, have noticeably pulled in their horns. Super Cars are still being built but they are not being aggressively merchandised like they were before—their place in the limelight is being taken by low-powered compacts.

Obviously, the climate is different for performance cars. Certainly changed from just a year ago. But does that mean that Detroit is being pressed toward a new frontier or that we have merely crested another wave in a repeating cycle of customer vacillation? History offers pregnant parallels. Turn back the pages of *Car and Driver*, back to 1957 when it was still called *Sports Cars Illustrated*, and read what one perceptive journalist had to say in a road test of an automobile advertised as, "The

Mighty Chrysler 300C. America's Most Powerful Car—375HP."

"… there's no doubt that the horse-power cycle is coming to the end of its course. State and federal governments are fed up with it and reaching for legal weapons to kill it. Detroit's current stock cars are so hot that it's questionable whether most operators are quick enough and competent enough to control them. Costs of purchase, operation and maintenance have become excessive. Most sane minds in Detroit, and there really are many, know that the time for housecleaning is overdue. It's a case of killing the goose that lays the loot-filled eggs before the goose kills you. And in an environment suddenly dedicated to "slow down and live," it's hard to see much of a future for projectiles like the 300C. … In fact, it's more than likely that the 300C is the last of its line, that there will be no 300D. This report on the most "super" of all Detroit super-stock models, on the Tyrannosaurus Rex of the automobile dinosaurs, is more than an ordinary road test. It's a look at a machine that stands as the culmination of an era that's ending."

That author was clearly premature in signing the coroner's report. The Chrysler 300 lived to see the letter L suffixed to its name and was succeeded by squadron after squadron of Detroit Super Cars whose capacity for rushing over the face of the earth made the old 300 seem like more of a family sedan. Let's go back to that forgotten road test again, back to the performance data on the specifications panel. "America's Most Powerful Car," the one thought to be beyond the capabilities of more than a few drivers, recorded a standing quarter-mile time of 16.9 seconds at 84 mph.

Early in September of 1970, in an air conditioned office overlooking the entrance to Chrysler's Jefferson Assembly Plant, public relations man Jim Stickford and Gordon

Cherry, Plymouth's Manager of Planning and Administration, were disappointed and apologetic when we told them that the new GTX we had just finished testing could do no better than 14.9 seconds at 95.4 mph at Detroit Dragway. Never mind that it was two full seconds and 11 mph faster than the legendary Chrysler 300—the GTX turned out to be a pretty lethargic Super Car by today's standards. "It was a very early production car," Cherry explained, "and you never can tell what parts those guys down on the line will use on the first few dozen cars." They knew that it didn't have a limited-slip differential, which was no help on the drag strip, and the new GTX, at 4,022 lbs, was somewhat heavier than past models. Still, they also knew it should have been faster.

But even though the GTX's acceleration was less than first-rate, by today's standards, it is still very much a Super Car. The insurance companies say so and Plymouth is not denying it. Cherry allows as how performance cars have recently fallen on hard times but he doesn't believe that the market for them has permanently dried up. "With the Road Runner and the GTX we were selling almost 100,000 performance cars per year. That has dropped off to about half now." He believes that increased unemployment and tight money (which makes it more difficult for youthful buyers to obtain financing) plus the recently increased insurance costs are responsible for the sluggish sales. With characteristic car manufacturer's optimism, he points out that an upswing in the economy will eliminate all of the problems—except for insurance cost—and that he expects to see sales pick up later in the year.

But even if sales don't pick up, Plymouth will continue to offer models like the Road Runner and the GTX. "Maybe if the volume dropped below 10,000 cars per year we'd cancel them out, but then only if we were pretty sure

those 10,000 customers would change into some other Plymouth model. If it looked like they would swing over to a competitor, of course we'd continue them. You can't give away sales."

Right now, Plymouth and Dodge have a stronger commitment to performance cars than anyone else in Detroit. With the exception of American Motors, Chrysler is the only car maker who has not announced an intention to lower the compression ratios of all engines to the point where they will operate on 91 octane fuel. "Not an easy decision," according to Cherry. "First off, we didn't have time to do it across the board so we concentrated where it would do the most good—the standard engines (which account for about 93% of Chrysler's sales). And there are some very strong reasons for not lowering the compression of performance engines—it hurts the power too much for one—so we decided to continue to offer the high compression engines as an option as long as customers want them."

The "option" part isn't strictly true in that the 440 4-bbl which is standard in the GTX has a 9.7-to-one ratio and does require premium fuel. The Road Runner 383, which is by far the biggest seller, has been lowered to 8.7, however, and it will run on regular. The 440 6-bbl and the 426 Hemi, optional on the Road Runner and

GTX, have not been changed.

While insurance companies concentrate primarily on the engine, there definitely is more than that to a performance car according to Cherry. Plymouth holds to the theory that the youthful buyers of this class of car usually go deeply in debt to buy it, consider it to be a strong social expression of their individual personalities and, therefore, want it to be easily recognizable. Hence such add-ons as styled wheels, scooped hoods and tape stripes. Unfortunately, the more years tape stripes are in use the harder it is for the stylists to

find a scheme that is both new and pleasing. But Plymouth hasn't stopped trying. You can draw your own conclusions about the GTX's front fender stripes and the Road Runner's segmented arrangement that angles down each rear roof pillar onto the rear quarter. Without them, however, the new Plymouth hardtop is a genuinely handsome car—one of those rare combinations of smoothly integrated curves that all of Detroit seems to be unable to generate more often than once every four or five years.

Actually, styling may be sufficient

Top: The GTX hood scoop—hungry for cool air.
Above: The rear spoiler was more for appearance than necessity.

ACCELERATION standing ¼ mile, seconds

	13	14	15	16	17	18	19	20
PLYMOUTH GTX								
454 CHEVELLE (1970)								
429 COBRA (1970)								
455 GTO (1970)								

BRAKING 80-0 mph panic stop, feet

	210	220	230	240	250	260	270	280
PLYMOUTH GTX								
454 CHEVELLE (1970)								
429 COBRA (1970)								
455 GTO (1970)								

FUEL ECONOMY RANGE mpg

	6	10	14	18	22	26	30	34
PLYMOUTH GTX NA								
454 CHEVELLE (1970) NA								
429 COBRA (1970)								
455 GTO (1970)								

PRICE AS TESTED dollars x 1000

	1	2	3	4	5	6	7	8
PLYMOUTH GTX NA								
454 CHEVELLE (1970)								
429 COBRA (1970)								
455 GTO (1970)								

PLYMOUTH GTX

Manufacturer: Plymouth Division
Chrysler Corporation
Detroit, Michigan 48231

Vehicle type: Front engine, rear-wheel-drive, 5-passenger 2-door hardtop

Price as tested: $ N.A.
(Manufacturer's suggested retail price, including all options listed below, Federal excise tax, dealer preparation and delivery charges, does not include state and local taxes, license or freight charges)

Options on test car: Power steering, power disc brakes, automatic transmission, vinyl roof, special steering wheel, tachometer, console, styled wheels, G60-15 tires, luggage rack

ENGINE
Type: V-8, water-cooled, cast iron block and heads, 5 main bearings
Bore x stroke.4.31 x 3.75 in, 109.2 x 95.2 mm
Displacement..................440 cu in, 7200 cc
Compression ratio.....................9.7 to one
Carburetion...................1 x 4-bbl Carter
Valve gear.Pushrod operated overhead valves, hydraulic lifters
Power (SAE)............370 bhp @ 4600 rpm
Torque (SAE)..........280 lbs/ft @ 3200 rpm

Specific power output........0.84 bhp/cu in, 51.5 bhp/liter
Max recommended engine speed...5500 rpm

DRIVE TRAIN
Transmission..............3-speed, Automatic
Max. torque converter.............2.02 to one
Final drive ratio.....................3.23 to one

	Gear Ratio	Mph/1000 rpm	Max. test speed
I	2.45	9.6	53 mph (5500 rpm)
II	1.45	16.2	89 mph (5500 rpm)
III	1.00	23.5	110 mph (4700 rpm)

DIMENSIONS AND CAPACITIES
Wheelbase.........................115.0 in
Track, F/R...................60.1/62.0 in
Length...........................203.2 in
Width.............................79.1 in
Height.............................53.0 in
Curb weight......................4022 lbs
Weight distribution, F/R........54.0/46.0%
Battery capacity..........12 volts, 70 amp/hr
Alternator capacity..............444 watts
Fuel capacity.....................21.0 gal
Oil capacity.......................4.0 qts
Water capacity...................15.5 qts

SUSPENSION
F: Ind., unequal length control arms, torsion bars, anti-sway bar
R: Rigid axle, semi-elliptic leaf springs

STEERING
Type..........Recirculating ball, power assist
Turns lock-to-lock.........................3.5
Turning circle curb-to-curb...........40.6 ft

BRAKES
F:.........10.7-in. vented disc, power assist
R:.. 10.0 x 2.5-in. cast iron drum, power assist

WHEELS AND TIRES
Wheel size.........................15 x 7.0-in
Wheel type.......Styled, stamped steel, 5-bolt
Tire make and size.........Goodyear G60-15
Tire type.........Fiberglass belted, tubeless
Test inflation pressures, F/R.......28/28 psi
Tire load rating.....1620 lbs per tire @ 32 psi

PERFORMANCE

Zero to	Seconds
30 mph	2.3
40 mph	3.4
50 mph	4.8
60 mph	6.5
70 mph	8.5
80 mph	10.8
90 mph	13.5
100 mph	16.2

Standing ¼-mile..........14.9 sec @ 95.4 mph
Top speed (at redline)..............130 mph
80-0 mph........................257 ft (0.83 G)
Fuel mileage......N.A. mpg on premium fuel

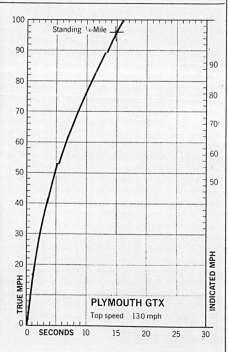

PLYMOUTH GTX
Top speed 130 mph

Standing ¼-Mile

recommendation for the GTX. As a car, it suffers only a few minor hardships from being in the "performance" category. Ride quality is probably its greatest deviation from normal-car character. The GTX has, as standard equipment, the stiffest suspension rates of any Plymouth intermediate, stiffer even than the station wagons, and the high spring-rates, combined with the wide Polyglas tires, add up to a relatively harsh ride—decidedly more so than in an equivalent Chevelle SS or Pontiac GTO. And there is also more road noise than in the competition. In trade for the hard ride and extra road noise you get a car that doesn't really handle any better than the run-of-the-mill Super Cars but, to the traditionalist, feels like it will. For most drivers, that is enough.

While, considering the current state of the art, one might be tempted to say that the suspension was deficient, there is little room for complaint about the powertrain. Engine idle is slightly rough but not any rougher than Super Cars were five years ago when there were no emission control systems to make things difficult. In fact, it seems that every phase of the engine's operation is well disciplined. Certainly the exhaust sound is. Nothing there to make you think of a gut-level performance car. It is quiet at all times and at full throttle is almost drowned out by the moan from the air intake, which in itself is not all that loud. The level of the engine's intrusiveness is in every way keeping with the car's performance

level—moderate.

One thing that works particularly well is the console-mounted gear selector for the 3-speed automatic. Plymouth calls it a Slap Stick which is an attempt to convey to you that it is a device which specialized in one-gear-at-a-time manual upshifts. When you are in low, just give the lever a whack and it shifts to second—another whack and it is in drive—all without the worry of moving one notch too far into neutral. Other manufacturers have shifters born of similar intentions but none of them work with the precision of this one.

With an eye toward easing the driver's task, Plymouth has worked on more than just the shifter—it has revised the whole driving position. Where the steering wheel was always too close to the driver and too high before, not unlike Captain America's ape-hangers, it is very well located now. In addition, there is an optional, smaller diameter (14 inches) wheel with a thick, padded rim that is enough to make you forget that you're in a Plymouth.

While the stylists were making improvements, there is another one which was probably made inadvertently. On the hard-tops, the windshield has an extreme rear-ward slope and the pillars slope along with it. This styling quirk is just enough so that you can drive along with the side windows down at any legal speed without having your ears buffeted off by the draft.

The instrument panel layout was obviously intentional and it deserves some credit also. It

manages to group a speedometer, tachometer, a full complement of gauges and a handful of knobs directly in front of the driver in a way that is both attractive and convenient. Unfortunately, the simulated replica of tree wood used to surround the dials is as bad as the instrument arrangement is good.

All in all, we would have to say that the Plymouth GTX is a step forward on a front where all others are retreating. In certain areas, styling and driver comfort, for example, it is vastly improved over the previous model and only in performance, primarily because of increased weight, has it lost ground.

And after a brief look at history, we have no intention of crawling out on a limb and predicting the imminent demise of the performance car. Such machines have survived too many doomsday reports to roll over and die now. Cars like the GTX have too much going for them. Not only are they more capable than a normal family sedan in situations that require evasive capability but they are also more interesting and fun to drive at the same time. And these are the qualities that are central to the car enthusiast. As long as there are car nuts there will be "performance" cars. Probably the biggest difference in the foreseeable future is that Plymouth will come up with something mew to supplement the GTX. In fact, Cherry said they had a couple ideas they were working on right now.

Above, left to right: The massive GTX 6-bbl Plymouth 440; the businesslike command center; mini-wing with GTX logo.

Reflections on Yates' Relatively Useless Axiom Number 47: "What is happening has already happened." The hazards of trying to stay "in" are well documented. It was bad enough when fashions spread around the nation by word-a-mouth, but in those days it only meant that by the time they started wearing spats in Des Moines, the smarties in Manhattan had long since switched over to wing-tips or something. As long as there was never any contact between the two worlds, everybody was content that he was operating in the vanguard of style. But today, with instant communication coupled to a merchandising world that is totally trend-oriented, you are really going to have to hustle if you have any illusions about staying in the area of where it's all happening. It goes something like this: Somebody within one of the groups that establishes our national life styles, i.e. entertainers, international socialites and fashion twits, the New Left, musicians, pop artists, the blacks, California teeny-boppers, etc. will show up in public with some zoomy fashion trick—Tony Curtis is wearing love beads! Johnny Carson makes the opera scene in a turtle-neck! Sammy Davis Jr. in a Nehru!

The stampede is on. Four million hustlers, salesmen with rhinestone pinkie rings, wholesalers, distributors, ad moguls, manufacturers (Tom Wolfe once referred to this genre as "short-arm fatties hustling nutball fads") flood the country with plastic love beads, Dacron turtlenecks and Nehrus in wrinkle-proof Kodel. Instant millions! Everybody in Des Moines is beautiful, hip, plugged-in, groovy. Except for one thing; the very act of seeking "in-ness" is self-defeating, and by the time the fashion has reached the ready-to-wear emporiums of Middle America, the trendy types have long since moved on to something entirely different and, usually, contradictory.

This is essentially the case with automobiles, but because of the expense of the item and the basic conservatism of its parent industry, trends grind their way across the nation like glaciers, taking years to arrive and years to thaw away. For example, it took the industry roughly ten years (1955–65) to recognize the enormous potential of the so-called Super Car market. Originally developed within the California hot rod cult and the East Coast sports car legions, the manifestation of the Super Car from Detroit was an amalgam of influences from both worlds. The car that really started it all—Pontiac's GTO—was essentially a hot rod, i.e. a small, otherwise mundane sedan stuffed with a gigantic engine, but it was laden with trappings like a wood-rim steering wheel, bucket seats and a discarded Ferrari name that came directly from the world of European sports cars.

As we all know, the GTO was a blockbuster in the showrooms, although it took the fusty General Motors hierarchy several years to recognize its impact. However, once the message sunk in, Detroit plunged into a self-parody of the slow-witted market overkill techniques that have characterized the industry almost since its beginning. They have now escalated the super car concept to the point of absurdity; 450 cubic inch engines are common, "shaker hoods," cornball, 1956-vintage racing stripes are everywhere, and you can get NASCAR-type hood pins and bogus-mag wheels on practically every brand of automobile except the Checker Marathon. They continue to grind out these ornate, over-powered, clumsy mastodons with the heady delusion that every kid in the U.S. wants a street racer. They may be right. At this very moment. But then again, remember Axiom Number 47.

Massive internal and external forces are conspiring to strike the super car as dead as a beached smelt. To begin with, the very fact that it is as popular as it is limits its future. "In-ness" and universality are directly contradictory, and the novelty of having a machine that will make your ears bleed every time you crack open the throttle has disappeared. That means something. Obviously Detroit has hastened this situation with its saturation marketing. As long as the kids could create super cars out of feckless, establishment 2-doors, they had meaning and status. But now that the cars themselves have become pre-packaged, die-cut baubles available to everybody, their uniqueness has gone. Add to this the increasing difficulties attendant with ownership of one of these wild boars, i.e. increasing insurance costs (whether justifiable or not), maintenance woes and wallet-busting operating expenses, and the demise of the super car—Detroit style—begins to come into focus.

Detroit is being forced to satirize its own products, à la the Judge, the Eliminator, the AMC Machine, etc. in order to stimulate even a modicum of interest in this brand of automobile. At the same time the once-booming "pony car" biz (Mustang, Camaro, etc.) has softened and is shifting rapidly to cheap, stark sedans like the Chevy II Nova, the Duster, etc. Therefore we have Detroit plastering its new super cars with every gross gimmick from spoilers to drag chutes in order to hypo interest in performance machines, while the more influential buyers are veering toward cooler, less obvious expressions of automotive fetishism.

In general sense, the only guys who are buying Detroit's gaudy, winged wonders are squares who still wear boot-camp haircuts and skinny ties. Out in that limbo where they operate, weirdo cars are still acceptable—in fact, they're still "happening" in a mass market sense—but among the trend-setters you'd be more "in" behind the wheel of a 1958 Mercury Turnpike Cruiser or a Studebaker Land Cruiser. At least those would be camp.

Take for example the California scene, where a great deal of America's car trends are established. The breathtaking boom in Volkswagens as bogus performance cars is highly significant; power means nothing in this context and a 36-hp VW rattling along on a set of Indy tires is a forceful satire on the entire concept of super cars. With this has come the popularity of the camper-buses and the dune buggies, both of which are rejections of the standard hot car that Detroit still thinks is so important to the youth market.

Like the song says, "Times they are a-changin'," and also coming is radical change of taste within the American enthusiast market. It is premature to determine exactly what form it will take, but a few trends appear to be taking shape:

(1) Four-wheeled sledge-hammers like the "Six-Packs" and the "Boss 429s" appear to be fading, although the market for well-balanced, proper-handling sports sedans, both domestic and imported, is justifiably strong.

(2) Appeal is building for dumb, out-dated, worthless cars of the recent past that represent simultaneous recognition and rejection of the entire faceless, mass-class consumer philosophy. In other words, we may be rapidly reaching a state where a 1961 Dodge Phoenix, with a slant-Six and push-button automatic transmission, will be so much more "in" than a 1970 "Super Bee Six-Pack" that you wouldn't even believe it. Total rejection of the New Car! I am an acknowledged lunatic in Detroit, so the suggestion that American car nuts are doing anything but slobbering like Pavlovian dogs over the new super cars will be written off as nothing more than my standard ravings. After all, when you are up to your desk top in market research that you've paid for to reinforce your own prejudices, who wants to hear anything from weirdo writers? As far as Detroit and their butch haircut customers in Des Moines are concerned, the super car is "what's happening," and I'm not wacky enough to think this treatise will have any effect on either group, nor am I suggesting that the super car phenomenon is going to die overnight. It took years to make the monsters and it'll take years to kill them.

Just don't forget Axiom Number 47.

When Mach I is set up to win 8,000 miles of rallying in stock trim, it's got to be a great car to get across town in.

Mach 1—pronounced Mach Won!

Winning is a habit with Mach 1. The latest triumph is the top rally award a car can win on this continent—the SCCA Manufacturer's Rally Championship for 1969. To win it you've got to run over 8,000 miles of rallies on all kinds of roads in all kinds of weather and finish every stage with split-second precision. That means sprinting acceleration; hanging tight when you corner, brakes that won't quit and power to ram your way through snow-clogged mountain passes. Mach 1 wins rally after rally because Mach 1's got what it takes: a balanced wide-tread chassis and sports-car design suspension, with front and rear stabilizer bars, extra-heavy-duty springs, shocks, and wide-rim wheels.

Power is what you get with any of Mach 1's great V-8's—a 351 2V is standard. Your first option is the brand-new free-breathing 351 4V Cleveland engine with canted valve heads and 300 horsepower that turns on

right now. From there on you option the 428 Cobra V-8 and its partner in power, the Cobra Jet Ram-Air. That's the one with the functional "Shaker" that pops up through the hood to ram cool air.

For '70 the Mach 1 looks as good as it goes. There's a unique black grille with special sports lamps, matte black hood, aluminum rocker panels, high-back buckets, full instrumentation, woodtoned panel and console, electric clock, and more. Get yourself a Mach 1 and really "shake up" the troops.

See your Ford Dealer for a free copy of the 1970 Performance Buyer's Digest or write to:

FORD PERFORMANCE DIGEST, Dept. CD-22, Box 747, Dearborn, Michigan 48121.

MUSTANG

After 8,000 miles of gruelling competition the Mustang team wrapped up the Manufacturers Rally Championship for 1969.

SAM POSEY AND THE C/D STAFF COMPARE
DETROIT'S 1970 PERFORMANCE CARS

SS 454 CHEVELLE, DUSTER 340, MUSTANG BOSS 302

TO THE ULTIMATE OF THE '60S

SHELBY AC COBRA

Through the windshield the horizon is tilted. Neck muscles strain against G-forces to support the weight of a crash helmet. Senses are bombarded with sounds—the painful scream of tires against asphalt, the belligerent roar of a 289 Ford—and smells; good British leather and traces of gasoline vapor. We arc halfway through the Hook, Lime Rock's unforgiving hairpin that is conquered with two carefully chosen apexes or not at all. The black Cobra snorts and bellows against an unseen force as Sam Posey works on the huge wooden steering wheel, correcting minute slides before they become malignant. He shouts over the auditory assault, "No doubt about it, this has the feel of a real racing car—very, very serious."

His description couldn't have been more accurate. The Shelby Cobra was as menacing as its name from the very first. With malice aforethought it attacked and annihilated the Corvettes in SCCA's A/production, and after that taste of blood a coupe-bodied version went on to win its class at Le Mans in 1964. So successful was it as a racer that it was the first car to break Ferrari's hold on the World Manufacturers Championship in the years after that title became based on competition among production automobiles. It is a single purpose car—a powerful, high-winding V-8 in a stark, lightweight English AC chassis—for men who equate truth with speed and agility, and ask for nothing more. Production ceased in 1966 but the Cobra's performance still stands as a high water mark for all to see. It is the yardstick by which all other performance cars must be measured.

Today a yardstick (and a long one at that) is essential if we are to comprehend the improvements Detroit is engineering into its performance cars. The need became obvious this past summer as we previewed the 1970 models. Small cars are being outfitted with big engines—medium-size cars have engines that are enormous. Wheels and tires are now as wide as what you would have found on pure racing cars a few years ago, and truly sophisticated handling packages (many with rear anti-sway bars) are standard equipment. The point was forcefully pounded home at the GM proving grounds when we discovered that a Buick GS455 (of all things), loaded down to 4,300 lbs with every conceivable comfort option, would still drive circles around an Opel GT, a "sports car," on the handling course. Detroit is building some very athletic automobiles, not just in acceleration but in handling and braking as well. Urged on by our natural curiosity about the sporting side of these devices we set out to ascertain the state of the art in Detroit.

Thanks to model proliferation, testing every one of Detroit's super cars is out of the question—it would take about five years for the task. Instead, we would take a sample, one car from each of the three distinct performance car categories, and see how they measured up to the Cobra yardstick. Which cars? Well, there had to be an intermediate sedan because that is what Detroit's super cars have been since the beginning. Chevrolet is fixing to sell a 450-horsepower SS454 Chevelle—the highest advertised horsepower rating in all of Detroit—and that is reason enough that it should be in the test. Walter Mackenzie, a gray-haired veteran of Chevrolet's diplomatic corps, was up for the idea as soon as we phoned him. He remembered the Cobra ("You mean that low,

skinny, lightweight thing?") and what it had done to the Corvettes and he wanted just one more chance. Production of the 450-hp Chevelle wasn't scheduled until January—but there were engines and there were cars—it was just a matter of putting the two together. Not to worry—there would be an SS 454 Chevelle for the test.

Of course, there had to be a sporty car. These scrappy coupes have hyped up the Trans-Am Series popularity to the point where it threatens to eclipse the Can-Am. Deciding on a representative from this class was more difficult. Eventually, all the big engine versions were dismissed in favor of the 5-liter, Trans-Am-inspired models because they specialize in carefully tailored overall performance rather than merely dazzling acceleration. We finally settled on the Boss 302 Mustang for the most straightforward of all reasons—we just like to drive it. We've been enchanted by its capabilities since we drove the first prototype in Dearborn (C/D, June '69) and Brock Yates has proven that a mildly modified Boss can be competitive in SCCA regional racing (C/D, January '69) while still remaining streetable. After all of this favorable experience we wanted to see how an absolutely stock Boss ranked on a Cobra yardstick.

That left one category to be filled—a category that we feel is the start of a trend. For a long time we've been questioning Detroit's logic in concentrating its performance efforts on the heavy intermediate-size cars when there were lighter models around which could do the same job but with smaller engines and, ultimately, less expense to the customer. Plymouth's junior Road Runner, the Duster

340, is a giant step in this sensible direction. By including a Duster in the test we could get an early reading on the validity of the concept and perhaps even encourage its growth. But in Detroit our motives were not so transparent. Plymouth felt picked upon. Remembering past C/D comparison tests designed to ferret out the most capable car in a given class, Plymouth figured it had been singled out for the booby prize. "What are you guys trying to do? How can a Duster compete against a 454 Chevelle?" The Cobra was obviously beyond comprehension. "Let us bring a Hemi Cuda. That'll show those bastids." But we finally convinced Plymouth that this wasn't the apples-to-pump-kins comparison test that it appeared to be. In fact, it wasn't a comparison test in the conventional sense at all. Rather, it was to be the definitive statement on the whole range of Detroit performance cars, using as reference what most enthusiasts consider to be the world's fastest production car, the Shelby Cobra.

And, of course, we had to have a Cobra. Because it was the 289 that established the Cobra's all conquering reputation we chose that model. The 427 is faster, to be certain, but in reality it only made the Cobra legend burn a bit more brightly. Besides, classifying the big-engined brute as a production car is something of a dubious practice since only about 200 of them were built.

Cobras are where you find them. Walter Perkins, a bright young engineer with a bumper crop of red hot corpuscles, had a well-oiled 1965 model—bright, shiny and unmodified—that he figured was more than a match for any Chevelle, 454 or otherwise. We would find out. So would Sam Posey our consulting arbitrator, who can be counted upon to hand down a decision in effusive pear-shaped tones. Posey is perfect for the job. That he is an intrepid competition driver is merely a proven fact, but his ability to drive to the ragged edge in anything with wheels and coolly describe its behavior in detail at the same time is a source of wonderment. And no one knows the way around Lime Rock better than he does. Any lingering doubts about that should have been erased by his two professional-series victories there in this past season alone; one in a Shelby-prepared Trans-Am Mustang and the other in

From top to bottom: 1970 Boss 302;
1970 Chevelle SS 454; 1965 AC Cobra 289.

CHEVELLE SS454

Price as tested: $4470.05

Options on test car: Chevelle coupe, $2809.00; SS package $445.55; 450-hp engine, $263.30; automatic transmission, $290.40; power steering, $105.35; bucket seats, $121.15; deluxe belts, $12.15; floor mats, $11.60; door edge guards, $4.25; vinyl roof, $94.80, console, $53.75; visor vanity mirror, $3.20; cushioned rim steering wheel, $34.80; AM/FM radio, $133.80; rear speaker, $13.20; bumper guards, $15.80, clock, $15.80; limited-slip differential, $42.15.

ENGINE
Bore x stroke.....................4.25 x 4.00 in
Displacement.........................454 cu in
Compression ratio...............11.0 to one
Carburetion........1 x 4-bbl Holley, 780 cfm
Power (SAE)...............450 hp @ 5200 rpm
Torque (SAE)..........500 lbs-ft @ 3600 rpm

DRIVE TRAIN
Final drive ratio....................3.70 to one

DIMENSIONS AND CAPACITIES
Wheelbase.............................112.0 in
Track.................F: 60.0 in, R: 59.8 in
Length.................................197.2 in
Width....................................75.4 in
Height...................................56.2 in
Curb weight.........................3885 lbs
Weight distribution, F/R..........57.1/42.9%

SUSPENSION
F: Ind., unequal-length control arms, coil springs, anti-sway bar
R: Rigid axle, trailing arms, coil springs, anti-sway bar

STEERING
Type..........Recirculating ball, power assist
Turns lock-to-lock................................2.9
Turning circle................................42.0 ft

BRAKES
F:................11.0-in vented disc, power assist
R:....9.5 x 2.2-in cast iron drum, power assist

WHEELS AND TIRES
Wheel size.............................14 x 7.0-in
Tire make and size..........Goodyear F70-14, polyester
Test inflation pressure....F: 35 psi, R: 35 psi

PERFORMANCE
Zero to	Seconds
40 mph	2.9
60 mph	5.4
80 mph	8.7
100 mph	13.0

Standing ¼-mile.....13.81 sec @ 103.80 mph
80-0 mph panic stop..........272 ft (0.79 G)

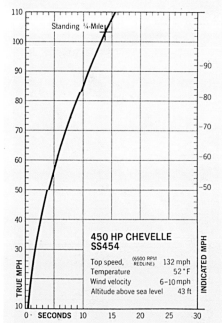

450 HP CHEVELLE SS454

Top speed, (6500 RPM REDLINE)	132 mph
Temperature	52°F
Wind velocity	6–10 mph
Altitude above sea level	43 ft

VALIANT DUSTER 340

Price as tested: $3455.70

Options on test car: Duster 340, $2547.00; bucket seats, $112.60; light package, $29.60; basic group, $82.60; decor group, $23.90; deluxe seat belts, $13.75; 4-speed transmission, $187.90; limited-slip differential, $42.35; special paint, $14.05; 50-amp alternator, $11.00; 59-amp battery, $12.95; tinted windshield, $20.40; day-night mirror, $7.10; dual horns, $5.15; pedal dress up, $5.45; undercoat, $16.60; door edge molding, $4.65; custom sill, $13.15; wheel lip molding, $7.60; belt molding, $13.60; bumper guards, $23.80, tach, $50.15; power steering, $85.15; vinyl roof, $83.95; vinyl side molding, $14.80; E70 tires, $26.45.

ENGINE
Bore x stroke.....................4.04 x 3.31 in
Displacement.........................340 cu in
Compression ratio...............10.5 to one
Carburetion........1 x 4-bbl Carter AVS
Power (SAE)...............275 hp @ 5000 rpm
Torque (SAE)..........340 lbs-ft @ 3200 rpm

DRIVE TRAIN
Final drive ratio....................3.91 to one

DIMENSIONS AND CAPACITIES
Wheelbase.............................108.0 in
Track.................F: 57.7 in, R: 55.6 in
Length.................................188.4 in
Width....................................71.6 in
Height...................................52.6 in
Curb weight.........................3368 lbs
Weight distribution, F/R..........55.0/45.0%

SUSPENSION
F: Ind., unequal-length control arms, torsion bars, anti-sway bar
R: Rigid axle, semi-elliptic leaf springs

STEERING
Type..........Recirculating ball, power assist
Turns lock-to-lock................................3.6
Turning circle................................41.0 ft

BRAKES
F:................10.8-in vented disc, power assist
R:....10.0 x 1.8-in cast iron drum, power assist

WHEELS AND TIRES
Wheel size.............................14 x 5.5-in
Tire make and size..........Goodyear E70-14
Test inflation pressure.....F: 35 psi, R: 35psi

PERFORMANCE
Zero to	Seconds
40 mph	3.0
60 mph	5.9
80 mph	9.9
100 mph	15.1

Standing ¼-mile.......14.39 sec @ 97.2 mph
80-0 mph panic stop..........287 ft (0.74 G)

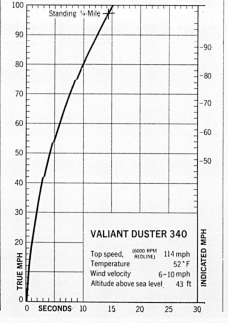

VALIANT DUSTER 340

Top speed, (6000 RPM REDLINE)	114 mph
Temperature	52°F
Wind velocity	6–10 mph
Altitude above sea level	43 ft

his Formula A McLaren-Chevrolet. With this kind of background our 4-car road test couldn't help but be revealing.

A varied group converged at Lime Rock on the appointed day—a handful of escapees from the C/D office; Posey and his stopwatch expert, John Whitman; Bill Howell, an engineering wizard from Chevrolet who can always be found stalking around in the pits at Trans-Ams making sure that Chevrolet isn't racing; Don Wahrman from Ford, one of Jacque Passino's disciples; and a couple of Detroit-owned PR men whose job is always to influence the outcome if possible. Plymouth had planned to send an engineering-type but the one chosen fell off a motorcycle at the last minute and couldn't make it. Perkins and Mrs. Perkins arrived with the Cobra and everything was set.

The cars had arranged themselves as to straight-line performance the day before at New York National. Perkins had kept the Cobra reputation alive by charging his machine through the quarter at 101.58 mph in 13.73 seconds—a scant 0.08 seconds ahead of the Chevelle—proving that there is no substitute for weight distribution. The Chevelle was decidedly more powerful, pushing its 3885-pound bulk through the traps at 103.80 mph, but with 57.1% of its weight on the front wheels it just couldn't quite get a good enough grip on the asphalt to move out ahead of the Cobra. The big 454 did prove itself however. It is a fairly straightforward derivative of the 435-hp Corvette 427 with a 0.24-inch longer stroke and a single 780 cubic-feet-per-minute Holley 4-bbl. instead of the Corvette's three 2-bbls. Because its solid-lifter valve train is very stable at high engine speeds, Howell felt that 6500 rpm wasn't an unreasonable redline—even though the Chevelle seemed to go just as quickly when shifted at 6000.

Just behind the Cobra and Chevelle in acceleration was the Duster. At 3,368 lbs it was the lightest of the Detroit cars—though still 1,046 lbs heavier than the Cobra. It also had the best weight distribution of all the Detroit iron with exactly 55% on the front. Its quarter-mile performance of 14.39 seconds at 97.2 was hampered by a balky shift mechanism but, even so, the Duster speaks well for the compact super car concept.

The Mustang turned out to be a disappointment. It was only a bit heavier than the Duster, 3,415 lbs with a full tank, but it was significantly less powerful, something we hadn't expected from an engine that was developed specifically for racing. When our best efforts were no better than 14.93 seconds at 93.45 mph we asked Wahrman to try, just to see if the factory knew something about driving Boss 302s that we didn't. In the best drag racer, gas-pedal-flat-to-the-floor tradition, he made two runs but neither bettered the Mustang's standings. The real point to be made here is that small displacement, high specific output engines suffer mightily in passing the exhaust emission and exhaust noise standards. Now that the SCCA allows production engines to be destroked down to the 5-liter maximum for the Trans-Am, the high performance 302s will soon disappear as a production option. In fact, the Boss 302 is the only one left right now.

That the acceleration portion of the test was out of the way meant that we had the whole day to evaluate handling and breaking at Lime Rock with Posey. Braking distances and cornering speeds would be measured, and to understand the behavior of each car as it approached the limit, one of the staff would ride along on all but the fastest laps to record Posey's observations. In the lead-off spot was the Chevelle.

We could have predicted Posey's first comment, which came, within 100 feet after pulling onto the track.

"Oh, look at that little louver. Whenever I accelerate a little trapdoor on the hood opens."

It is a great piece of entertainment. With the "Cowl Induction" option, Chevrolet's version of a hood scoop, a little backwards-facing hatch at the rear of the hood opens whenever manifold vacuum drops below a predetermined value. In goes cold air and up goes horsepower or something like that. But Posey's next observation was far more serious.

"The rear view mirror is placed exactly where I want to look for a right turn. I have to scrunch down if I want to see."

This has been a problem in many Detroit cars since the federal safety standards requiring larger rear view mirrors went into effect. Now you have a blind spot in

SHELBY AC COBRA

Price as tested: $6167.00

Options on test car: dress-up group, $172.00 (price does not include chrome wire wheels or hardtop).

ENGINE
Bore x stroke	4.00 x 2.87 in
Displacement	289 cu in
Compression ratio	10.5 to one
Carburetion	1 x 4-bbl Autolite
Power (SAE)	271 hp @ 6000 rpm
Torque (SAE)	312 lbs-ft @ 3400 rpm

DRIVE TRAIN
Final drive ratio	3.77 to one

DIMENSIONS AND CAPACITIES
Wheelbase	90.0 in
Track	F: 51.5 in, R: 52.5 in
Length	151.5 in
Width	61.0 in
Height	49.0 in
Curb weight	2322 lbs
Weight distribution, F/R	48.5/51.5%

SUSPENSION
F: Ind., lower wishbones, upper transverse leaf spring
R: Ind., lower wishbones, upper transverse leaf spring

STEERING
Type	Rack and pinion
Turns lock-to-lock	2.75
Turning circle	34.0 ft

BRAKES
F:	11.6-in disc
R:	10.8-in disc

WHEELS AND TIRES
Wheel size	15 x 6.0-in
Tire make and size	Goodyear F70-15, polyester
Test inflation pressure	F: 30 psi, R: 30 psi

PERFORMANCE
Zero to	Seconds
40 mph	2.7
60 mph	5.2
80 mph	8.5
100 mph	13.4
Standing ¼-mile	13.73 sec @ 101.58 mph
80-0 mph panic stop	256 ft (0.84 G)

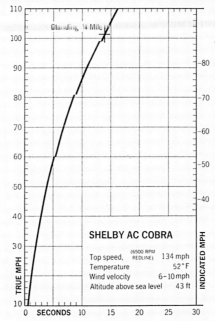

SHELBY AC COBRA

	(6500 RPM REDLINE)
Top speed,	134 mph
Temperature	52°F
Wind velocity	6-10 mph
Altitude above sea level	43 ft

MUSTANG BOSS 302

Price as tested: $4318.45

Options on test car: fastback coupe with Boss package (includes: 290-hp engine, bucket seats, 4-speed transmission, front disc brakes, racing mirrors, collapsible spare, quick-ratio steering, competition suspension, front spoiler, carpets, gauges, fiberglass belted tires), $3720.00; rear spoiler, $20.00; limited-slip differential, $43.00; 3.91 rear axle, $13.00; convenience check group, $32.00; sport slats, $65.00; AM/FM stereo radio, $214.00; decor group, $78.00; tinted glass, $32.00; deluxe belts, $15.00; HD battery, $13.00; tachometer $54.00.

ENGINE
Bore x stroke	4.00 x 3.00 in
Displacement	302 cu in
Compression ratio	10.6 to one
Carburetion	1 x 4-bbl Holley
Power (SAE)	290 hp @ 5800 rpm
Torque (SAE)	290 lbs-ft @ 4300 rpm

DRIVE TRAIN
Final drive ratio	3.91 to one

DIMENSIONS AND CAPACITIES
Wheelbase	108.0 in
Track	F: 59.5 in, R: 59.5 in
Length	187.4 in
Width	71.7 in
Height	50.2 in
Curb weight	3415 lbs
Weight distribution, F/R	55.9/44.1%

SUSPENSION
F: Ind., unequal-length control arms, coil springs, anti-sway bar
R: Rigid axle, semi-elliptic leaf springs, anti-sway bar

STEERING
Type	Recirculating ball
Turns lock-to-lock	3.6
Turning circle	38 ft

BRAKES
F:	11 3 in vented disc, power assist
R:	10.0 x 2.0- n cast iron drum, power assist

WHEELS AND TIRES
Wheel size	15 x 7.0-in
Tire make and size	Goodyear F60-15, Polyglass
Test inflation pressure	F: 28 psi, R: 28 psi

PERFORMANCE
Zero to	Seconds
40 mph	3.3
60 mph	6.5
80 mph	11.1
100 mph	17.0
Standing ¼-mile	14.93 sec @ 93.45 mph
80-0 mph panic stop	296 ft (0.72 G)

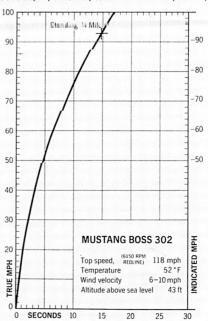

MUSTANG BOSS 302

	(6150 RPM REDLINE)
Top speed,	118 mph
Temperature	52°F
Wind velocity	6-10 mph
Altitude above sea level	43 ft

front instead of behind, which is a most unsatisfactory trade-out. And there were more comments about the interior.

"The driving position is really quite good but I can't brace my knees against the side panel—it is too far away. I just have to hold on to the steering wheel."

The observations continued in a calm, analytic flow, but there was absolutely nothing calm about what he was doing with the Chevelle. Three-digit numbers on the speedometer, airborne over the brow of the hill, 6000 rpm on the tach—the straights were now brief bursts of wide-open throttle and the curves abrupt changes of heading.

"The brakes are good for only about two laps and then they begin to fade. While they're working they are predictable, though. The biggest problem is the abrupt downshifts in the automatic transmission which breaks the tires loose and throws the rear end out. To get good control I have to shift manually at some point where I can stand a little twitch."

When it came to getting around corners the Chevelle proved to be quite agile in Posey's hands.

"The engineers who did this thing understand their problem—all that weight up front—and I think they've coped very well. The track is rough and the bumps are not throwing it off badly. It under-steers but the understeer kind of cancels out the bumps. When the front tires are at the limit the rears aren't working so hard, just enough so they get some power to the ground and contend with the bumps too. Now, if we were teetering through these corners in an oversteer posture the car would be very sensitive to them."

From the lap times it was obvious that he was getting along well with the Chevelle. Already he was down to 1:10:4, which is a very good time for a street car. How would the other super car, the Duster, do? It was time to find out.

"For a gearshift here, hell, it looks like a stick for pole vaulting. And the funny little round knob. I don't know why they tried to make it look like wood. It is one of the most conspicuously fake things I've ever set my eyes on. Look at the little tach. It's tiny. I do like looking out over the orange hood though—

gives me just a hint of being a McLaren driver. I'm a little apprehensive about all of this noise. We are going to have to shout."

After the smooth, quiet Chevelle the Duster was a vivid contrast. It rattled and buzzed at anything approaching speed and just generally broadcasted the same vibrance that made the Model A Ford seem so sophisticated in its day. As he started to work on faster lap times Posey wasn't optimistic.

"The power steering has nowhere near the road feel of the Chevelle and the car is not reacting well to the Gs. The suspension doesn't feel like the final solution. I don't detect the subtle hand of Colin Chapman in the geometry. What's happening is that as the body rolls in the turns it uses up all of the suspension travel and comes right in solid against the rubber bumpers. At that instant the weight transfer is complete on that wheel and the tire takes a terrible beating."

And, all the while the poor confused little Duster is being hurled around the track in a fashion it never dreamed possible. Through the Hook and into the Esses, tail out, tires howling and the lion-hearted 340 moaning spasmodically as Sam played the throttle for just the right amount of torque.

"It is both understeering and oversteering simultaneously, which is to say that it's sliding right off the road. The carburetor isn't helping either. It cuts out at the most inopportune times. Also, I'm having a lot of trouble with the shift, particularly into third."

The shifter problem is unfortunate. Chrysler buys the Hurst linkage, but because of confusion on the part of the executives as to which is most important, a solid, dependable shift or total absence of noise, the engineers are forced to rubber isolate the shifting mechanism to the point where its usefulness in changing gears is merely coincidental. And the tall lever contributes its share to the confusion by making the throw unreasonably long. Even though the Duster was having its problems Sam wasn't ready to give up.

"Notice that the tires are leaving black marks in the turns which suggests that they need more pressure."

With a best lap of 1:13:95 the Duster didn't appear to be much of a threat to the Cobra.

Still, with more air in the tires it figured to improve. As the pressures were being raised from 30 to 35 psi we went on to the Mustang.

"The instruments may be at the end of the Holland Tunnel down there. They are big enough but still difficult to read because of the complex markings. The driving position is a bit peculiar. The steering wheel is plenty close but the floor is too far away to brace my left foot satisfactorily. A telescoping steering column would be a good idea. This car has far more lateral support than the others and it feels very solid and secure."

We had been impressed by the same sensation when driving the Mustang on the road. It is quiet and exudes quality, very much like an expansive European GT car. The stiff suspension and high shock absorber control give it a very purposeful feel, and because the body doesn't quiver or rattle when you hit a bump the overall impression is most satisfying.

"With the manual steering it feels very heavy up front, particularly after the Duster which, although it didn't generate high lateral forces, was very easy to toss around. The steering effort is extremely high—certainly higher than any race car."

Within a few laps the Mustang's virtues and vices, which tend to be extreme, were laid out for inspection.

"The brakes are fabulous. I can go in way deeper before I have to brake with this car than I could with the other cars. And the pedal feel is excellent. Here, I can control the braking with pressure on the pedal where in the other cars the pressure stays about the same and the braking seems to depend on how far down I push the pedal. That is very tricky to do accurately, especially when you are going fast. But boy, does it understeer. Look, you'd think I was going into the pretzel business with my arms. I've got the wheel really cranked over and it just isn't getting the job done. The only way I can get the tail out is to trick it by hitting a bump at just the right time or setting it up with the brakes. Funny, I expect more of this car in handling than it's giving me. And it's busting my hands. Every time we hit a bump in the turns the wheel kicks back so hard that I can hardly hold on to it with my arms crossed up the way they have to be."

With a best lap of 1:12:35 the Mustang had been quicker than the Duster, but only with considerable effort. Once back in the pits the hardships of manual steering and extreme understeer were obvious for all to see. Sam's hands, in the crotch between the thumb and first finger, were bruised and swollen from being battered by the steering wheel spokes. The front tires hadn't escaped either. The outer tread rib was badly shredded—so bad, in fact, that it looked like the tread might start to peel. This brings up an interesting point about wide tires like the Mustang's F60–15s. Chevrolet is reluctant to use them, particularly on cars like the Chevelle, because the front suspension camber pattern is such that it lifts the inside of the tread patch in hard cornering to the point where the front tires are operating at a disadvantage relative to the rears—which exaggerates understeer. Curiously, the Chevelle wasn't wearing bias-belted tires (which are standard equipment this year) but rather last year's Goodyear bias-ply, polyester cord Wide Tread GTs. As a point of interest, the Cobra and the Chevelle both had exactly the same type of tires.

With the preliminaries out of the way it was time to explore the limits of Detroit performance. The Chevelle was charging around the track, its ears laid back and its hood louver snapped open to battle position. In compliance with California noise laws the exhaust has been restricted to a benevolent rumble, but the air rushing into the carburetor to feed those 454 cubic inches sounded like it was trying to take half the landscape with it. The Chevelle is a big car, enormous on Lime Rock, a tight, twisty, 1.53-mile circuit normally inhabited by Formula Vees and other assorted fruit-cup racers, but it didn't matter. Across the start-finish line at 110 mph, hard on the brakes for the Hook, wheels cocked in for the turn and clipping the infield grass at the apex—it seemed right at home. And it was doing very well, too. With a best lap of 1:08:00 it was the fastest non-race car that Jim Haynes, the track manager, could remember. The cornering speeds were good too—66.0 mph through the Hook and 61.4 mph through the Esses, a section with a left/right transition that is difficult for softly sprung passenger cars.

The Duster, now with 35 psi in its tires, began to show a new personality. At the end of the test Posey had revised his earlier opinion.

"Somehow, as the laps went by, this turned out to be the car that was a ball to drive. The steering is very, very light. Tremendous drift angles are possible, as are huge oversteers through the Esses with armloads of opposite lock. The car assumed nutty postures all the way around the course. It seemed to sort of get up on its tiptoes with the body rocking back and forth in a spectacular way and go really fast once I got used to it."

Of course, it still wasn't nearly as quick as the Chevelle, lapping at 1:11:7 and averaging 63.9 mph through the Hook and 60.2 through the Esses. But it was fun—a commodity that Posey didn't find much of in the Mustang.

"With the wide tires and stripes and louvers it looked so exciting in the pits. Perhaps because of my Trans-Am victory here in May with the Shelby car I had such high expectations for this one, but they just dwindled away as the laps went by. All I got out of it was sore hands. I'd rather just stand here and look at it."

Historic warriors: AC Cobra 289, foreground, and Chevrolet Corvette Stingray.

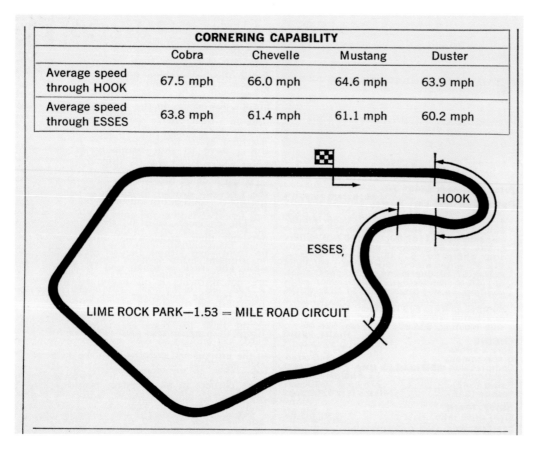

CORNERING CAPABILITY				
	Cobra	Chevelle	Mustang	Duster
Average speed through HOOK	67.5 mph	66.0 mph	64.6 mph	63.9 mph
Average speed through ESSES	63.8 mph	61.4 mph	61.1 mph	60.2 mph

LIME ROCK PARK—1.53 = MILE ROAD CIRCUIT

HOOK

ESSES

At the beginning of the test we expected the Boss 302 to give the Cobra real chase, but with its 1:11:2 lap times it was only slightly quicker than the Duster. Of interest, however, was that its excellent transient handling made it only 0.3 mph slower through the Esses than the Chevelle.

With the Chevelle having established itself as the toughest of the Detroit representatives, the question now was how would it fare against the formidable Cobra. That confrontation could be put off no longer. Posey was already buckling himself into the cockpit.

"The most incredible feeling of immediacy exists in this car. Everything is up close to you. None of the remoteness found in the other cars. There was a feeling, in the others, that you had to penetrate the styling concepts to figure out which controls did what. Everything here is very obvious."

The Cobra is a shockingly single purpose car. No frills, no extra sound deadener, only the implements (tube frame, 4-wheel disc brakes, fully independent suspension) required for rapid transit. The flat instrument panel has simple, round, white-on-black gauges—one

to monitor every factor you might need to check, including oil temperature. The external body sheetmetal extends right into the cockpit to form the top of the instrument panel and the windshield clamps down on the cowl, in traditional British sports car fashion, just inches in front of your nose. If there is any doubt, at a skeletal 2,322 lbs stuffed with a 271-hp Ford V-8, the Cobra is the archetypal high performance car.

"Oh, listen to the exhaust. If we were rating these cars on the basis of sound, this one would be the winner. The clutch is a heavy mutha. So is the steering, but it's very direct—much less lock required than in the other cars. And the suspension is very, very stiff. You feel every bump. Ah, see how nicely the tail comes out. This car has the feel of a racing car. The others didn't."

Because of its undisguised race car personality Posey adjusted to the Cobra in only a few laps. Partly because of its rearward weight bias—51.5% on the rear wheels—and partly because of its suspension rates, the Cobra was the only one of the cars that oversteered, and he used it to good

advantage. In corners the Cobra adopted a curious posture. Because of its equal length arms, the independent suspension cambers the wheels in the same direction as body roll—which is exactly the wrong way. This, combined with the wide swinging tail, would have been humorous, except that the Cobra was ferociously eating up the circuit. Although the brakes began to fade after several laps the Cobra still made its point. With a best lap of 1:06:95 it was quicker than the Chevelle by slightly more than a full second. And, despite its suspension histrionics, the cornering speeds were faster too—by 2.5 mph in the Hook and 2.4 mph in the Esses.

Although lap times are a reliable indicator of a car's balance between handling and useful power, it doesn't tell the whole story about brakes, primarily because you never come to a complete stop on a road course. Fade and controllability of the braking process are measured but stopping ability is not. For that reason, the braking test had some interesting conclusions. The Cobra stopped quickest, requiring 256 feet (0.84G) from 80 mph. It was also the most controllable. The Chevelle was next at 272 feet (0.79G). Although it stopped in a straight line the braking was heavily biased toward the front wheels which meant that, to realize the full potential of the rears, the fronts had to be fully locked up, which will (and did) badly flat-spot the front tires. The Duster stopped in 287 feet (0.74G) with the rears tending to lock slightly before the fronts. The Mustang suffered from extreme rear wheel lock up—something that didn't show up significantly in the road course part of the test because a racing driver always avoids that situation if possible. Rear wheel lock up is a highly unstable situation which causes a car to skid sideways—which happened to the Mustang on one of its stops. Its best stop was 296 feet (0.72G)—an unseeming contrast to its stellar performance on the road course.

A point that Posey feels very strongly about, and so do we, is that controls, like brakes, should be sensitive to effort rather than travel. This problem shows up frequently with the strong power assists that are necessary in Detroit's heavy cars. The Mustang's brakes are very good in this respect while the Chevelle's

leave much room for improvement. And somewhat the same problem exists with power steering. The Duster's steering is so highly assisted that you sense the direction of the front wheels, not by feel, but by the position of the steering wheel.

After two solid days of testing we can see that improvement is required before Detroit can knock the Cobra off its "world's fastest car" pedestal—but not nearly as much as you may have thought. Those tweedy-capped purists who have been accusing Detroit's performance cars of being ill-handling hogs capable of little more than straight-line travel have had their legs kicked out from under them by the Chevelle. Naturally, the Chevelle was quicker in the straights, but it also made the fastest cornering speeds—significantly faster than the Boss 302, in fact, which has a reputation for good handling. After the test Posey commented on the Chevelle. "It's typically GM—wouldn't have offended anybody. It's quiet and well behaved—almost innocuous… I can't even remember what the dashboard looked like. But it has striking performance that you'd never suspect in traffic."

The Duster, although not the fastest, is certainly the most amusing. It's whimsical and has a kind of disposable air about it. Breaking it would not be a catastrophe—you just won't get your deposit back. For the price it delivers

a full measure of performance but it has been badly compromised by confused priorities (the shift linkage) and inept stylists. Not only are the stylists responsible for many unnecessarily cheap looking details in the interior (fake wood knob, for example), but by their decree the Duster has been lowered on its suspension. This little trick for snuggling the Duster down against the ground has left the suspension jounce travel in an impoverished condition, detrimental to both ride and handling. Still, the Duster is a good start toward a compact super car—the basic mechanical parts definitely do the job—and with some work could be every bit as satisfying as the Chevelle.

Most of the Boss 302's problems could be cured by power steering (which is available) and less understeer. After driving the prototype Boss in Dearborn last spring we thought Ford had finally cured the understeer problem but, apparently, we were wrong. With its strong styling and quality feel the Mustang is an appealing road car, but that is quite apart from the implication of "Boss."

For now Perkins can continue along carefree paths, snuffing Corvettes in gymkhanas and autocrosses, confident in the knowledge that his aluminum-bodied Anglo-American hand grenade has got Detroit pretty well covered. But he is definitely not as anxious for the 1971 Chevelle as we are.

Clockwise from top: AC Cobra 289; Mustang Boss 302 detail; Chevelle SS 454 detail.

BROCK YATES

THE INSURANCE SQUEEZE

The insurance industry has decided that the present generation of performance
cars should be the last—and they are trying to make their decision stick

As I drove into the office this morning a 1970 Roadrunner, painted in that fluorescent color that has come to be known as "Gang-Green," passed me doing about 85 on the frozen open metal roadbed of the Brooklyn Bridge. The driver was, I guess, in his late twenties, shades, 'burns, the collar of a fleece-lined, suede jacket turned up against what could only be imagined as cold. In all, nothing overtly extraordinary—except in my mind, where I couldn't get rid of the feeling that I had just seen a 1970 version of J. Paul Getty go by. Careening past me, over an antiquated ice-slickened span on the way to buying out Apple—or maybe paying off Michael J. Brody's debts—confident, as only the truly rich can be, that the perils which face mere mortals are of no consequence to him. And maybe only I of the drones that witnessed his passing was fully aware of what his garish automobile represented. A goddamn chartreuse metalflake icon announcing its owner's complete disregard, or disinterest in the nickel-dime budgets that the rest of us slogging across that bridge dealt with. I knew—by his car, his New York City license plate, by the way he drove—that he had to be paying at least $1,000 a year for compulsory automobile liability insurance.

One thousand dollars a year for the right to drive a car that probably didn't cost more than three times that amount. That, is money! And if you aren't aware of it yet you'd better get used to showing a little more than fear when a Roadrunner, or Z/28, or even a 360 Javelin hauls up alongside because you, friend, are in the presence of real wealth. Forget about the Coupe de Villes and all the other traditional totems—anybody with a clean credit record and a life-expectancy of over 36 months can lump around in one of those things. It's the guy in the high-performance car, with the throaty V-8 vibrating inside, who's the genuine article.

Which means, Super Car owners, that all you have to do is hang in there for a few months, keep making your payments, and instant respect will be yours in the years ahead. Because if things keep going the way the insurance companies want, you're probably going to be driving a 6-cylinder sedan and congratulating yourself that you haven't been forced to go to a Four.

What safety standards, lower speed limits, smog regulations, engine governors and radar traps haven't been able to do, your friendly insurance agent can, and is doing. Smiling at you from behind rate charts and application forms that may well have been written by Noel Coward (Estimate how many drinks you have a week:—glasses of wine,—bottles of beer,—cocktails,—highballs—when was the last time you heard anyone order a "highball"?), this friendly member of the Rotary, Elks, Junior Chamber of Commerce, PTA, is telling you—and Detroit—that the present generation of performance cars is the last.

Detroit's slide rule and demographic savants will never know what hit them. While their research may continue to show that the interest in high performance cars should be as healthy as ever, out in the showrooms the people that make up that market will be kicking tires and slamming doors of 6-cylinder sedans as the marketing man's beloved stripped and spoilered creation sits gathering dust behind the water cooler. A dazzling tribute to man's inability to understand priorities in an age of technology or properly interpret statistics.

Until the insurance companies decided to ante-up and deal themselves into the automotive marketing game, Detroit has had little choice but to continue making high-performance cars, even in the face of growing legislation and crusader pressure to ease off, simply because there has been an immense

market for such vehicles—drivers who have demanded good engine response, handling and styling and have been willing to pay for it. In a few years, if the insurance companies have their way, the concept of actually enjoying a car and buying one with that reason in mind, will be as anachronistic as being a roller derby fan. By threatening to put exorbitant surcharges on automobile insurance for "high-performance" cars (particularly compulsory liability coverage) the insurance companies will effectively destroy the market for such vehicles. The result, as one marketing man for a major auto maker put it, is obvious: "We figured the high-performance market may have been approaching its natural plateau in the past two or three years ... until then we could only guess at its size. Now, most of the companies see that it represents about 15–25% of the total market and we've invested a lot of time and money in developing the present generation of performance vehicles, as well as figuring out where we can go next. ... But if the bottom suddenly drops out, and this insurance situation is certainly the type of thing that could make that happen, then all that we've done isn't going to be worth a damn. ... We won't make cars that the market can't afford to drive."

A marketing specialist for a rival automaker was more adamant. "Washington feels safe in passing legislation dealing with cars ever since we got painted as the villains in the piece. We don't particularly like it but we have to live with it. Only now the insurance industry, which is in business to make a profit just like us, is exploiting the same image and hiding behind the fact that law requires liability insurance, to tell us what kind of cars we can make. ... And to base it on published horsepower ratings, they might just as well base it on the color of the car and how many stripes it's got.

In fact, they'd probably be better off."

He's worried. Yet Detroit's case is weakened by the fact that much of its "development" for high performance cars has centered around producing more horsepower. Handling, in general, has not been the prime engineering goal, and even the most insular Super Car fan will admit that there are examples of the breed that exhibit the all-competent agility of a 747 taxiing to its loading ramp.

On the other hand, the insurance companies are under fire themselves and a year-long investigation of insurance premiums and repair costs by the Senate Judiciary Anti-Trust & Monopoly Subcommittee under the chairmanship of Senator Philip A. Hart (D., Michigan) has brought matters to a head. The industry claims that in 1968 (the most recent year for which figures are available) it earned $11.4-billion in premiums, $800-million more than the previous year—and double the figure for a decade earlier. At the same time the industry claims to have lost $1.7-billion in claims over the course of the previous ten years, although contradictory testimony by the secretary-treasurer of Ohio AFL-CIO pointed out, "… The profits the industry is talking about are underwriting profits and not net profits. As you know, underwriting profits do not include investment income from case loss reserves or unearned premium reserves." There may be dispute about the accounting procedures but the insurance companies, working through a lobby that is generally conceded to be second in effectiveness only to the oil industry's, are currently in a much stronger position in Washington than the auto companies and they plan to make the most of it by demanding that cars they consider unsafe (read "unprofitable") cannot be marketed. Their argument is based on the fact that in every state licensed drivers must be able to prove a financial capability to make certain minimum reparation in liability suits. Insurance is the most common method of establishing such proof and the insurance companies rankle at being forced to write policies on high-risk individuals—particularly in states where "assigned risk" pools (now euphemistically called "State Insurance Plans") are in operation. In addition, the industry must

contend with 50 different sets of standards as the federal government, to this point at least, has completely left operations and requirements in the hands of state review boards.

Naturally the insurance industry wants to simplify its problems, and to reduce the immense overhead stemming from the current system which requires separate forms, large legal staffs, different rate structures, etc. in each state. Several plans have been proposed with the most popular being a no-fault type of liability coverage which would reduce legal fees and overhead (currently calculated at 40% of the amount collected in premiums).

This, then, was the prevailing atmosphere in late 1969 when Dean W. Jeffers, president of Nationwide Mutual (the fifth leading auto insurer behind State Farm, Allstate, Travelers and Aetna) revealed that his company was going to assess a 50% surcharge penalty to the owners of 1970 model cars in the "overpowered" class. In other words, Nationwide plans to base liability premiums on the car rather than the individual.

In presenting his case before Hart's Anti-Trust Committee, Jeffers did not hide the Nationwide's intent. With the new rates, consumers concerned about their auto insurance would think seriously before purchasing these motorized missiles. ... If consumers begin to lose interest in such high-powered cars, obviously the auto manufacturers will be induced to decrease the output of such cars.

Hart concurred, winning the everlasting hatred of many of his Michigan constituents. "All of us who are insured but don't have super cars are really picking up the difference." He went on to say that the manufacturers, insurers and the government have a joint responsibility to prevent usage of vehicles that may be instruments of destruction. Once Nationwide broke the ice several of the other automobile liability companies, Allstate for one, have picked up on the favorable reception and are requesting similar rate changes. (Previously Allstate had been requiring a 20% Super Car surcharge in some states.)

Although Jeffers did not spell out for the Committee what exactly he meant by

overpowered cars, describing them instead as cars with engines providing "substantially more power than needed for smooth acceleration, comfortable driving, and safe passing," it turns out that the rate structure is based purely on a published horsepower to weight scale. Cars with a power/weight ratio of 11-to-one or under will cost their owners an extra 50%. The same surcharge holds true for cars with a power/weight ratio of less than 13-to-one, but only when equipped with manual 4-speed transmissions. (See accompanying chart for models that can be penalized.)

Even within the insurance industry there is disagreement with performance car surcharges. State Farm, the nation's largest insurer of automobiles, has announced that while under-25 drivers of Super Cars are not being accepted as readily as before, their driving records are being examined and penalties will not be assessed on "good" drivers. A spokesman for Liberty Mutual, the seventh leading insurer and the company that has most actively sponsored safety research and driver training clinics, commented, "Any intelligent approach to auto insurance considers the driver first. It may be heresy but *I'm not at all sure that there is a reliable set of statistics to prove a greater risk factor between a Volkswagen and a Super Car* (italics ours—Ed.). Off hand, the only car I know we won't insure is a Corvette in New York City. That's because it has an average life on the street of under two hours before it's stolen—not because it's a safety risk."

With 55,000 deaths, over 4 million injuries and an estimated loss of $14.2-billion a year resulting from automobile accidents, it is hard to blame the insurance industry for trying to cover its bet that you won't be involved. Yet, by arbitrarily demanding that the owners of performance cars must pay a surcharge for the right to drive such vehicles, Nationwide is incorrectly placing the blame. The people who buy performance cars obviously take a greater interest in driving than the owners of "transportation appliances." They are more knowledgeable and more aware of the capabilities of a car, and, by singling them out for punitive measures, the insurance industry is contradicting its own findings. Dr. Thomas

L. Wenck, himself an insurance specialist at Michigan State University, believes that "the solution to the insurance industry's and society's problem is to remove the accident-causing drivers from the road. ... Six percent of the drivers cause 50% of all accidents, and 50% of the accidents in which there are fatalities involve drinking drivers. Yet the insurance industry is expected, and sometimes required, to insure these drivers."

To counter seemingly contradictory statements and studies such as Wenck's, the insurance industry has established the Insurance Institute for Highway Safety, directed by Dr. William Haddon, Jr. Haddon, whose calm demeanor earned him the grudging respect of Detroit when he was the first Administrator of the National Traffic and Safety Bureaus, has acquired a new shrill tone in addition to a new title. A recent article in *The Washington Post* quoted him as saying, "(Super Cars are) fine on the race track but it's almost criminal irresponsibility to use these on the public streets.

"Because of advertising techniques, the image that is being sold at great expense to the American public is that you don't have safe transportation; you have thrills on the American highway."

Haddon's blanket indictment of performance cars carries with it an implication of righteous justification, but he continues, "Insurance loss rates are greatly higher on these cars; whether it's because of the way these cars are built or that they are used too fast, *we don't know*."

It's a battle being staged by a pair of giants right now: an insurance industry that collects over $11-billion a year in premiums and an auto industry that sells $23-billion worth of cars and trucks a year. The consumer, the guy who is paying for both, seems helpless. As opposed to, say, the National Rifle Association, which actively and effectively lobbies in Washington, the automobile enthusiast has no organized voice to speak with where it counts. The closest he comes is Detroit's lobbyists, who confidentially concede that the present administration cannot be expected to take action against the influential insurance companies. As one said, "In Washington's

power-dealing politics the insurance industry currently wields considerably more clout than the automakers and if the performance market must be sacrificed to keep the wolf away from Detroit's door, so be it."

But what of the enthusiast who finds that not only Super Cars but vehicles like Z/28s, 302 Mustangs, 340 Barracudas, Corvettes, Porsches and Jaguars are being surcharged out of the market? These people are looking for well-balanced cars, not a vicarious ride atop a remote-controlled Saturn V. For this group there appears little hope and little understanding.

When a company can be selective with optional equipment (such as an automatic transmission) in establishing its rates, the intelligent performance car buyer sees a faint glimmer of hope—is the converse true? Is there equipment that he should order that will give him a break—disc brakes, for instance?

When asked this question, the reply from an officer of a company which has announced a high performance surcharge replied, "The rate structure is not refined enough to take such items as brakes or tires into account." So much for well-balanced cars.

The structure also does not take into account any luxury convenience equipment that may adversely affect a car's inherent safety factor. Items such as automatic speed control devices—which are under investigation to determine whether they might make driving too easy by lulling drivers into a sense of removed boredom—have yet to appear on the actuarial tables.

Based on Nationwide's power/weight scale, approximately 30% of Detroit's 1970 models will catch their owners up in the surcharge net. This surcharge, of course, is computed on top of the insurance industry's traditional surcharge criteria which falls into 10 basic categories: where you live (high density areas tend to mean higher liability rates, although lower collision rates); sex (men get the higher rate); age (according to industry statistics over half of all accidents are accounted for by under-25 drivers); marital status ("singles tend to be more irresponsible"); how a car is used (if you drive it to work every day you put on more mileage and thus increase the probability of an

accident); frequency of claims; cost of previous claims; number of cars in a family, whether or not you've taken driver education; "safety reasons" (health, vision, etc.); and occupation (with farmers getting the best break).

And based on the insurance industry's figures, America's 105,000,000 drivers spend an average of $110 a year in insurance premiums, which is a fairly modest tariff. However, when the under-25 owner of a 1970 Super Car in New York City reports that his compulsory liability insurance will cost him $1,200 this year, or when a casualty claims worker on Wall Street reports that he can't get new insurance for his XK-E because his broker was cancelled when the insurer he dealt with discovered a high claim loss ratio, then one begins to doubt what course is left open for the person who enjoys driving.

Reinforcing this distrust, and contrary to the advertisement's portrayal of the insurance man as a "friend who's always there to help," the prospective policyholder often meets with disillusionment. For example, agents for the five leading auto liability companies, asked to reply to an inquiry about the cost of insuring a Super Car, curtly dismissed the potential policyholder with comments like "we do not accept cars of this type ... we suggest that you contact the 'state insurance plan' office" or did not reply at all. It is apparent that auto insurance agents view high performance enthusiasts with the same affection that a life insurance agent holds for tertiary syphilis patients.

However, a quick survey of independent agents, who act as brokers for a number of different companies and can therefore "shop" for the prospective policyholder, may indicate a path to follow for the immediate future. There are nearly 800 different companies that offer automobile liability coverage and many, including some of the largest, don't subscribe to the surcharge theory for high performance cars. These independent agents, particularly if they are personal acquaintances or are enthusiasts themselves, often have the advantage of being able to place a customer without resorting to the assigned risk pools, where it is difficult to get anything but minimum coverage at maximum rate.

But that may be little more than a temporary expedient. The insurance industry, which hauls out ledger books full of figures to answer any question posed to it, and has built up an obfuscating vocabulary of jargon that would make a NASA controller green with envy, has clearly said that performance cars are on the way out. And the auto industry has shown little inclination to take up the fight on behalf of a market that it once prized. Already bell-weather speeches by several policy makers in Detroit have made it clear that the "youth market," (which has become synonymous with the "high performance market," even though the industry's own figures show the median age of "performance car" buyer is 27) should no longer be catered to with the enthusiasm that prevailed in the last half of the Sixties. "Soft pedal the 'kiddie ads'." is the hot tip in Motown, and, despite the fact that most of those "kiddies" average a higher income than the faithful bread-and-butter sedan buyers, they had better begin looking at ATVs and dune buggies because high performance is likely to be measured in gradient-climbing-ability in the years to come. Projects that are almost a reality, like the mid-engined and rear-engined cars, will

be economically unthinkable if a buyer has to allot 20% extra on top of the purchase price for something that does him no good unless he stuffs his car into a bridge abutment—and Detroit realizes it.

The prospect of seeing the end of performance cars is dismaying, but to accept the reasoning behind the insurance company's thinking is preposterous. If the government and the insurance companies continue to blame accidents on the machinery of driving, rather than on the driver himself, it's unlikely that any significant progress will ever be made in reducing highway fatalities. But the political climate makes it unlikely that any change in theory is forthcoming. It sits much better with a Congressman's constituents to read "Representative Doe accuses the $23-billion a year auto industry of building killer cars" than to discover that Representative Doe wants his constituents to take a driver's examination every five years.

So the highways remain public for everyone to use, including the chronic alcoholic, the senile, the feeble, the nearly blind, the speed freak and the cold tablet swallowers who may be driving with impaired depth perception. And driver education courses continue to

consist of little more than learning where to insert an ignition key and mastering the intricacies of the "k-turn." But Washington and the insurance industry blast away at high performance cars as if every driver on the road was as qualified as Mario Andretti while comparable statistics on standard cars prove that this is not the case.

Glider pilots aren't allowed to jump behind the controls of 707s—as a result, it's safer to fly than to drive. But the lesson hasn't been learned, and in another decade when the performance car concept is a dull memory and all those dull gray men in their dull gray sedans continue to splatter each other into bright red heaps, everyone will continue to wring his hands and wonder why.

It's time to accept the fact that cars built to collapse like marshmallows aren't the answer. No amount of mechanical tinkering is going to begin to solve the problem unless some human engineering is done first.

ROAD TEST
PLYMOUTH BARRACUDA

The end of the road is in sight and no one, it seems, is looking for the detour.

Even brief exposure behind the wheel will reveal Plymouth's secret: the Barracuda is a sheep in wolf's clothing. It's easy to be fooled at first by the 150-mph speedometer; the trick tachometer with its numbers rotated racer-style to place the 6500 rpm redline at the 11 o'clock position; and the business-like Hurst shifter standing at attention, its Bowie-knife grip ready for whatever rapid gear changing may be necessary to win. And down there where no casual observer can see is a powerplant so notorious that its displacement has been boldly announced in chrome numerals on that scooped performance hood (highlighted, if you so desire, by stripes). The wheel wells are filled with white-letter tires to guarantee delivery of the goods to the ground, and peering out under the bumper is a pair of drainpipe-sized exhaust tips that insure a hasty release of spent gases so as not to put a short rein on the operation. Inside, high back bucket seats promise a secure command post from which all conquering will take place. The whole package reeks of performance… performance that allowed your insurance agent to move into the high-rent subdivision and kept police summons books looking thin. But with the exception of Ronnie Sox's car, there will be precious little conquering by the emasculated 1972 Plymouth Barracuda. If outside it looks like the street eliminator, underneath you will find a back-of-the-pack impostor.

A quick study of the option list will reveal the extent of the current predicament as Plymouth—and all Detroit—tries to find a path for the future in a tangled thicket of safety-emission-insurance requirements. Gone from the Barracuda are the killer V-8s, those monsters like the Hemi, 440, and 383 series. Laid to rest with them are the stump-puller axles, cold air packages and multiple carburetion setups. Sixty series tires and

wide wheel rims are also noticeably absent. Seeing these omissions, it's apparent that Plymouth is offering only a thin shell of last year's car for the shrinking sporty car market. By substituting parts from other models and simplifying the assembly operations with fewer options, Plymouth plans to make money on the Barracuda even as sales for the entire sporty car segment plummet.

All very logical for Plymouth, but what about the buyer seeking a real sporty car for his $4,000? First off, styling mavens will no longer find convertibles or low-line bench seat coupes complicating their decisions. And the quarter-mile freaks have already begun to concentrate on used car lots for earlier engines less compromised by emission development. But it's the enthusiast seeking versatility for every phase of performance who's really been boxed in. Previously, Plymouth offered the potent 340 engine in such packages as the AAR 'Cuda to satisfy such demands. They've even been wise enough to promote the Duster and Road Runner with the wonder motor. In each case, some of the blinding acceleration of Chrysler's giant performance V-8s was wisely exchanged for additional capabilities in cornering and braking. Handling in the Barracuda was never anything to call to Jim Hall's attention, but the lighter powerplant placed less burden on the overworked front tires than the more brutish Mopar engines. And, as a result of premium components inside the 340, throttle response compensated for most other deficiencies, in that there were more revs available than anyone could want or need. Only a cautious throttle foot could restrain that free-swinging tach needle.

That's the way it was. Now, the 340 occupies the top rung of the horsepower ladder and its 240 net hp at 4800 rpm (as opposed to 1971's conservative rating of

275 gross hp at 5000 rpm) only hints at the disappointment in store. The fact of the matter is the 340 lives, but in name only. Plymouth gave rein to the accounting department and the bean counters slipped out the good parts before our very eyes. Beginning with 1971 models, the low restriction exhaust manifolds with large passages and gentle bends were dropped in favor of cheaper log restrictors (manifolds) from the 360 cu.in. V-8 (a family sedan motor). But, the real below-the-belt whack was delivered in 1972 and now we are short-changed for our cylinder head money. The 360 heads have been volunteered for duty in the 340 and, in this application, the best that can be said is that they do a fine job of sealing in the anti-freeze. Compression has tumbled from a 10.5-to-one ratio to a regular-gas 8.5. Intake valves have shrunk from a 2.02-inch diameter to a nail-like 1.88, and, in place of the large area high-volume ports, the 340 now wheezes through congested passages. The engineers are the first to admit that none of these parts belong in a performance engine but they mistakenly let the cost accountants know about "interchangeability." As a result, for '72 Plymouth is selling lackluster 360 components under the 340's nameplate and whereas the 340 engine was once a highly responsive small V-8, now it can no longer be considered a performance engine.

If tire-smoking burnouts are your bag, you'll be pleased to learn that this feat of ego-tripping is still possible with the 4-speed transmission and, as always, the unsilenced air cleaner will deliver impressive sounds, but there will be little other response as you step into the secondaries. Asthma sets in above 5000 rpm and the free-breathing, rev-forever nature of the 340 is just a memory. In its place you'll be getting 15.5-second and 91.4 mph ET slips (compared to 14.3-sec. @ 99.5 mph for

the 1970 AAR 'Cuda). Just to show that we're good guys, we will point out where the bean counters have missed an excellent chance at further cost savings—by not attacking that real racer tach. It is calibrated to 8000, but use of even two-thirds of that scale is senseless thrashing of parts.

One genuinely desirable component has slipped through, courtesy of the emissions budget. An electronic ignition package is standard on the 340, justified by the emissions benefits from constant dwell angle and less spark scatter. Everyone will gain from increased reliability since breaker points have been ash-canned in favor of a maintenance-free magnetic pulse generator in the distributor. This ingenious device supplies a signal at firing intervals which is amplified by a semi-conductor module to control a conventional ignition coil. An rpm limiter is sealed into the system and at a preset limit of 6400 rpm the control module interrupts all messages to the coil, ceasing ignition until the revs drop.

While the engine received vivid attention there is little evidence of a proportionate

effort for other areas where the Barracuda could have gained. In fact, the contrary seems to be the case. Last year's Rallye suspension with anti-sway bars front and rear does remain standard for the 340 package—but the 60-series tires and wide rims have gotten the axe. Consequently, the car's ultimate cornering power has diminished with this year's 70-series tires on 5.5-inch rims. Suddenly we are back to 1968 and the fast-backed fish. Transition from a desirable handling stance to a tail-out attitude now begins at a lower speed, and any major power applications while cornering must include a corresponding steering correction. A faster steering ratio would ease the driving chores but a variable-ratio, high-effort power steering gear is a development Chrysler hasn't justified at this point. Catalytic mufflers and air bags come first.

In braking, at least, the Barracuda still provides excitement. It's not from eyeball-popping deceleration but the lack of directional stability due to rear wheel lock-up on the first maximum-effort stop. On the second try, you'll find that fade has diminished

the proportioning inconsistencies. More pedal effort is required but at least you'll be facing the right direction when you finally come to a halt. If you care to continue, the performance quickly deteriorates further as fade takes its toll on the whole system.

We feel Plymouth's actions are particularly unwise. Their attempts to generate broad appeal for the Barracuda by compromising every aspect has been a stone around the car's neck since its beginning. Early Barracudas shared so many Valiant components that the styling had sufficient sporty appeal only for 80-year-old widows. The new body was handicapped by dated styling concepts and an engine compartment suitable for the greatest mass of cast iron to leave the foundry.

If sporty car interest must fade, the obvious response would be a more competitive entry with glowing advantages over the sales leaders. The 340 engine was just such an advantage and many judged it to be the very best small block engine one could buy. But Plymouth has allowed the major attraction of the car to wither with only an accounting department justification.

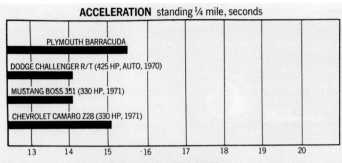

PLYMOUTH BARRACUDA
DODGE CHALLENGER R/T (425 HP, AUTO, 1970)
MUSTANG BOSS 351 (330 HP, 1971)
CHEVROLET CAMARO Z28 (330 HP, 1971)

13 14 15 16 17 18 19 20

BRAKING 80-0 mph panic stop, feet

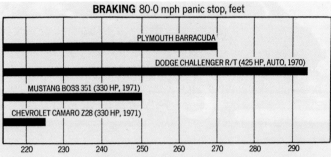

PLYMOUTH BARRACUDA
DODGE CHALLENGER R/T (425 HP, AUTO, 1970)
MUSTANG BOSS 351 (330 HP, 1971)
CHEVROLET CAMARO Z28 (330 HP, 1971)

220 230 240 250 260 270 280 290

FUEL ECONOMY RANGE mpg

PLYMOUTH BARRACUDA
DODGE CHALLENGER R/T (425 HP, AUTO, 1970)
MUSTANG BOSS 351 (330 HP, 1971)
CHEVROLET CAMARO Z28 (330 HP, 1971)

6 10 14 18 22 26 30 34

PRICE AS TESTED dollars x 1000

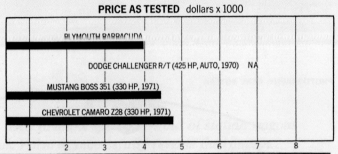

PLYMOUTH BARRACUDA
DODGE CHALLENGER R/T (425 HP, AUTO, 1970)   NA
MUSTANG BOSS 351 (330 HP, 1971)
CHEVROLET CAMARO Z28 (330 HP, 1971)

1 2 3 4 5 6 7 8

PLYMOUTH BARRACUDA

Manufacturer: Chrysler-Plymouth Division
Chrysler Corporation
Detroit, Michigan 48231

Vehicle type: Front engine, rear-wheel-drive, 4-passenger coupe

Price as tested: $3937.39
(Manufacturer's suggested retail price, including all options listed below, Federal excise tax, dealer preparation and delivery charges, does not include state and local taxes, license or freight charges)

Options on test car: Base Barracuda, $2867.00; 340 engine, $284.05; 4-speed transmission, $198.10; F70-14 tires, $99.50; Power steering, $106.95; Power disc brakes, $64.00; Performance axle package, $61.45; Rallye instrument panel, $87.04; Console, $53.05; AM radio, $61.10; Sport hood, $20.25; Inside hood release, $9.75; Wheel covers, $25.15.

ENGINE
Type: V-8, water-cooled, cast iron block and heads, 5 main bearings
Bore x stroke .... 4.04 x 3.31 in, 102.5 x 84.0 mm
Displacement .... 340 cu in, 5580cc
Compression ratio .... 8.5 to one
Carburetion .... 1 x 4-bbl Carter
Valve gear .... Pushrod operated overhead valves, hydraulic lifters
Power (SAE net) .... 240 bhp @ 4800 rpm

Torque (SAE net) .... 290 lbs-ft @ 3600 rpm
Specific power output .... 0.71 bhp/cu in, 43.0 bhp/liter
Max recommended engine speed .... 6500 rpm

DRIVE TRAIN
Transmission .... 4-speed, all-synchro
Final drive ratio .... 3.55 to one

Gear	Ratio	Mph/1000rpm	Max. test speed
I	2.47	8.6	55 mph (6400 rpm)
II	1.77	12.0	72 mph (6000 rpm)
III	1.34	15.9	95 mph (6000 rpm)
IV	1.00	21.3	125 mph (5900 rpm)

DIMENSIONS AND CAPACITIES
Wheelbase .... 108.0 in
Track, F/R .... 59.7/61.6 in
Length .... 186.6 in
Width .... 74.9 in
Height .... 50.9 in
Ground clearance .... 5.2 in
Curb weight .... 3520 lbs
Weight distribution, F/R 56.8/43.2%
Battery capacity .... 12 volts, 46 amp-hr
Alternator capacity .... 574 watts
Fuel capacity .... 19.0 gal
Oil capacity .... 5.0 qts
Water capacity .... 16.0 qts

SUSPENSION
F: Ind., unequal length control arms, torsion bars, anti-sway bar
R: Rigid axle, semi-elliptic leaf springs, anti-sway bar

STEERING
Type .... Recirculating ball, power assist
Turns lock-to-lock 3.6
Turning circle curb-to-curb .... 41.3 ft

BRAKES
F: .... 10.7-in ventilated disc, power assist
R: .... 10.0 x 2.5-in cast iron drum, power assist

WHEELS AND TIRES
Wheel size .... 14 x 5.5-in
Wheel type .... Stamped steel, 5-bolt
Tire make and size .... Goodyear, F70-14
Tire type .... Tubeless, bias ply
Test inflation pressures, F/R .... 26/26 psi
Tire load rating .... 1500 lbs per tire @ 32 psi

PERFORMANCE

Zero to	Seconds
30 mph	2.8
40 mph	3.9
50 mph	5.2
60 mph	6.9
70 mph	8.8
80 mph	12.1
90 mph	14.9
100 mph	19.5

Standing ¼-mile .... 15.5 sec @ 91.7 mph
Top speed (observed) .... 125 mph
80-0 mph .... 270 ft (0.79 G)
Fuel mileage .... 10-15 mpg on regular fuel
Cruising range .... 190-285 mi

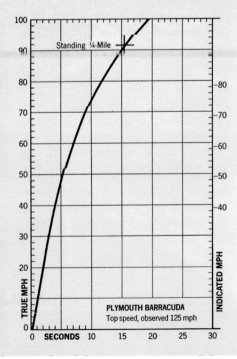

PLYMOUTH BARRACUDA
Top speed, observed 125 mph

PHOTOGRAPHY CREDITS

Pages 9, 10, 49, 75, 109, 110, 116: all rights reserved; page 15: Al Francekevich; front cover, back cover and poster, pages 1, 2-3, 4, 8, 11, 13, 16, 17, 18, 19, 25, 26, 29, 30, 32, 34, 42, 43, 44, 52, 53, 54, 56, 58 (right), 64, 89, 90, 113, 119, 121, 125, 129, 131: Mike Mueller; page 37: Alfred Fisher, Noel Werrett; pages 38, 39: Alfred Fisher; page 49: Mike Brady; page 57: Irv Tybel; page 58 (left): Courtesy of General Motors Historical Collection; page 83: Noel Werrett; page 91: Hi-Tech Software; page 95: Classic Car Studio; page 137: Humphrey Sutton; page 138: Courtesy of Chrysler Corporate Historical Collection.

When *Car and Driver* clearly identified the writers and photographers of stories reproduced in this book, we mention them on this page. Although efforts have been made to identify the copyright holders of all material published here, we apologize for any error or omission and will insert appropriate credit in subsequent editions.

Copyright © 2008 Filipacchi Publishing, a division of Hachette Filipacchi Media U.S., Inc.

First published in 2008 in the United States of America by
Filipacchi Publishing
1633 Broadway
New York, NY 10019

Car and Driver is a registered trademark of Hachette Filipacchi Media U.S., Inc.

Design: Patricia Fabricant
Photo research: Erika Koning
Production: Ed Barredo

ISBN 10: 1-933231-37-8
ISBN 13: 978-1-933231-37-2

Library of Congress Control Number: 2008924234

Printed in China